Editorial project:
© 2023 **booq** publishing, S.L.
c/ Domènech, 7-9, 2º 1ª
08012 Barcelona, Spain
T: +34 93 268 80 88
www.booqpublishing.com

ISBN: 978-84-9936-638-8 [EN]
ISBN: 978-84-9936-624-1 [ES]

© Éditions du Layeur
Dépôt Légal : novembre 2023
Espagne, en novembre 2023

ISBN : 978-2-38378-059-5

Editorial coordinator:
Claudia Martínez Alonso

Art director:
Mireia Casanovas Soley

Editor:
Cayetano Cardelús Vidal

Layout:
Cristina Simó Perales

Translation:
© **booq** publishing, S.L.

Printing in Spain

The evolution of concrete over the centuries in the field of construction reached a significant turning point at the beginning of the 20th century, when it went beyond its original vocation as a structural material to become a versatile component that could be used simultaneously as an exterior finish. The consolidation of the reinforced concrete system and the development of prefabricated elements based on it thus opened up a new avenue for the development of architectural expression.

The great versatility and mouldability offered by precast fair-faced concrete structures and elements, supported by the evolution of the material as a result of its technological development, provides architectural professionals with almost unlimited design freedom. Its special materiality is complemented by a wide range of finishes, textures and colours, whose unique qualities often provide a starting point for the architectural approach to projects.

Traditionally considered an environmentally unfriendly material despite its recognised robustness, durability and low maintenance, many companies are currently developing research aimed at creating concretes that integrate environmentally beneficial components and are manufactured using less polluting processes.

This volume contains works from the five continents in which the suggestive materiality of exposed concrete is manifested not only in the structural elements but also as a building envelope, a space-defining or simple compositional element, but which in all cases stands as the fundamental element in the global design of the project.

Die Entwicklung des Betons im Laufe der Jahrhunderte im Bereich des Bauwesens erreichte zu Beginn des 20. Jahrhunderts einen bedeutenden Wendepunkt, als er über seine ursprüngliche Bestimmung als Konstruktionsmaterial hinaus zu einem vielseitigen Bauteil wurde, das gleichzeitig als Außenverkleidung verwendet werden konnte. Die Konsolidierung des Stahlbetonsystems und die Entwicklung von vorgefertigten Elementen auf seiner Grundlage eröffnete einen neuen Weg für die Entwicklung des architektonischen Ausdrucks.

Die große Vielseitigkeit und Formbarkeit der vorgefertigten Strukturen und Elemente aus Sichtbeton, unterstützt durch die Weiterentwicklung des Materials als Ergebnis der technologischen Entwicklung, bietet den Architekten eine fast unbegrenzte Gestaltungsfreiheit. Seine besondere Materialität wird durch eine breite Palette von Oberflächen, Texturen und Farben ergänzt, deren einzigartige Qualitäten oft den Ausgangspunkt für den architektonischen Ansatz der Projekte bilden.

Da Beton trotz seiner anerkannten Robustheit, Langlebigkeit und Wartungsarmut traditionell als umweltfeindliches Material gilt, forschen viele Unternehmen derzeit an der Entwicklung von Betonen, die umweltfreundliche Komponenten enthalten und mit weniger umweltbelastenden Verfahren hergestellt werden.

Dieser Band enthält Arbeiten aus den fünf Kontinenten, in denen die suggestive Materialität des Sichtbetons nicht nur in den strukturellen Elementen, sondern auch als Gebäudehülle, als raumbestimmendes oder einfaches kompositorisches Element zum Ausdruck kommt, das jedoch in allen Fällen als grundlegendes Element im Gesamtdesign des Projekts steht.

L'évolution du béton au cours des siècles dans le domaine de la construction a connu un tournant important au début du XX^e siècle, lorsqu'il a dépassé sa vocation première de matériau structurel pour devenir un composant polyvalent pouvant être utilisé simultanément comme finition extérieure. La consolidation du système du béton armé et le développement d'éléments préfabriqués sur cette base ont ainsi ouvert une nouvelle voie pour le développement de l'expression architecturale.

La grande polyvalence et la facilité de moulage offertes par les structures et les éléments préfabriqués en béton apparent, soutenues par l'évolution du matériau résultant de son développement technologique, offrent aux professionnels de l'architecture une liberté de conception presque illimitée. Sa matérialité particulière est complétée par une large gamme de finitions, de textures et de couleurs, dont les qualités uniques constituent souvent un point de départ pour l'approche architecturale des projets.

Traditionnellement considéré comme un matériau peu respectueux de l'environnement malgré sa robustesse reconnue, sa durabilité et son faible entretien, de nombreuses entreprises développent actuellement des recherches visant à créer des bétons qui intègrent des composants bénéfiques pour l'environnement et qui sont fabriqués selon des procédés moins polluants.

Ce volume contient des œuvres provenant des cinq continents dans lesquelles la matérialité suggestive du béton apparent se manifeste non seulement dans les éléments structurels, mais aussi en tant qu'enveloppe du bâtiment, élément de définition de l'espace ou simple élément de composition, mais qui, dans tous les cas, constitue l'élément fondamental de la conception globale du projet.

La evolución del hormigón a lo largo de los siglos dentro del ámbito de la construcción alcanzó un significativo punto de inflexión a principios del siglo XX, momento en el que sobrepasó su original vocación como material estructural para transformarse en un versátil componente que podía ser utilizado simultáneamente como acabado exterior. La consolidación del sistema de hormigón armado y el desarrollo de elementos prefabricados basados en él abrían de esta manera una nueva vía al desarrollo de la expresión arquitectónica.

La gran versatilidad y la moldeabilidad que ofrecen las estructuras y los elementos prefabricados de hormigón visto, apoyadas en la evolución del material derivada de su desarrollo tecnológico, ponen a disposición de los profesionales de la arquitectura una libertad de diseño casi ilimitada. Su especial materialidad se ve complementada con un amplio abanico de acabados, texturas y colores, cuyas singulares cualidades ofrecen en muchas ocasiones un punto de partida al enfoque arquitectónico de los proyectos.

Tradicionalmente considerado como un material poco ecológico a pesar de su reconocida robustez, durabilidad y bajo mantenimiento, muchas empresas desarrollan en la actualidad investigaciones destinadas a crear hormigones integradores de componentes beneficiosos para el medio ambiente y fabricados mediante procesos menos contaminantes.

El presente volumen contiene obras de los cinco continentes en los que la sugestiva materialidad del hormigón visto se manifiesta no sólo en los elementos estructurales, sino también como envolvente de los edificios, definidor de espacios o simple elemento compositivo, pero que en todos los casos se erige como el elemento fundamental del diseño global del proyecto.

# ÂNGELA ROLDÃO Arquitetura

**Ângela Roldão**

instagram.com/angelaroldaoarquiteta

Ângela Roldão Arquitetura is a brazilian office based in Belo Horizonte. Ângela Roldão, who gratuated from UFRJ (the same university where Oscar Niemeyer studied, in Rio de Janeiro) has studied and worked both in Brazil and in Germany and has been working for almost forty years in the architecture and interior design field. The studio has projects in several cities in Brazil and abroad, and has been published in many websites, books and magazines all over the world. The will to innovate and create a modern and minimalist architecture are inseparable characteristics of the office's work. "When it comes to architecture, we always study a lot and venture a little further" - said Ângela. As each project is unique, we believe that it is essential to surprise, as the late brazilian architect Ruy Ohtake said: "if it does not mark an era or cause surprise and emotion, my work makes no sense".

Ângela Roldão Arquitetura ist ein brasilianisches Büro mit Sitz in Belo Horizonte. Ângela Roldão, Absolventin der UFRJ (der gleichen Universität, an der auch Oscar Niemeyer studierte, in Rio de Janeiro), hat sowohl in Brasilien als auch in Deutschland studiert und gearbeitet und ist seit fast vierzig Jahren in den Bereichen Architektur und Innenarchitektur tätig. Das Studio hat Projekte in mehreren Städten Brasiliens und im Ausland realisiert und wurde in vielen Websites, Büchern und Zeitschriften auf der ganzen Welt veröffentlicht. Der Wille zur Innovation und zur Schaffung einer modernen und minimalistischen Architektur sind untrennbare Merkmale der Arbeit des Büros. „Wenn es um Architektur geht, studieren wir immer viel und wagen uns ein bisschen weiter vor" - sagt Ângela. Da jedes Projekt einzigartig ist, glauben wir, dass es wichtig ist, zu überraschen, wie der verstorbene brasilianische Architekt Ruy Ohtake sagte: „Wenn es keine Epoche markiert, keine Überraschung und keine Emotionen hervorruft, hat meine Arbeit keinen Sinn".

Ângela Roldão Arquitetura est un cabinet brésilien basé à Belo Horizonte. Ângela Roldão, diplômée de l'UFRJ (la même université où Oscar Niemeyer a étudié, à Rio de Janeiro), a étudié et travaillé au Brésil et en Allemagne et exerce depuis près de quarante ans dans le domaine de l'architecture et du design d'intérieur. Le studio a des projets dans plusieurs villes au Brésil et à l'étranger, et a été publié sur de nombreux sites web, dans des livres et des magazines du monde entier. La volonté d'innover et de créer une architecture moderne et minimaliste sont des caractéristiques indissociables du travail du cabinet. « En ce qui concerne l'architecture, nous étudions toujours beaucoup et nous aventurons un peu plus loin » — a déclaré Ângela. Comme chaque projet est unique, nous croyons qu'il est essentiel de surprendre, comme l'a dit le regretté architecte brésilien Ruy Ohtake : « Si cela ne marque pas une époque, ne suscite pas de surprise et d'émotion, mon travail n'a aucun sens ».

Ângela Roldão Arquitetura es una oficina brasileña con sede en Belo Horizonte. Ângela Roldão, licenciada por la UFRJ (la misma universidad donde estudió Oscar Niemeyer, en Río de Janeiro) ha estudiado y trabajado tanto en Brasil como en Alemania y lleva casi cuarenta años trabajando en el campo de la arquitectura y el diseño de interiores. El estudio tiene proyectos en varias ciudades de Brasil y del extranjero, y ha publicado en numerosos sitios web, libros y revistas de todo el mundo. La voluntad de innovar y crear una arquitectura moderna y minimalista son características inseparables del trabajo del estudio. «Cuando se trata de arquitectura, siempre estudiamos mucho y nos aventuramos un poco más» —dice Ângela. Como cada proyecto es único, creemos que es esencial sorprender, como dijo el difunto arquitecto brasileño Ruy Ohtake: «si no marca una época o causa sorpresa y emoción, mi trabajo no tiene sentido».

# CONCRETE HOUSE

**Nova Lima, Minas Gerais, Brazil**

Photos: © Jomar Bragança

The Concrete House is the result of an effort to create a beautiful and functional residential project from a simple and rational structure of exposed concrete. The house was designed as a concrete and glass box. The first floor is where services and leisure are located. On the second floor is where the house truly is! Access is via the stairs in the entrance hall, with double height ceilings, which is introduced by a portico over a large pivot door. Upstairs are the dining, living and bedrooms, the kitchen, office and an inner courtyard. Between the rooms, a beautiful central external patio, with a tree in the middle. On the same floor, a concrete plan separates the intimate part of the house.
From the front facade it is possible to see the mountains through the entire building. The visual permeability of the glass enclosures made it possible to share the privileged view of the house with the street.

Das Concrete House ist das Ergebnis der Bemühungen, aus einer einfachen und rationalen Struktur aus Sichtbeton ein schönes und funktionales Wohnprojekt zu schaffen. Das Haus wurde als eine Box aus Beton und Glas entworfen. In der ersten Etage befinden sich Dienstleistungen und Freizeiteinrichtungen. In der zweiten Etage befindet sich das eigentliche Haus! Der Zugang erfolgt über die Treppe in der Eingangshalle mit doppelter Deckenhöhe, die durch einen Säulengang über eine große Drehtür eingeleitet wird. Im Obergeschoss befinden sich die Ess-, Wohn- und Schlafzimmer, die Küche, das Büro und ein Innenhof. Zwischen den Zimmern befindet sich ein schöner, zentraler Innenhof, in dessen Mitte ein Baum steht. Auf der gleichen Etage trennt ein Betonplan den intimen Teil des Hauses.
Von der vorderen Fassade aus kann man durch das gesamte Gebäude hindurch die Berge sehen. Durch die visuelle Durchlässigkeit der Glaseinfassungen konnte die privilegierte Aussicht des Hauses mit der Straße geteilt werden.

La Concrete House est le résultat d'un effort pour créer un projet résidentiel beau et fonctionnel à partir d'une structure simple et rationnelle en béton apparent. La maison a été conçue comme une boîte en béton et en verre. Le premier étage abrite les services et les loisirs. Le deuxième étage est là où se trouve la vraie maison ! L'accès se fait par l'escalier dans le hall d'entrée, avec des plafonds à double hauteur, introduit par un portique sur une grande porte pivotante. À l'étage se trouvent la salle à manger, le salon et les chambres, la cuisine, le bureau et une cour intérieure. Entre les pièces, un magnifique patio extérieur central, avec un arbre au milieu. Au même étage, un plan en béton sépare la partie intime de la maison.
De la façade avant, il est possible de voir les montagnes à travers tout le bâtiment. La perméabilité visuelle des enclos en verre a permis de partager la vue privilégiée de la maison avec la rue.

La Concrete House es el resultado de un esfuerzo por crear un proyecto residencial bello y funcional a partir de una estructura sencilla y racional de hormigón visto. El edificio fue diseñado como una caja de hormigón y vidrio. En la planta baja se sitúan las zonas de servicio y de ocio, pero es en la segunda planta donde realmente se sitúa la casa. Una puerta pivotante bajo un pórtico da acceso al hall de entrada a doble altura, que contiene la escalera principal. En el piso superior están el comedor, el salón y los dormitorios, la cocina y el despacho. Situado entre las habitaciones, un hermoso patio exterior contiene un árbol en su centro. En la misma planta, un plano vertical de hormigón delimita la parte más privada de la casa.
A través de la fachada frontal es posible ver las montañas desde de todo el edificio. La permeabilidad visual de los cerramientos acristalados permitió compartir la vista privilegiada de la casa con la calle.

**Awards:**
**Archello's Best Projects of 2022**

**Project team:**
Architect: Ângela Roldão
Collaborating architects: Thalita Mattos, Marina Rebelo

**Construction period:**
2021-2022

**Total built area:**
711 $m^2$

**General contractor:**
Construtora Privilège - Rogério Labriola

**Consultants:**
Window consultancy:
Bianca Di Franco Michell
Landscaping: Thiers Matos
Lighting design: Junia Carsalade

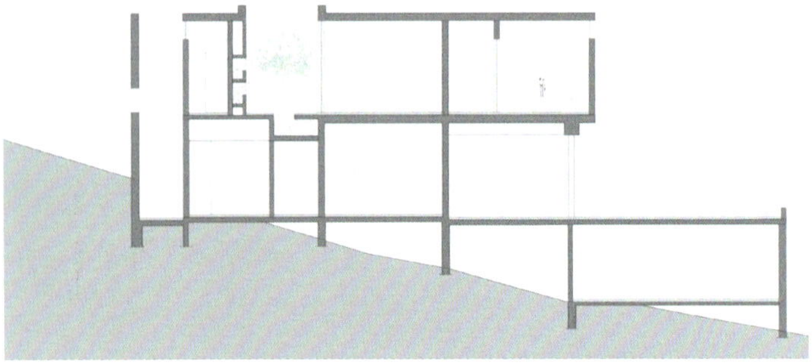

A-A section

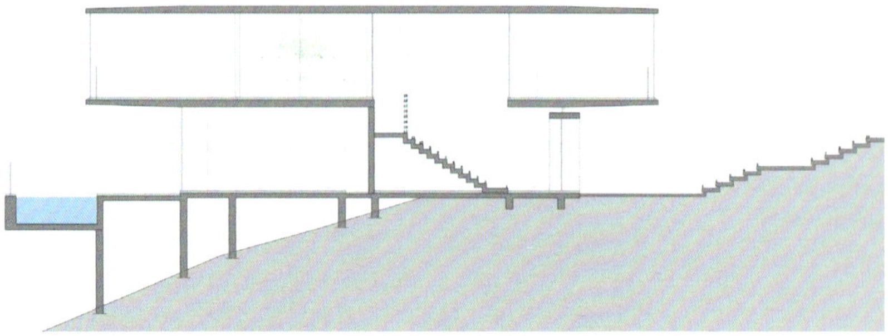

B-B section

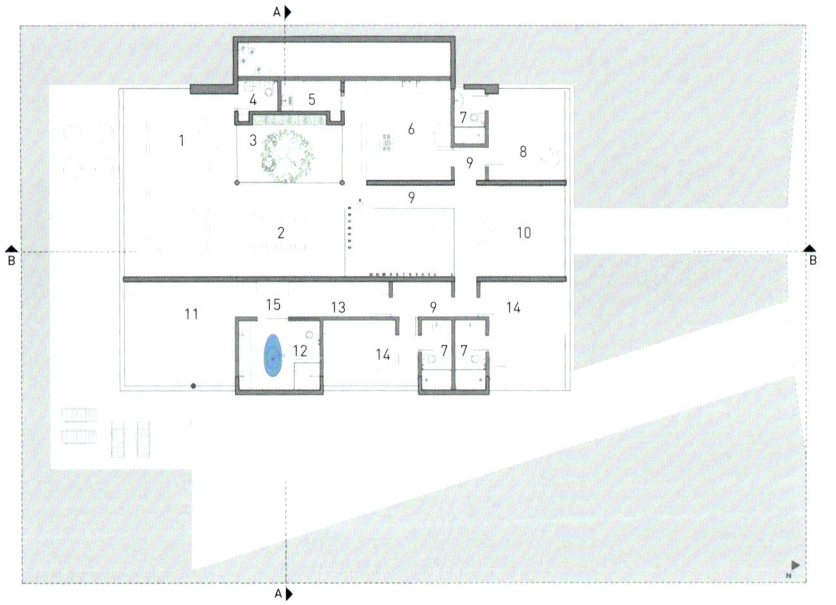

First floor plan

1. Living room
2. Dining room
3. Terrace
4. Toilet
5. Pantry
6. Kitchen
7. Bathroom
8. Library/study
9. Walkway
10. Living room
11. Master bedroom
12. Master bathroom
13. Closet
14. Bedroom
15. Corridor

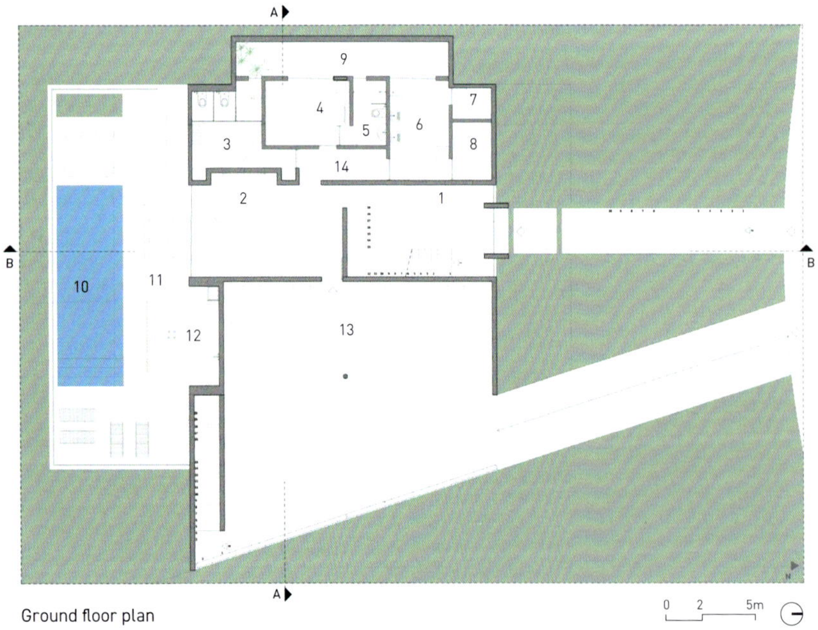


Ground floor plan

1. Hall
2. Living room
3. Dressing room
4. Guest room
5. Guest bathroom
6. Laundry
7. Pantry
8. Store
9. Terrace
10. Pool
11. Veranda
12. Gourmet kitchen
13. Garage
14. Corridor

# CAGE Atelier

**Ricardo Cardoso Ramos**

www.cageatelier.pt

CAGE is more than an Atelier. Created in 2016, based in Coimbra and Lisbon, CAGE is a mixed of experiences with Architecture and Design being the main areas of intervention. The relation with the client is our main focus when we are producing our work. We need to know them and what are their concerns and expectations. We believe that this areas needs to leave together and can share contents and have another relations with what the world can give to us.

CAGE ist mehr als ein Atelier. CAGE wurde 2016 gegründet und hat seinen Sitz in Coimbra und Lissabon. CAGE ist eine Mischung aus Erfahrungen, wobei Architektur und Design die Hauptinterventionsbereiche sind. Die Beziehung zum Kunden ist unser Hauptaugenmerk bei der Produktion unserer Arbeit. Wir müssen sie kennen und wissen, was ihre Anliegen und Erwartungen sind. Wir glauben, dass diese Bereiche gemeinsam verlassen werden müssen, um Inhalte zu teilen und eine andere Beziehung zu dem zu haben, was die Welt uns geben kann.

CAGE est plus qu'un atelier. Créé en 2016, basé à Coimbra et Lisbonne, CAGE est un mélange d'expériences avec l'architecture et le design comme principaux domaines d'intervention. La relation avec le client est notre principal objectif lorsque nous produisons notre travail. Nous devons les connaître et savoir quelles sont leurs préoccupations et leurs attentes. Nous pensons que ces domaines ont besoin de rester ensemble, de partager des contenus et d'avoir d'autres relations avec ce que le monde peut nous offrir.

CAGE es más que un Atelier. Creado en 2016, con sede en Coimbra y Lisboa, CAGE es una mezcla de experiencias siendo la Arquitectura y el Diseño las principales áreas de intervención. La relación con el cliente es nuestro principal foco cuando estamos produciendo nuestro trabajo. Necesitamos conocerlos y saber cuáles son sus preocupaciones y expectativas. Creemos que estas áreas necesitan salir juntas y pueden compartir contenidos y tener otras relaciones con lo que el mundo puede darnos.

# CONCRETE 11

Lisbon, Portugal

Photos: © Ivo Tavares Studio

CONCRETE 11 was born from the desire to live in harmony with both downtown Lisbon and the surrounding nature. An urban house that offers the same level of connection with nature as a country house.
Urban and landscape integration was ensured through the materials used on the facades, which camouflage the house in the terrain. The steep slope of the plot allowed the building to function as two superimposed layers: one embedded in the ground serving as a base and another floating above it, materialized in a white concrete volume with horizontal openings that house the common areas of the residence. The interior design creates a relaxed and welcoming atmosphere, giving the house unique, modern, and serene characteristics. The customization of all aspects of the design provided the owners with a home they can proudly call their own.

**Project team:**
Cage Atelier

**Construction period:**
2020-2022

**Total built area:**
540 m$^2$

CONCRETE 11 entstand aus dem Wunsch, sowohl im Zentrum von Lissabon als auch in der umgebenden Natur im Einklang zu leben. Ein Stadthaus, das die gleiche Verbindung zur Natur bietet wie ein Landhaus.
Die städtische und landschaftliche Integration wurde durch die für die Fassaden verwendeten Materialien gewährleistet, die das Haus in der Umgebung verschmelzen lassen. Die steile Hanglage des Grundstücks ermöglichte es dem Gebäude, als zwei übereinanderliegende Schichten zu funktionieren: eine, die in den Boden eingebettet ist und als Basis dient, und eine andere, die darüber schwebt und in einem weißen Betonvolumen mit horizontalen Öffnungen materialisiert ist, die die Gemeinschaftsbereiche des Hauses beherbergen. Das Innendesign schafft eine entspannte und einladende Atmosphäre und verleiht dem Haus gleichzeitig einzigartige, moderne und ruhige Merkmale. Die Anpassung aller Aspekte des Designs ermöglichte es den Eigentümern, ein Zuhause zu besitzen, auf das sie stolz sein können.

CONCRETE 11 est né du désir de vivre en harmonie avec le centre de Lisbonne et la nature environnante. Une maison de ville qui offre le même niveau de connexion avec la nature qu'une maison de campagne.
L'intégration urbaine et paysagère a été assurée par les matériaux utilisés sur les façades, qui fondent la maison dans le terrain. La forte pente de la parcelle a permis au bâtiment de fonctionner comme deux couches superposées : une encastrée dans le sol servant de base, et une autre flottant au-dessus en forme de volume en béton blanc avec des ouvertures horizontales abritant les espaces communs de la maison. La conception intérieure crée une atmosphère détendue et accueillante tout en conférant à la maison des caractéristiques modernes et sereines. La personnalisation de tous les aspects de la conception a permis aux propriétaires de posséder fièrement une maison qui leur est propre.

CONCRETE 11 nace del deseo de vivir en armonía tanto con el centro de Lisboa como con la Naturaleza que la rodea. Una casa urbana que ofrece el mismo nivel de conexión con la Naturaleza que una casa de campo.
La integración urbana y paisajística se garantizó a través de los materiales utilizados en las fachadas, que camuflan la casa en el terreno. La acusada pendiente de la parcela hizo posible que el edificio funcionara como dos capas superpuestas: una que se incrusta en el terreno y sirve de base y otra que levita sobre la primera y que se materializa en un volumen de hormigón blanco con huecos horizontales que alberga las zonas comunes de la vivienda. El diseño de los interiores genera un ambiente relajado y acogedor, dotando al mismo tiempo a la casa de unas características únicas, modernas y serenas. La personalización de todos los aspectos del diseño proporcionó a los propietarios un hogar que pueden llamar orgullosamente suyo.

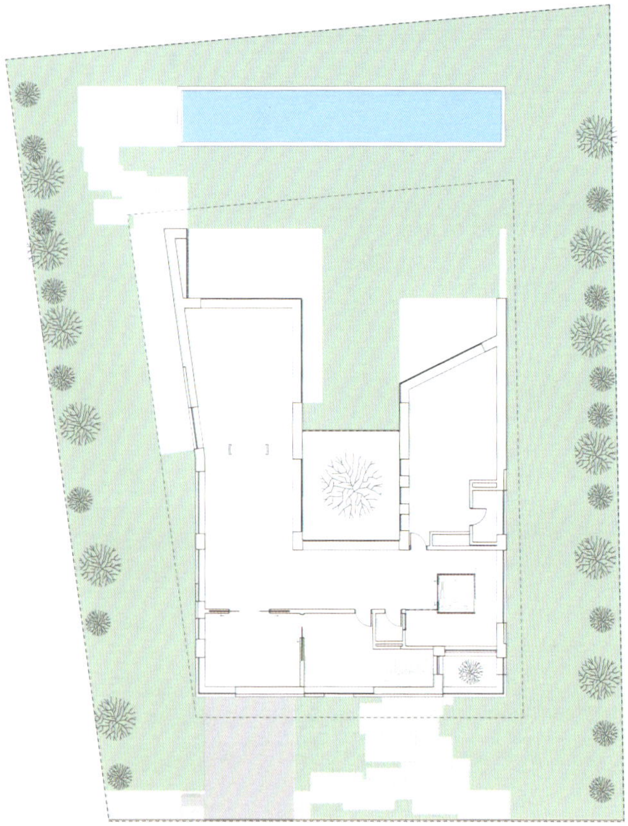

First floor plan

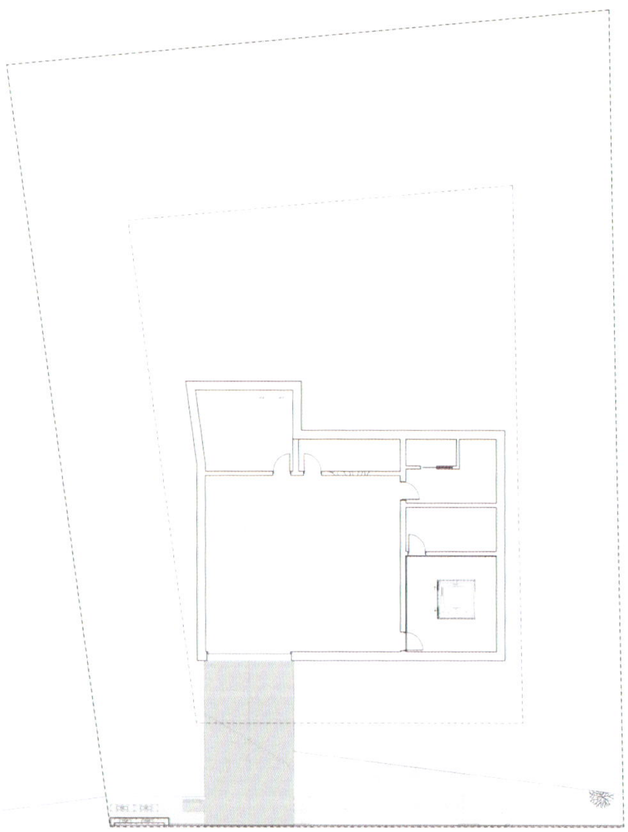

Basement plan

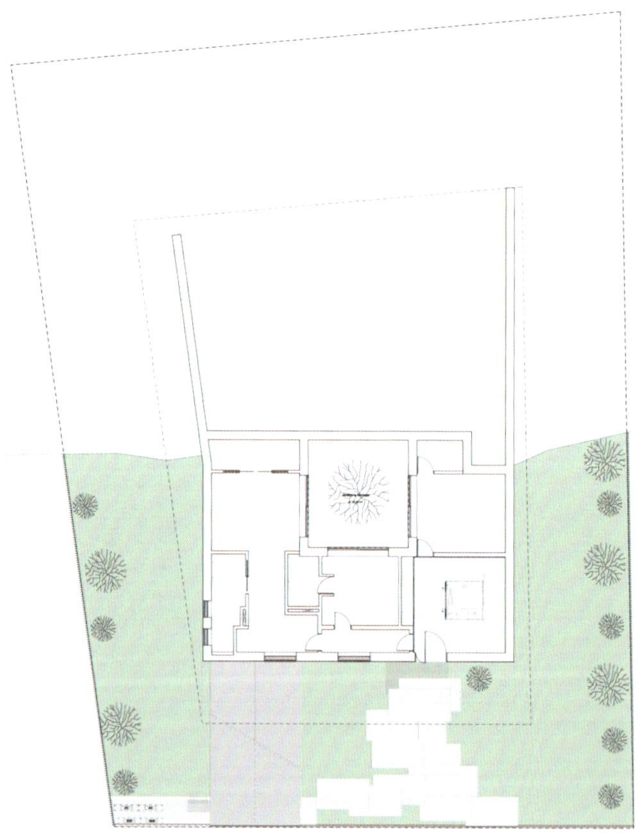

Ground floor plan

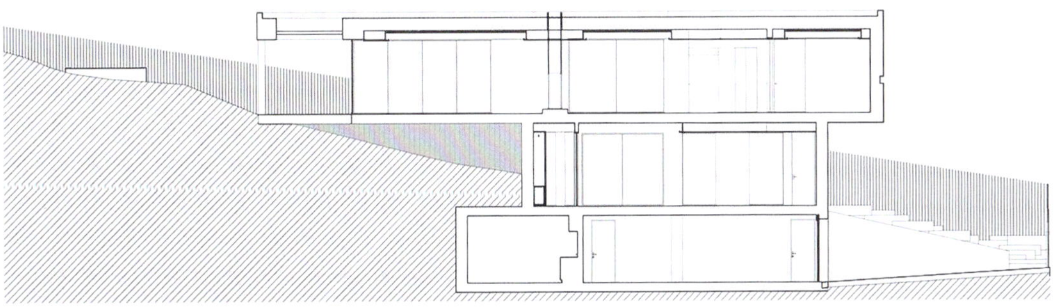

Section

## CAIO PERSIGHINI Arquitetura & Design

Caio Persighini

www.caiopersighini.com

Present since 2013, Studio Caio Persighini Arquitetura & Design develops architectural projects with the aim of providing clients with access to a unique and singular architecture.

Based on the conviction that architecture can exist in any place, proportion, budget or individual, we are guided to face the precepts and prototypes that incessantly disguise other possibilities. We spare no creative capacity to provide great meaning in places where architecture is not expected to be found.

We strive to express architecture in the places we work and, in the desires and principles of the people and institutions we serve.

Das seit 2013 bestehende Studio Caio Persighini Arquitetura & Design entwickelt architektonische Projekte mit dem Ziel, den Kunden Zugang zu einzigartiger und einzigartiger Architektur zu verschaffen.

Ausgehend von der Überzeugung, dass Architektur an jedem Ort, in jeder Proportion, mit jedem Budget und jeder Person existieren kann, lassen wir uns von den Vorgaben und Prototypen leiten, die immer wieder andere Möglichkeiten verschleiern. Wir scheuen keine schöpferische Kraft, um den Orten, an denen man keine Architektur erwartet, eine große Bedeutung zu verleihen.

Wir bemühen uns, die Architektur an den Orten, an denen wir arbeiten, und in den Wünschen und Prinzipien der Menschen und Institutionen, denen wir dienen, zum Ausdruck zu bringen.

Présent depuis 2013, le Studio Caio Persighini Arquitetura & Design développe des projets architecturaux dans le but d'offrir aux clients l'accès à une architecture unique et singulière.
Partant de la conviction que l'architecture peut exister dans n'importe quel lieu, proportion, budget ou individu, nous sommes guidés pour affronter les préceptes et les prototypes qui déguisent sans cesse d'autres possibilités. Nous n'épargnons aucune capacité créative pour donner un sens fort à des lieux où l'architecture n'est pas attendue.
Nous nous efforçons d'exprimer l'architecture dans les lieux où nous travaillons, ainsi que dans les désirs et les principes des personnes et des institutions que nous servons.

Presente desde 2013, Studio Caio Persighini Arquitetura & Design desarrolla proyectos arquitectónicos con el objetivo de proporcionar a los clientes el acceso a una arquitectura única y singular.
Partiendo de la convicción de que la arquitectura puede existir en cualquier lugar, proporción, presupuesto o individuo, nos guiamos para hacer frente a los preceptos y prototipos que disfrazan incesantemente otras posibilidades. No escatimamos capacidad creativa para dotar de gran significado a lugares donde no se espera encontrar arquitectura.
Nos esforzamos por expresar la arquitectura en los lugares donde trabajamos y en los deseos y principios de las personas e instituciones a las que servimos.

# CASA PATIO

**Araraquara, São Paulo, Brazil**

Photos: © Favaro JR.

This project arose from an in-depth reading of the plot and its topography. Its width and slight slope generated a house developed on different levels and with a central open space that constituted one of the premises of the commission.
The use of in-situ concrete not only determines the materiality of the building, but also takes into account the constructive dynamics, the architectural reasoning and the structure. The circulation in the house is extremely dynamic and fluid. The foyer functions as the distribution centre of the house and from it the central courtyard can be seen, framed between the two parallel blocks of the building. The social area is conceived as an open space that extends outwards. The use of brise-soleils in the rooms adapts the "muxarabi" principle, which allows residents to enjoy the surrounding landscape but prevents exposure to views from the outside.

Dieses Projekt entstand aus einer eingehenden Betrachtung des Grundstücks und seiner Topografie. Die Breite des Grundstücks und die leichte Neigung des Geländes führten zu einem Haus, das auf verschiedenen Ebenen und mit einer zentralen Freifläche entwickelt wurde, die eine der Prämissen des Auftrags darstellte.
Die Verwendung von Ortbeton bestimmt nicht nur die Materialität des Gebäudes, sondern berücksichtigt auch die konstruktive Dynamik, die architektonischen Überlegungen und die Struktur. Die Zirkulation im Haus ist äußerst dynamisch und fließend. Das Foyer fungiert als Verteilerzentrum des Hauses, von dem aus man den zentralen Innenhof sehen kann, der zwischen den beiden parallelen Blöcken des Gebäudes eingefasst ist. Der Sozialbereich ist als offener Raum gestaltet, der sich nach außen erstreckt. Durch die Verwendung von Brise-Soleils in den Zimmern wird das „Muxarabi"-Prinzip adaptiert, das den Bewohnern den Blick auf die umgebende Landschaft ermöglicht, aber den Blick nach außen verhindert.

Ce projet est né d'une lecture approfondie du terrain et de sa topographie. Sa largeur et sa légère pente ont généré une maison développée sur différents niveaux et avec un espace central ouvert qui constituait l'une des prémisses de la commission.
L'utilisation du béton coulé sur place ne détermine pas seulement la matérialité du bâtiment, mais prend également en compte la dynamique constructive, le raisonnement architectural et la structure. La circulation dans la maison est extrêmement dynamique et fluide. Le foyer fonctionne comme le centre de distribution de la maison et, de là, on peut voir la cour centrale, encadrée entre les deux blocs parallèles du bâtiment. La zone sociale est configurée comme un espace ouvert qui s'étend vers l'extérieur. L'utilisation de brise-soleil dans les chambres adapte le principe du « muxarabi », qui permet aux résidents de profiter du paysage environnant tout en empêchant l'exposition aux vues de l'extérieur.

Este proyecto surge de la lectura en profundidad de la parcela y su topografía. Su anchura y su ligera pendiente generaron una vivienda desarrollada en diferentes niveles y con un espacio abierto central que constituía una de las premisas del encargo.
El uso de hormigón in situ no sólo determina la materialidad del edificio, sino que también tiene en cuenta la dinámica constructiva, el razonamiento arquitectónico y la estructura. La circulación en la casa es extremadamente dinámica y fluida. El vestíbulo funciona como centro de distribución de la casa y desde él se contempla el patio central, enmarcado entre los dos bloques paralelos del edificio. La zona social se configura como un espacio abierto que se prologa hacia el exterior. La utilización de brise-soleils en las habitaciones adapta el principio del «muxarabi», que permite a los residentes disfrutar del paisaje circundante pero impide la exposición a las vistas desde el exterior.

**Project team:**
Laisi Fassini, Bruna Caires, Felipe Orocini

**Construction period:**
2022

**Total built area:**
268 m$^2$

**Structural engineer:**
Rodolpho Maia

**Management/execution:**
Raphael Oprime

**Landscaping:**
Angela Bonancin

**Constructor:**
Ailton Felipe de Oliveira

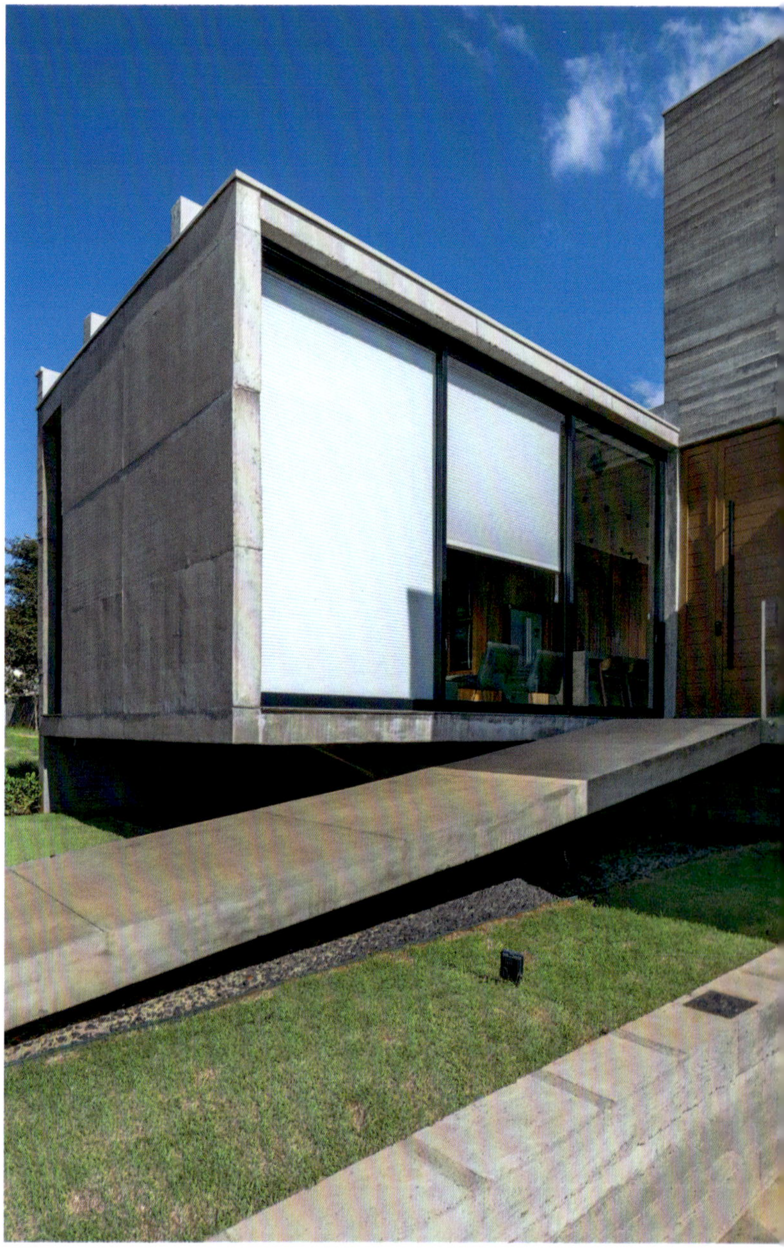

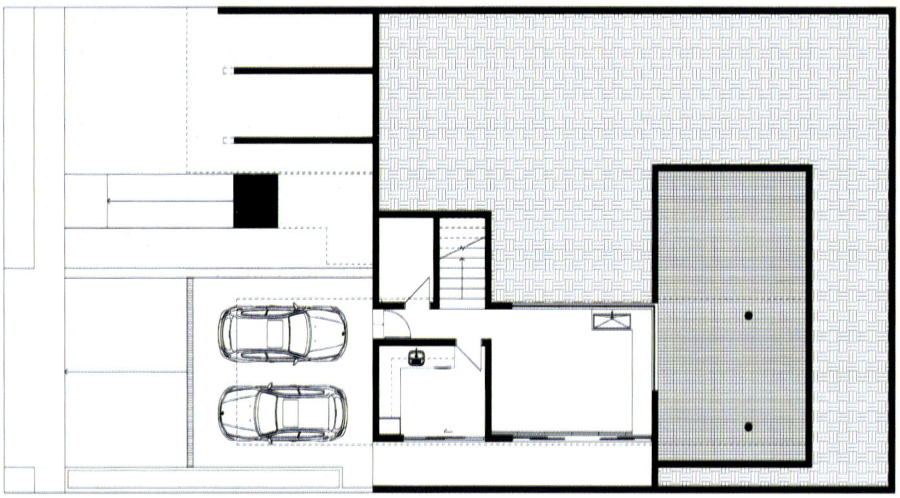

Ground floor plan

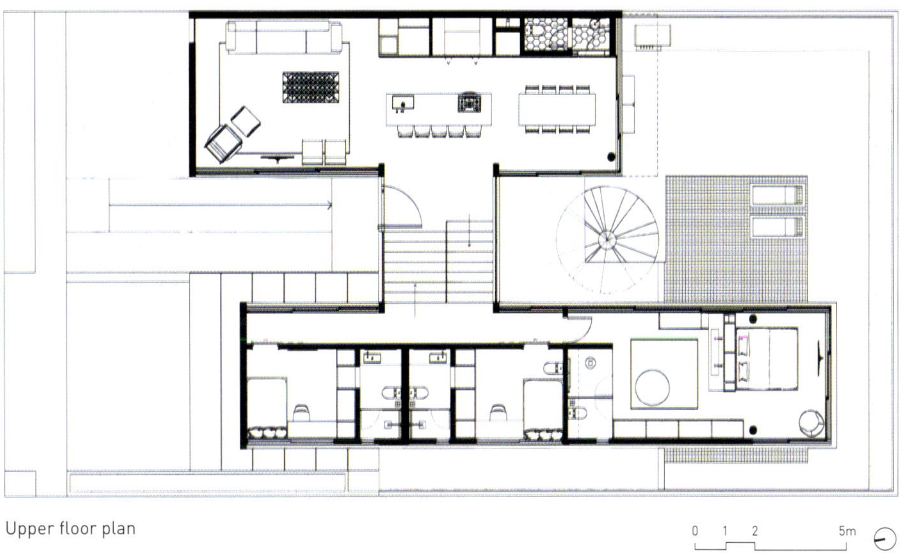


Upper floor plan

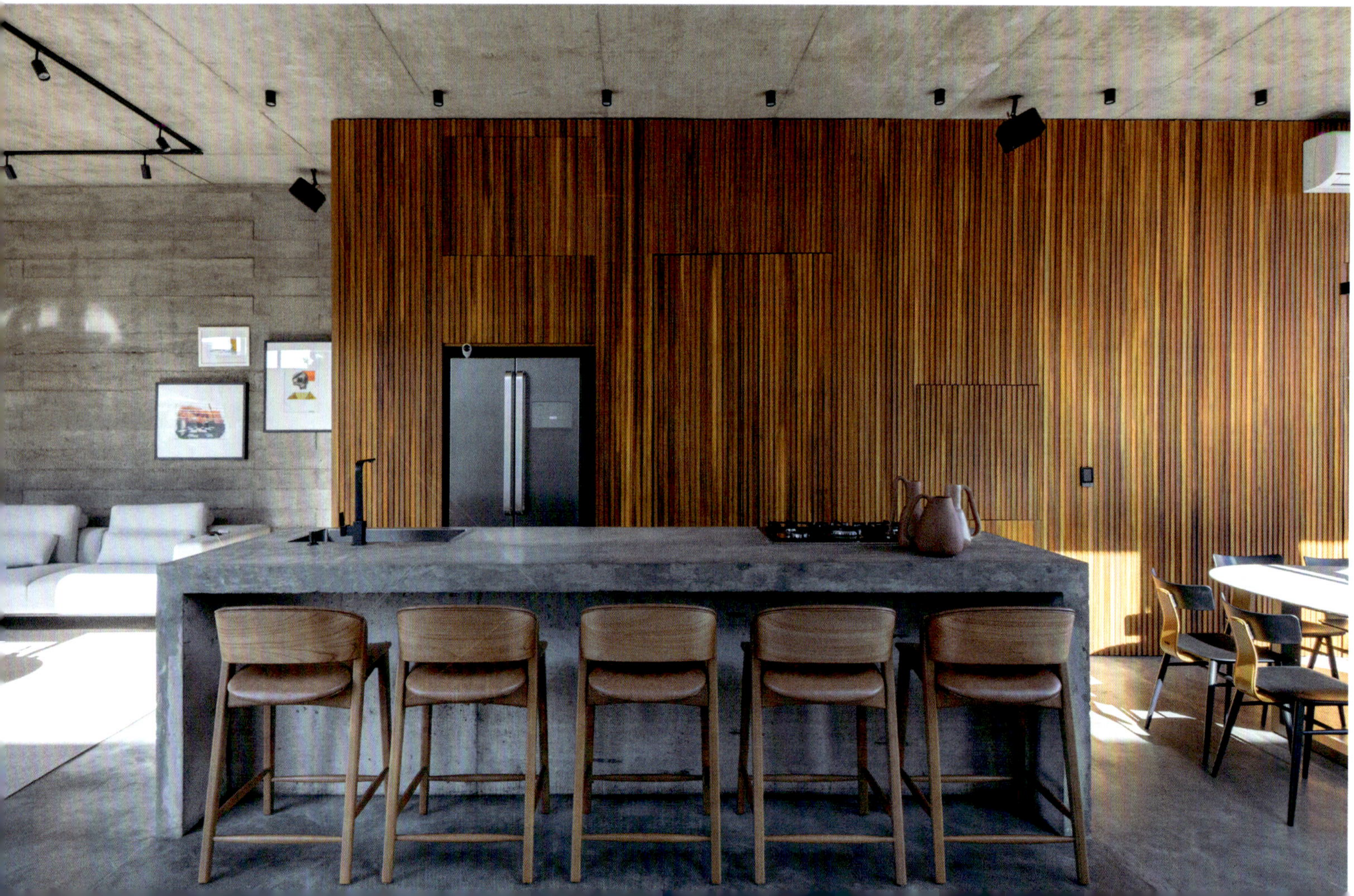

## Design Group COLLABO

**JOUNG Moon Chul**

www.dgcollabo.com

JOUNG Moon Chul was born in Seoul, South Korea, in 1972. Graduated from the E.S.A.G-PENNINGHEN, School of Interior Architecture in Paris in 2001. Graduated from the L'École nationale supérieure d'architecture de Paris-La Villette (ENSAPLV) in 2007.

He worked Wilmote & Associes and Architecture Studio in Paris, (2006-2008). He created Design Group COLLABO in South Korea in 2012. In South Korea he worked on numerous house and commercial spaces. Neungpo commercial (Geojedo 2014-2015), House DAM (Gyeonggido, 2014-2015), Siyeonjae house (Seoul, 2015-2016), 36th Seoul Metropolitan Government Architecture Award for Excellence, Gyeongwonjae house (Seoul, 2016-2017) House L.M. (Incheon 2018-2019) Rock Fild (Incheon 2019-2020) House H (Gyeonggido, 2021-2022), Vazzo Terrace (Busan 2021-2022).

JOUNG Moon Chul wurde 1972 in Seoul, Südkorea, geboren. Abschluss an der E.S.A.G-PENNINGHEN, Schule für Innenarchitektur in Paris im Jahr 2001. 2007 schloss er sein Studium an der L'École nationale supérieure d'architecture de Paris-La Villette (ENSAPLV) ab.

Er arbeitete bei Wilmote & Associes und Architecture Studio in Paris (2006-2008). 2012 gründete er die Design Group COLLABO in Südkorea. In Südkorea arbeitete er an zahlreichen Wohn- und Geschäftsräumen. Neungpo commercial (Geojedo 2014-2015), House DAM (Gyeonggido, 2014-2015), Siyeonjae house (Seoul, 2015-2016), 36th Seoul Metropolitan Government Architecture Award for Excellence, Gyeongwonjae house (Seoul, 2016-2017) House L.M. (Incheon 2018-2019) Rock Fild (Incheon 2019-2020) House H (Gyeonggido, 2021-2022), Vazzo Terrace (Busan 2021-2022).

JOUNG Moon Chul est né à Séoul, en Corée du Sud, en 1972. Diplômé de l'E.S.A.G-PENNINGHEN, École d'architecture d'intérieur à Paris en 2001. Diplômé de l'École nationale supérieure d'architecture de Paris-La Villette (ENSAPLV) en 2007.

Il a travaillé chez Wilmote & Associes et Architecture Studio à Paris (2006-2008). Il a créé le Design Group COLLABO en Corée du Sud en 2012.

En Corée du Sud, il a travaillé sur de nombreuses maisons et espaces commerciaux. Neungpo commercial (Geojedo 2014-2015), Maison DAM (Gyeonggido, 2014-2015), Maison Siyeonjae (Séoul, 2015-2016), 36e Prix d'excellence en architecture de la Ville métropolitaine de Séoul, Maison Gyeongwonjae (Séoul, 2016-2017), Maison L.M. (Incheon 2018-2019), Rock Fild (Incheon 2019-2020), Maison H (Gyeonggido, 2021-2022), Terrasse Vazzo (Busan 2021-2022).

JOUNG Moon Chul nació en Seúl (Corea del Sur) en 1972. Se graduó en la Escuela de Arquitectura Interior E.S.A.G-PENNINGHEN de París en 2001 y en la Escuela Nacional Superior de Arquitectura de París-La Villette (ENSAPLV) en 2007.

Trabajó en Wilmote & Associes y en Architecture Studio de París, (2006-2008). Creó el grupo de diseño COLLABO en Corea del Sur en 2012.

En Corea del Sur trabajó en numerosas casas y espacios comerciales. Neungpo Commercial (Geojedo 2014-2015), Casa DAM (Gyeonggido, 2014-2015), Casa Siyeonjae (Seúl, 2015-2016), 36º Premio de Arquitectura a la Excelencia del Gobierno Metropolitano de Seúl, Casa Gyeongwonjae (Seúl, 2016-2017) Casa L.M. (Incheon 2018-2019) Rock Fild (Incheon 2019-2020) Casa H (Gyeonggido, 2021-2022), Terraza Vazzo (Busan 2021-2022).

# HOUSE L.M.

**Chanradong, Seo-gu, Incheon, Republic of Korea**

Photos: © JaeYoun Kim

This residence is located facing a golf course oriented to the south. To maximize panoramic views from the interior, the functional program extends along the southern facade, where a play of false walls and concrete slats frames the views and controls the entry of natural light.
On the other facades, openings are minimized, offering a more monolithic appearance. The north facade is fragmented into three parts that break the monotony of the block, one of which guides access to the interior of the house and obstructs views from the street. This gesture creates a journey from the exterior that represents an exciting visual and spatial change culminating in the open, elevated area of the staircase and the views over the living room's landscape. Inside, the staircase becomes a place of interaction that provides small yet diverse visual experiences.

Diese Immobilie befindet sich gegenüber einem nach Süden ausgerichteten Golfplatz. Um den Panoramablick vom Innenraum aus zu maximieren, wird das Funktionsprogramm entlang der Südfassade eingesetzt, wo eine Reihe von Zwischenwänden und Betonlamellen die Aussicht einrahmen und dazu beitragen, den Einfall von natürlichem Licht zu steuern.
An den übrigen Fassaden sind die Öffnungen auf ein Minimum reduziert und bieten ein eher monolithisches Erscheinungsbild. Die Nordfassade ist in drei Teile gegliedert, die die Monotonie des Blocks aufbrechen, von denen einer den Zugang zum Inneren der Wohnung regelt und den Blick von der Straße aus verhindert. Diese Geste erzeugt einen Weg von außen, der eine spannende visuelle und räumliche Veränderung darstellt, die in der offenen Höhe des Treppenhauses und in den Ausblicken auf die Landschaft vom Wohnzimmer aus gipfelt. Im Inneren wird die Treppe zu einem Ort der Interaktion, der kleine, aber vielfältige visuelle Erfahrungen ermöglicht.

Cette maison est située en face d'un terrain de golf orienté au sud. Afin de maximiser les vues panoramiques depuis l'intérieur, le programme fonctionnel est déployé le long de la façade sud, sur laquelle un jeu de faux murs et de lames de béton encadre les vues et permet de contrôler l'entrée de la lumière naturelle.
Sur le reste des façades, les ouvertures sont réduites au minimum, offrant un aspect plus monolithique. La façade nord est fragmentée en trois parties qui rompent la monotonie du bloc, dont l'une guide l'accès à l'intérieur de la maison et empêche les vues depuis la rue. Ce geste génère un parcours depuis l'extérieur qui représente un changement visuel et spatial passionnant qui culmine dans la hauteur ouverte de l'escalier et dans les vues sur le paysage depuis le salon. À l'intérieur, l'escalier devient un lieu d'interaction qui offre des expériences visuelles petites mais variées.

Esta vivienda se ubica frente a un campo de golf orientado hacia el sur. Para potenciar al máximo las vistas panorámicas desde el interior, el programa funcional se despliega a lo largo de la fachada sur, sobre la que un juego de falsos muros y lamas de hormigón enmarca las visuales y ayuda a controlar la entrada de luz natural.
En el resto de fachadas las aberturas se reducen al mínimo, ofreciendo un aspecto más monolítico. La fachada norte se fragmenta en tres partes que rompen la monotonía del bloque, una de las cuales guía el acceso al interior de la vivienda e impide las vistas desde la calle. Este gesto genera un recorrido desde el exterior que representa un emocionante cambio visual y espacial que culmina en el ámbito abierto en altura de la escalera y en las vistas sobre el paisaje de la sala de estar. En el interior, la escalera se convierte en un lugar de interacción que proporciona pequeñas pero diversas experiencias visuales.

**Project team:**
Cheol Kwan KIM

**Construction period:**
2018-2020

**Total built area:**
390.51 m$^2$

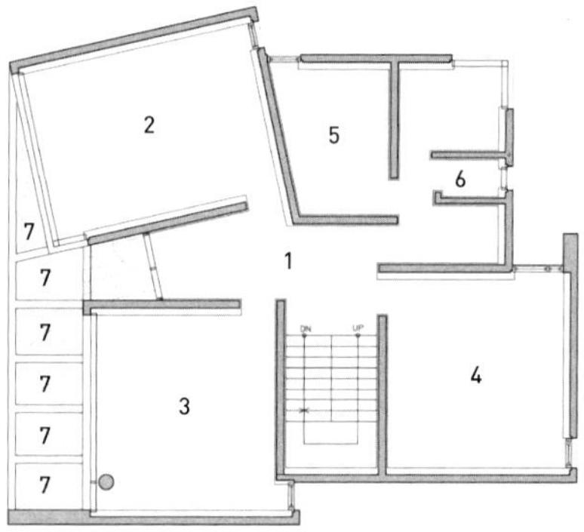

Second floor plan

1. Corridor 02
2. Bedroom 02
3. Bedroom 03
4. Audio room
5. Dressroom 02
6. Toilet
7. Void

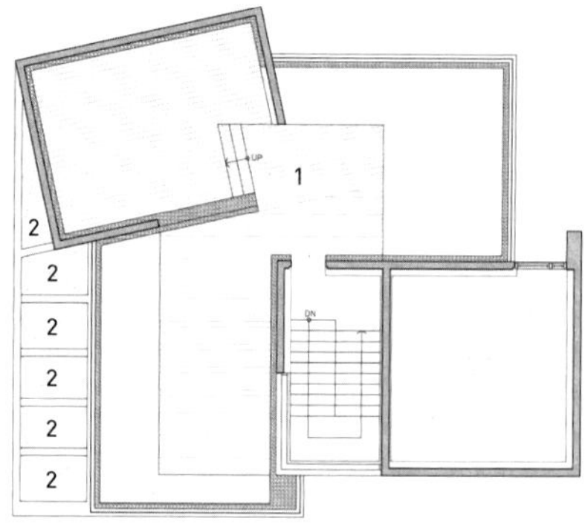

Third floor plan

1. Rooftop terrace
2. Void

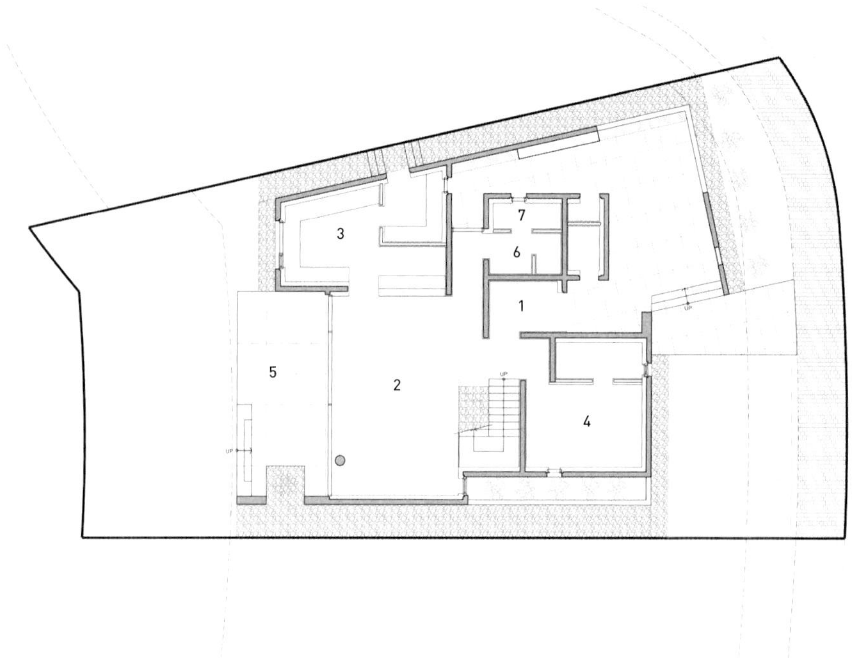

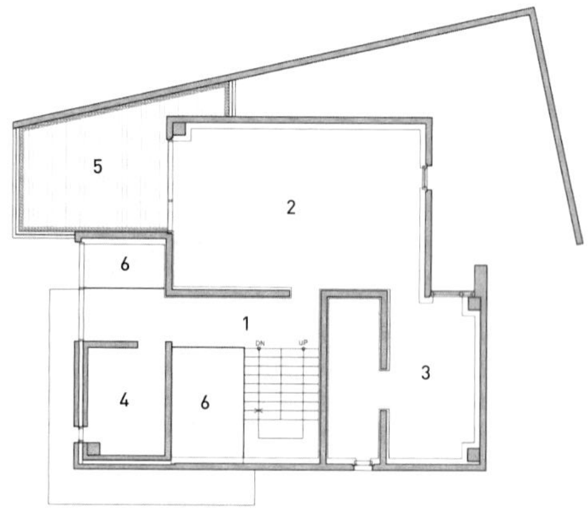

First floor plan

1. Corridor 01
2. Bedroom 01
3. Dressroom 01
4. Prayer room
5. Terrace
6. Void

Ground floor plan

1. Entrance
2. Living room
3. Kitchen
4. Guest room
5. Terrace
6. Toilet
7. Laundry room

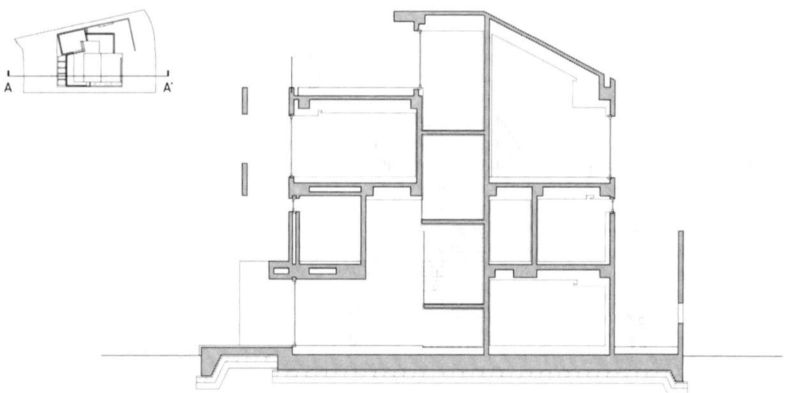

A-A' section

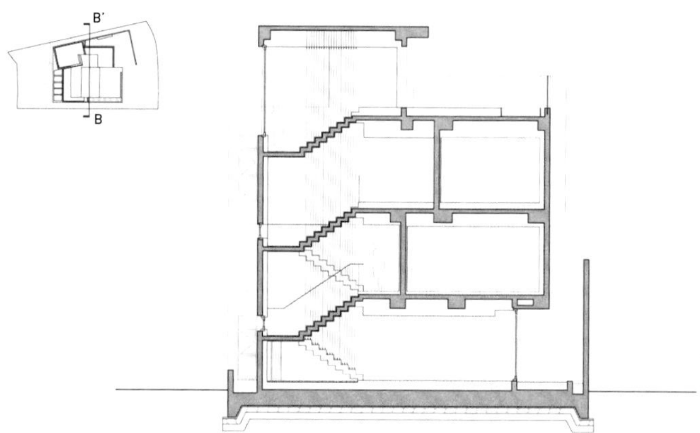

# GRAUX & BAEYENS architecten

**Basile Graux, Koen Baeyens**

www.graux-baeyens.be

GRAUX & BAEYENS architecten was established in 2005 in Ghent, Belgium, by Koen Baeyens and Basile Graux. The practice operates in the field of contemporary architecture, interior and product design and has developed a distinct architectural vision during the last 20 years.

GBA strives to create ideas that result in one clear concept that emerge through continuous questioning and production. From the start, they resolutely opted for a total approach: from urban scale to the interior and its details. This approach results in a sometimes atypical plan and structure, surprising but always with strongly coherent, recognizable and functional spatialities.

The context of building in a saturated Flanders inspires GBA to create its own architectural language, giving answers to the contemporary urban complexity with an apparent simplicity.

GRAUX & BAEYENS architecten wurde 2005 in Gent, Belgien, von Koen Baeyens und Basile Graux gegründet. Das Büro ist im Bereich zeitgenössischer Architektur, Innenarchitektur und Produktdesign tätig und hat in den letzten 20 Jahren eine eigenständige architektonische Vision entwickelt.

GBA strebt danach, Ideen zu entwickeln, die in einem klaren Konzept münden, das durch kontinuierliches Hinterfragen und Produzieren entsteht. Von Anfang an haben sie sich entschieden für einen ganzheitlichen Ansatz: von der städtischen Ebene bis hin zum Interieur und seinen Details. Dieser Ansatz führt manchmal zu einem untypischen Plan und einer Struktur, die überraschend, aber immer mit stark kohärenten, wiedererkennbaren und funktionalen Raumgestaltungen sind.

Der Kontext des Bauens in einem gesättigten Flandern inspiriert GBA dazu, eine eigene architektonische Sprache zu entwickeln, die Antworten auf die zeitgenössische urbane Komplexität mit einer scheinbaren Einfachheit bietet.

GRAUX & BAEYENS architecten a été créé en 2005 à Gand, en Belgique, par Koen Baeyens et Basile Graux. La pratique opère dans le domaine de l'architecture contemporaine, du design d'intérieur et de produits, et a développé une vision architecturale distincte au cours des 20 dernières années.

GBA s'efforce de créer des idées qui aboutissent à un concept clair émergeant grâce à une interrogation et une production continues. Dès le départ, ils ont résolument opté pour une approche globale : de l'échelle urbaine à l'intérieur et à ses détails. Cette approche se traduit parfois par un plan et une structure atypiques, surprenants mais toujours avec des spatialités fortement cohérentes, reconnaissables et fonctionnelles.

Le contexte de construction dans une Flandre saturée inspire GBA à créer son propre langage architectural, apportant des réponses à la complexité urbaine contemporaine avec une apparente simplicité.

GRAUX & BAEYENS architecten fue fundado en 2005 en Gante, Bélgica, por Koen Baeyens y Basile Graux. El estudio opera en el campo de la arquitectura contemporánea, el diseño de interiores y productos y ha desarrollado una visión arquitectónica distintiva durante los últimos 20 años.

GBA se esfuerza por crear ideas que resulten en un concepto claro que emerja a través de una continua interrogación y producción. Desde el principio, optaron decididamente por un enfoque integral: desde la escala urbana hasta el interior y sus detalles. Este enfoque da como resultado a veces un plan y una estructura atípicos, sorprendentes pero siempre con espacialidades fuertemente coherentes, reconocibles y funcionales.

El contexto de construcción en una Flandes saturada inspira a GBA a crear su propio lenguaje arquitectónico, ofreciendo respuestas a la complejidad urbana contemporánea con una aparente simplicidad.

# HOUSE B - T

## Meilegem, Belgium

Photos: © Dennis De Smet

The premise of this project was the clients' request to build a house to live in for the rest of their lives, designed with a brutalist aesthetic of exposed concrete.
The building presents itself as an expressive ensemble composed of three plateaus that form spacious terraces and provide protection from the sun, with large windows situated between them. The robustness of its exterior cladding and the size of the platforms are combined with interventions more in line with the residents' scale. The ground floor houses auxiliary spaces and a dwelling for a potential caregiver or family, while the first floor accommodates the owners' residence, which features an attractive open space containing the common areas. The raw concrete finishes both indoors and outdoors blend stylishly with elegant details and finishes, as well as the natural materials of the specially designed furniture and windows for the project.

Die Prämisse dieses Projekts war die Bitte der Kunden, ein Haus zu bauen, in dem sie den Rest ihres Lebens verbringen könnten, gestaltet mit einer brutalistischen Ästhetik aus sichtbarem Beton.
Das Gebäude präsentiert sich als ein ausdrucksstarkes Ensemble, bestehend aus drei Plateaus, die geräumige Terrassen bilden und vor der Sonne schützen, sowie großen Fenstern dazwischen. Die Robustheit seiner äußeren Verkleidung und die Größe der Plattformen werden mit Eingriffen kombiniert, die besser zur Größe der Bewohner passen. Das Erdgeschoss beherbergt Nebenräume und eine Wohnung für einen möglichen Betreuer oder eine Familie, während das erste Obergeschoss die Wohnung der Eigentümer beherbergt, in der sich ein attraktiver offener Raum befindet, der die gemeinsamen Bereiche umfasst. Die groben Betonoberflächen im Innen- und Außenbereich harmonieren stilvoll mit eleganten Details und Oberflächen sowie mit den natürlichen Materialien der speziell für das Projekt entworfenen Möbel und Fenster.

La prémisse de ce projet était la demande des clients de construire une maison pour y vivre le reste de leur vie, conçue avec une esthétique brutaliste en béton apparent.
Le bâtiment se présente comme un ensemble expressif composé de trois plateaux formant de vastes terrasses qui offrent une protection contre le soleil, avec de grandes fenêtres situées entre elles. La robustesse de son revêtement extérieur et la taille des plates-formes sont combinées avec des interventions plus adaptées à l'échelle des résidents. Le rez-de-chaussée abrite des espaces auxiliaires et une habitation pour un éventuel gardien ou une famille, tandis que le premier étage loge la résidence des propriétaires, avec un espace ouvert attrayant contenant les espaces communs. Les finitions en béton brut à l'intérieur et à l'extérieur se marient avec élégance avec des détails et des finitions raffinés, ainsi qu'avec les matériaux naturels des meubles et des fenêtres spécialement conçus pour le projet.

La premisa de este proyecto fue la petición de los clientes de construir una casa para vivir el resto de sus vidas, diseñada con una estética brutalista de hormigón visto.
El edificio se presenta como un expresivo conjunto compuesto por tres mesetas que forman amplias terrazas y protegen del sol y por los grandes ventanales situados entre ellas. La robustez de su revestimiento exterior y el tamaño de las plataformas se combinan con actuaciones a escala más acorde con los residentes. La planta baja aloja espacios auxiliares y una vivienda para un eventual cuidador o una familia, mientras que la planta primera alberga la vivienda de los propietarios, en la que se despliega un atractivo espacio abierto que contiene las zonas comunes. Los acabados de hormigón en bruto interiores y exteriores combinan con estilo con detalles y acabados elegantes y con los materiales naturales de los muebles y ventanas especialmente diseñados para el proyecto.

**Project team:**
Graux & Baeyens architecten

**Construction period:**
2019-2021

**Total built area:**
409 m$^2$

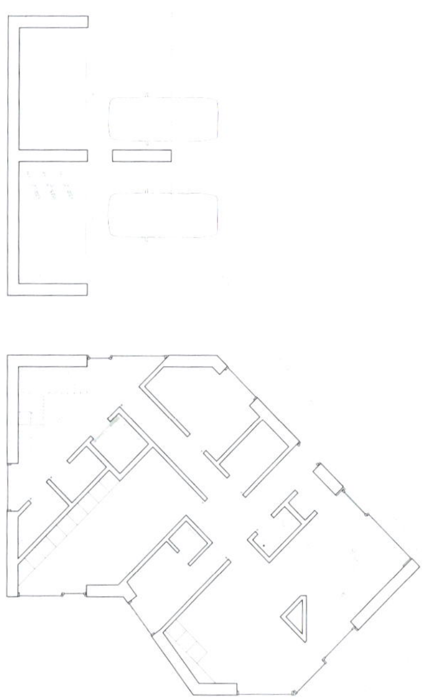

Ground floor plan

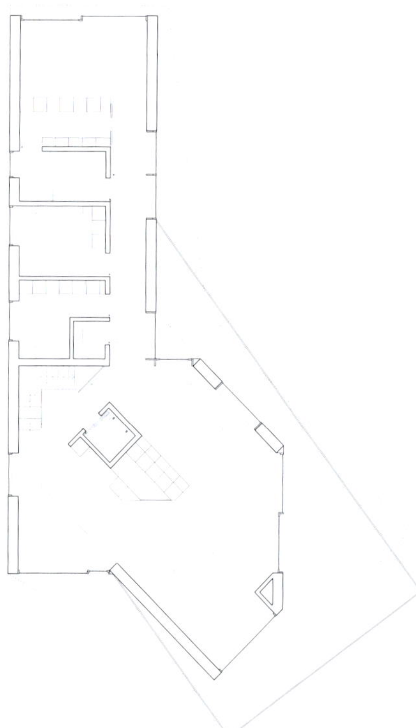

First floor plan

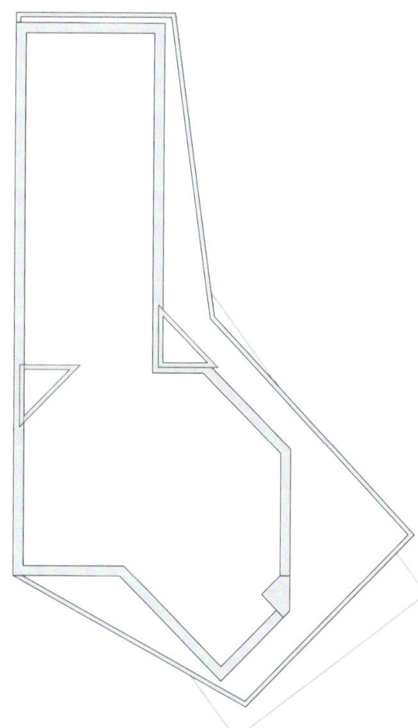

Roof plan

# HOUSE N-DP

Mechelen, Belgium

Photos: © Filip Dujardin

This house stands out for the seemingly random play of asymmetrical concrete canopies that open and close the façade, creating a pleasant effect of introverted openness.
The dynamism created by the canopies and the sophisticated arrangement of triangular floors culminates in a creative process that responds to the environmental constraints. Each floor is set back from the previous one and overlaps at a slightly offset angle to generate privacy and a sense of security. This fan-like movement towards the interior also creates a playful effect that counteracts the monolithic appearance of the building. Inside, the furniture was custom designed. The balanced use of a palette of discreet materials extends to the smallest details, alternating the warm texture of clay plaster on walls and ceilings with raw concrete and wood finishes, which are also used on the exterior facades.

**Project team:**
Graux & Baeyens architecten

**Construction period:**
2016-2018

**Total built area:**
474 m²

Dieses Haus zeichnet sich durch das scheinbar zufällige Spiel asymmetrischer Betonvordächer aus, die die Fassade öffnen und schließen und einen angenehmen Effekt der introvertierten Öffnung erzeugen. Die Dynamik, die durch die Vordächer und die ausgeklügelte Anordnung der dreieckigen Etagen entsteht, führt zu einem kreativen Prozess, der auf die Umweltbedingungen reagiert. Jede Etage ist gegenüber der vorherigen zurückversetzt und überlappt sich leicht versetzt, um Intimität und Sicherheit zu schaffen. Diese fächerförmige Bewegung nach innen erzeugt auch einen spielerischen Effekt, der dem monolithischen Erscheinungsbild des Gebäudes entgegenwirkt. Im Inneren wurde die Möblierung maßgeschneidert. Die ausgewogene Verwendung einer Palette dezenter Materialien erstreckt sich bis in die kleinsten Details und wechselt zwischen der warmen Textur von Lehmputz an Wänden und Decken und dem rohen Beton sowie der Holzoberfläche, die auch an den äußeren Fassaden verwendet wird.

Cette maison se distingue par le jeu apparemment aléatoire de marquises asymétriques en béton qui ouvrent et ferment la façade, créant un agréable effet d'ouverture introvertie.
Le dynamisme créé par les marquises et l'agencement sophistiqué des étages triangulaires couronnent un processus créatif qui répond aux contraintes environnementales. Chaque étage est en retrait par rapport au précédent et se chevauche à un angle légèrement décalé pour créer de l'intimité et un sentiment de sécurité. Ce mouvement en éventail vers l'intérieur crée également un effet ludique qui contrebalance l'aspect monolithique du bâtiment. À l'intérieur, le mobilier a été conçu sur mesure. L'utilisation équilibrée d'une palette de matériaux discrets s'étend jusqu'aux plus petits détails, alternant la texture chaleureuse du plâtre d'argile sur les murs et les plafonds avec le béton brut et la finition en bois utilisés également sur les façades extérieures.

Esta casa destaca por el juego aparentemente aleatorio de marquesinas asimétricas de hormigón que abre y cierra la fachada, creando un agradable efecto de apertura introvertida.
El dinamismo creado por las marquesinas y la sofisticada disposición de las plantas triangulares culmina un proceso creativo que responde a los condicionantes del entorno. Cada planta se retranquea con respecto a la anterior y se superpone en un ángulo ligeramente desplazado para generar intimidad y sensación de seguridad. Este movimiento en abanico hacia el interior crea también un efecto lúdico que contrarresta el aspecto monolítico del edificio. En el interior, el mobiliario se diseñó a medida. El uso equilibrado de una paleta de materiales discretos se extiende a los detalles más pequeños, alternando la cálida textura del enlucido de arcilla en paredes y techos con el hormigón en bruto y el acabado de madera que también se utilizan en las fachadas exteriores.

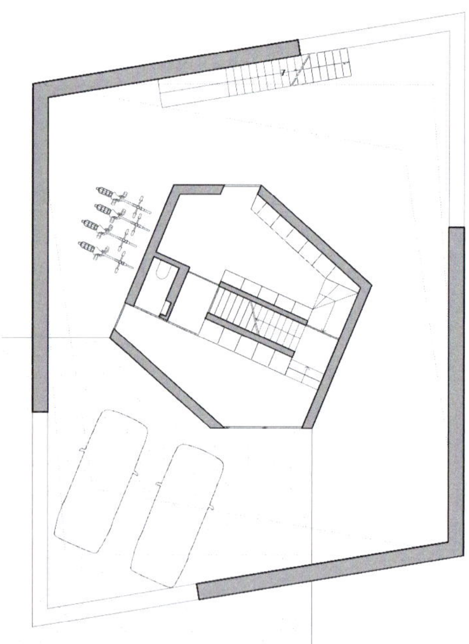

Ground level plan

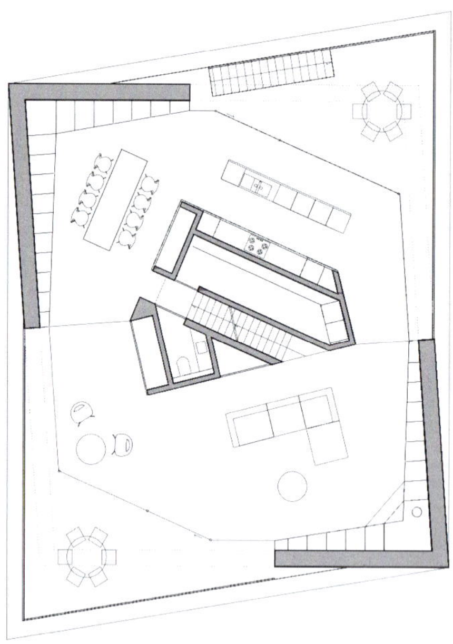

First level plan

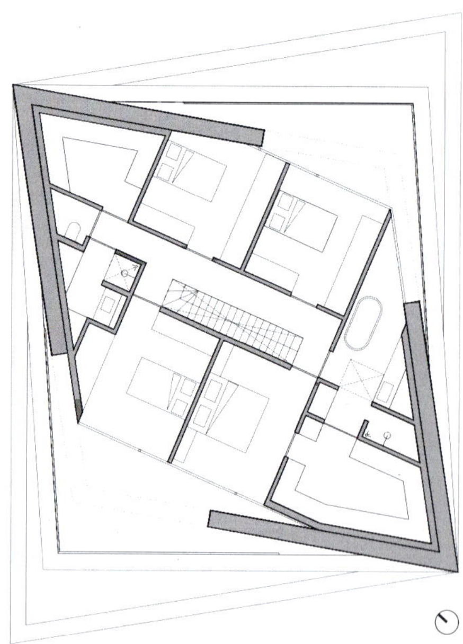

Second level plan

## HGAA Architects

**Nguyễn Văn Thu**

www.hgaa.vn

HGAA started out with a group of young passionate architects who have worked together since 2012. In2017, after 5 years of collaborating on various projects, we officially came to a decission of establishing an architecture office where we can collaboratively build and develop a meaningful architectural brand in Vietnam.
We are always looking for new and unique solutions in different construction conditions in order to build creative projects which is close to nature, creating a better living environment for people, contributing to the shift of Vietnamese people mindset about architectural concepts. Consequently, it can lead to a Social image changing through architectural works. Our design philosophy focuses on creativity, suitability, sustainability, efficiency and meaning, honoring the respectful values of human being, nature and society.

HGAA wurde von einer Gruppe junger leidenschaftlicher Architekten gegründet, die seit 2012 zusammenarbeiten. Im Jahr 2017, nach 5 Jahren der Zusammenarbeit an verschiedenen Projekten, kamen wir offiziell zu dem Entschluss, ein Architekturbüro zu gründen, in dem wir gemeinsam eine bedeutende Architekturmarke in Vietnam aufbauen und entwickeln können.
Wir sind immer auf der Suche nach neuen und einzigartigen Lösungen für unterschiedliche bauliche Gegebenheiten, um kreative, naturnahe Projekte zu realisieren, die ein besseres Lebensumfeld für die Menschen schaffen und zu einem Umdenken der vietnamesischen Bevölkerung in Bezug auf Architekturkonzepte beitragen. Folglich kann dies zu einem gesellschaftlichen Imagewandel durch architektonische Arbeiten führen. Unsere Entwurfsphilosophie konzentriert sich auf Kreativität, Angemessenheit, Nachhaltigkeit, Effizienz und Sinnhaftigkeit und ehrt die respektvollen Werte von Mensch, Natur und Gesellschaft.

HGAA a débuté avec un groupe de jeunes architectes passionnés qui travaillent ensemble depuis 2012. En 2017, après 5 ans de collaboration sur divers projets, nous avons officiellement pris la décision d'établir un bureau d'architecture où nous pouvons construire et développer en collaboration une marque architecturale significative au Vietnam.
Nous sommes toujours à la recherche de solutions nouvelles et uniques dans différentes conditions de construction afin de construire des projets créatifs qui sont proches de la nature, créant un meilleur environnement de vie pour les gens, contribuant à l'évolution de la mentalité des Vietnamiens sur les concepts architecturaux. Par conséquent, cela peut conduire à un changement d'image sociale par le biais d'œuvres architecturales. Notre philosophie de conception se concentre sur la créativité, l'adéquation, la durabilité, l'efficacité et le sens, en honorant les valeurs de respect de l'être humain, de la nature et de la société.

HGAA comenzó con un grupo de jóvenes arquitectos apasionados que han trabajado juntos desde 2012. En 2017, después de 5 años de colaboración en varios proyectos, llegamos oficialmente a la decisión de establecer una oficina de arquitectura donde podamos construir y desarrollar en colaboración una marca arquitectónica significativa en Vietnam.
Siempre estamos buscando soluciones nuevas y únicas en diferentes condiciones de construcción con el fin de construir proyectos creativos que estén cerca de la naturaleza, creando un mejor entorno de vida para las personas, contribuyendo al cambio de mentalidad de los vietnamitas sobre los conceptos arquitectónicos. En consecuencia, puede conducir a un cambio de imagen social a través de las obras arquitectónicas. Nuestra filosofía de diseño se centra en la creatividad, la idoneidad, la sostenibilidad, la eficiencia y el significado, honrando los valores respetuosos del ser humano, la naturaleza y la sociedad.

# BẮC GIANG HOUSE

Dĩnh Kê, Bắc Giang, Vietnam

Photos: © Duc Nguyen

**Project team:**
Trần Mai Phương, Nguyễn Minh Đức

**Construction period:**
2021-2022

**Total built area:**
115 m²

The project for this house arises as a response to the urban context and the residential architecture model in many Vietnamese cities. This typology has not received the attention and investments it deserves and is governed by conventional construction models that do not generate habitable spaces of true quality.
The project experiments with exposed concrete, a durable and spatially expressive material that is rarely used in Vietnam. Its goal was to find a simple and sustainable solution that also achieves a balance between architecture and nature. The building is structured in two blocks offset from each other to create interstitial gardens, so that all spaces in the house are oriented towards a green area. The gardens are not merely decorative elements but are integrated into the house and grow with it, harmoniously combining and completing themselves with the exposed concrete envelope.

Das Projekt dieses Hauses entstand als Antwort auf den städtischen Kontext und das Modell der Wohnarchitektur in vielen vietnamesischen Städten. Diese Typologie hat nicht die gebührende Aufmerksamkeit und Investition erhalten und folgt konventionellen Baustilen, die keine qualitativ hochwertigen Lebensräume schaffen.
Das Projekt experimentiert mit einer Sichtbetonstruktur, einem haltbaren und räumlich ausdrucksstarken Material, das in Vietnam jedoch wenig verwendet wird. Ziel war es, eine einfache und nachhaltige Lösung zu finden, die gleichzeitig eine Balance zwischen Architektur und Natur schafft. Das Gebäude ist in zwei versetzte Blöcke unterteilt, um Zwischengärten zu schaffen, sodass alle Räume des Hauses auf einen grünen Bereich ausgerichtet sind. Die Gärten sind kein rein dekoratives Element, sondern integrieren sich in das Haus und wachsen mit ihm, wodurch sie harmonisch mit der Sichtbetonhülle kombiniert und ergänzt werden.

Le projet de cette maison est né en réponse au contexte urbain et au modèle d'architecture résidentielle de nombreuses villes vietnamiennes. Cette typologie n'a pas reçu l'attention et les investissements appropriés et repose sur des modèles de construction conventionnels qui ne génèrent pas des espaces de vie de véritable qualité.
Le projet expérimente avec une structure en béton apparent, un matériau durable et expressif d'un point de vue spatial mais peu utilisé au Vietnam. L'objectif était de trouver une solution simple et durable tout en équilibrant l'architecture et la nature. Le bâtiment est divisé en deux blocs décalés pour créer des jardins interstitiels, de sorte que tous les espaces de la maison soient orientés vers une zone verte. Les jardins ne sont pas simplement un élément décoratif, mais s'intègrent à la maison et grandissent avec elle, se fondant harmonieusement avec l'enveloppe en béton apparent.

El proyecto de esta casa surge como una respuesta al contexto urbano y al modelo de arquitectura residencial de muchas ciudades vietnamitas. Esta tipología no ha recibido la debida atención e inversiones y se rige por unos modelos constructivos convencionales que no generan espacios habitables de verdadera calidad.
El proyecto experimenta con una estructura de hormigón visto, material duradero y espacialmente expresivo pero poco utilizado en Vietnam. Su objetivo fue buscar una solución sencilla y sostenible que a su vez consiguiera un equilibrio entre arquitectura y naturaleza. El edificio se estructura en dos bloques desplazados entre si para crear jardines intersticiales, de manera que todos los espacios de la casa se orienten hacia una zona verde. Los jardines no suponen un mero elemento decorativo, sino que se integran en la casa y crecen con ella, combinándose y completándose armoniosamente con la envolvente de hormigón visto.

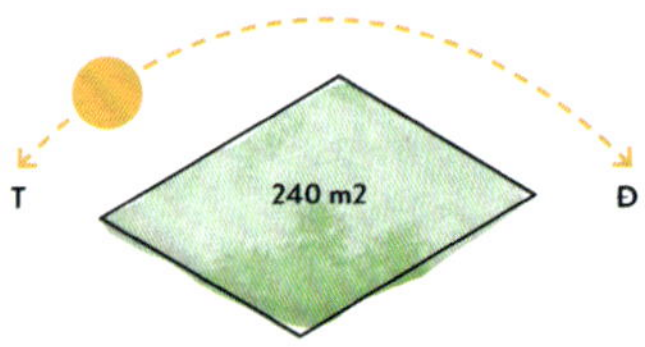


1. Site study
The land has an area of 240m², front facing southwest.

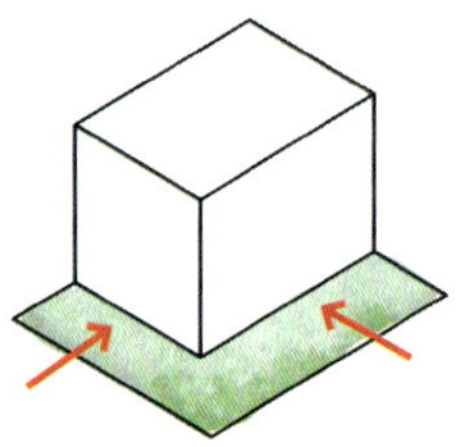

2. Set back
Push the building to the north corner, createa setback to the south, help take advantage of the main wind direction and plant trees to block the west direction.

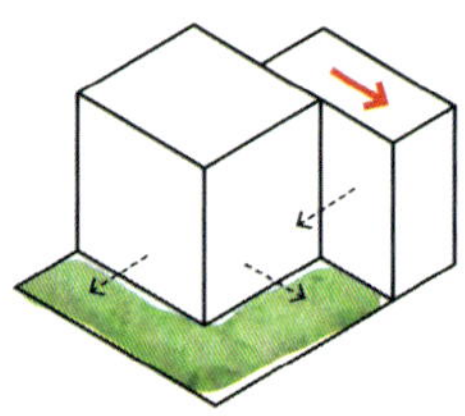

3. Shifting
Pulling blocks creates alternating green spaces, both with views of nature and helping to ventilate and light.

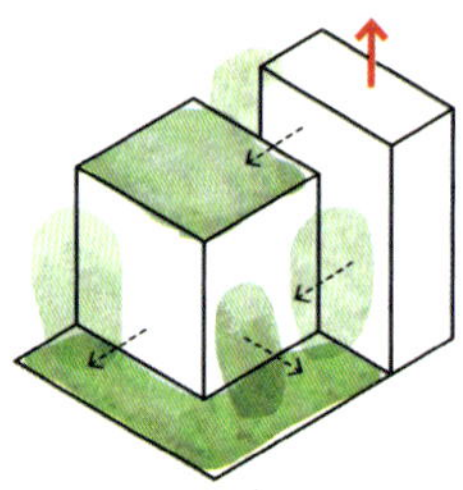

4. Pulling
The block gradually rises inside, helping to utilize the roof area for a garden and making the building less heavy and massive.

Concept diagrams

Axonometic

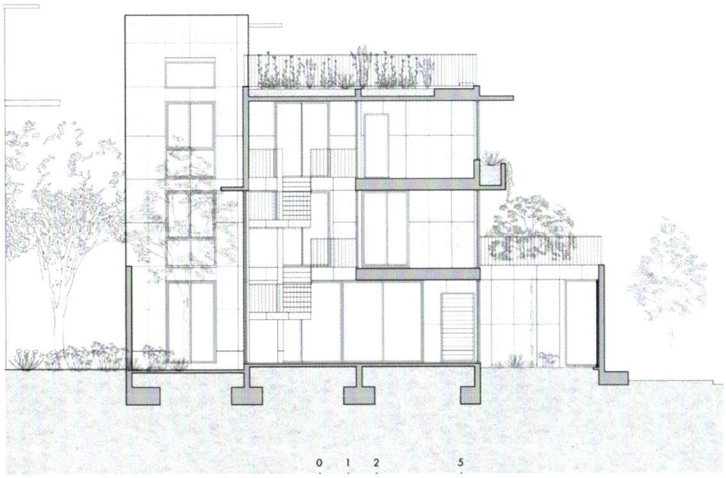


Section 1-1

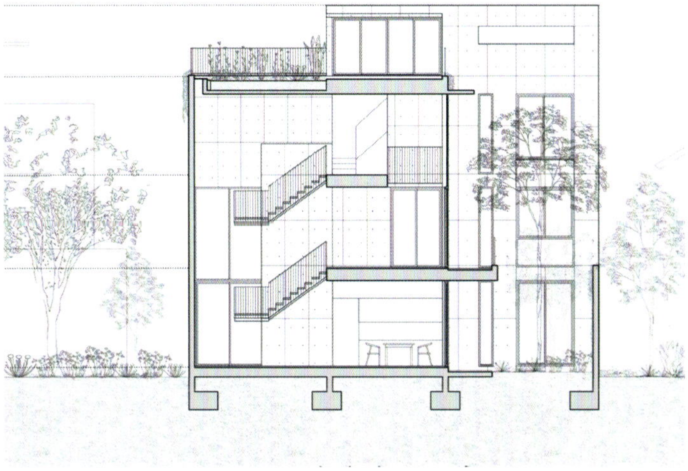

Section A-A

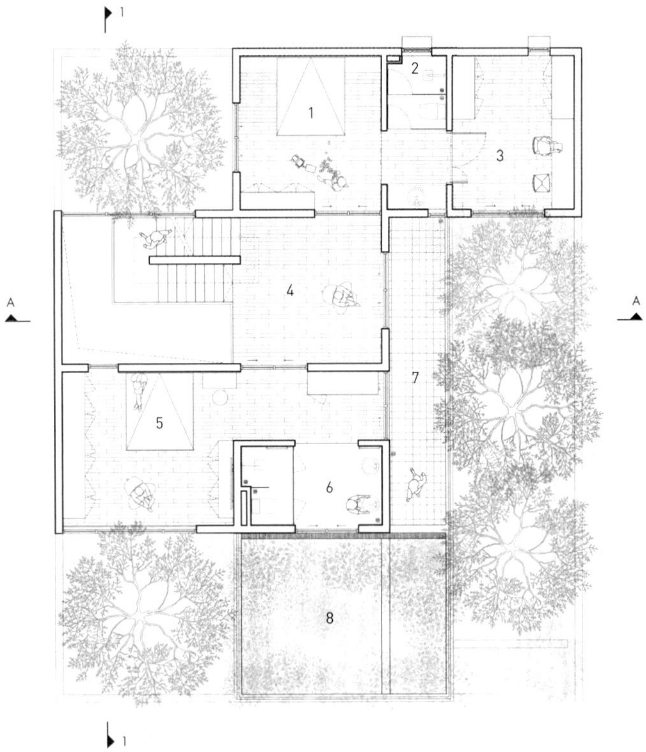

Second floor plan

1. Bedroom 2
2. Restroom
3. Dressing room
4. Hall way
5. Bedroom master
6. Restroom master
7. Bacony
8. Garden

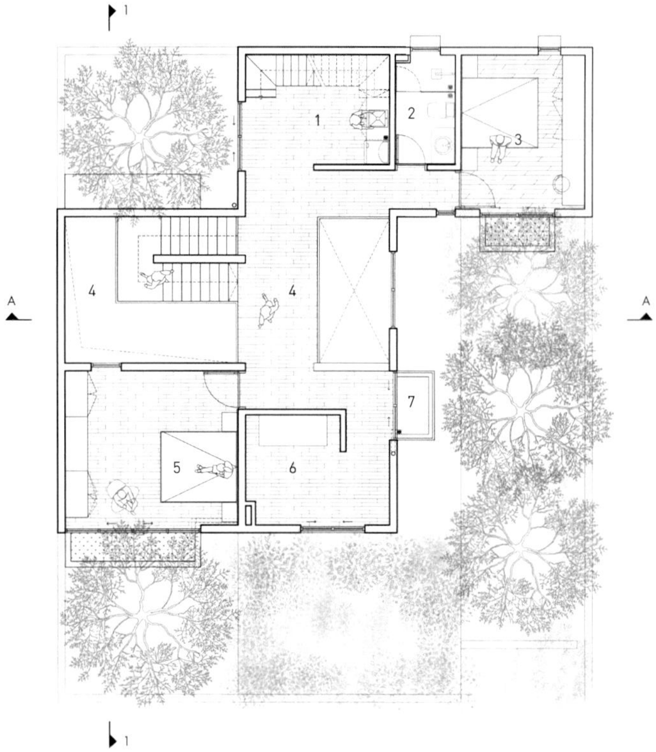

Third floor plan

1. Kitchen
2. Restroom
3. Bedroom 3
4. Void
5. Bedroom 4
6. Altar room
7. Bacony

Section in perspective

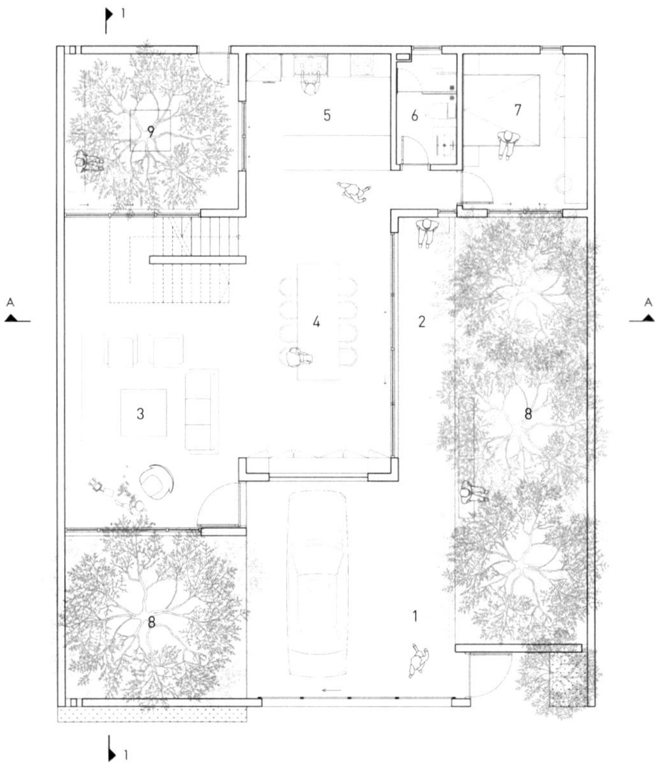

First floor plan

1. Garage
2. Eaves
3. Living room
4. Dining room
5. Kitchen
6. Restroom
7. Bedroom 1
8. Garden
9. Backyard

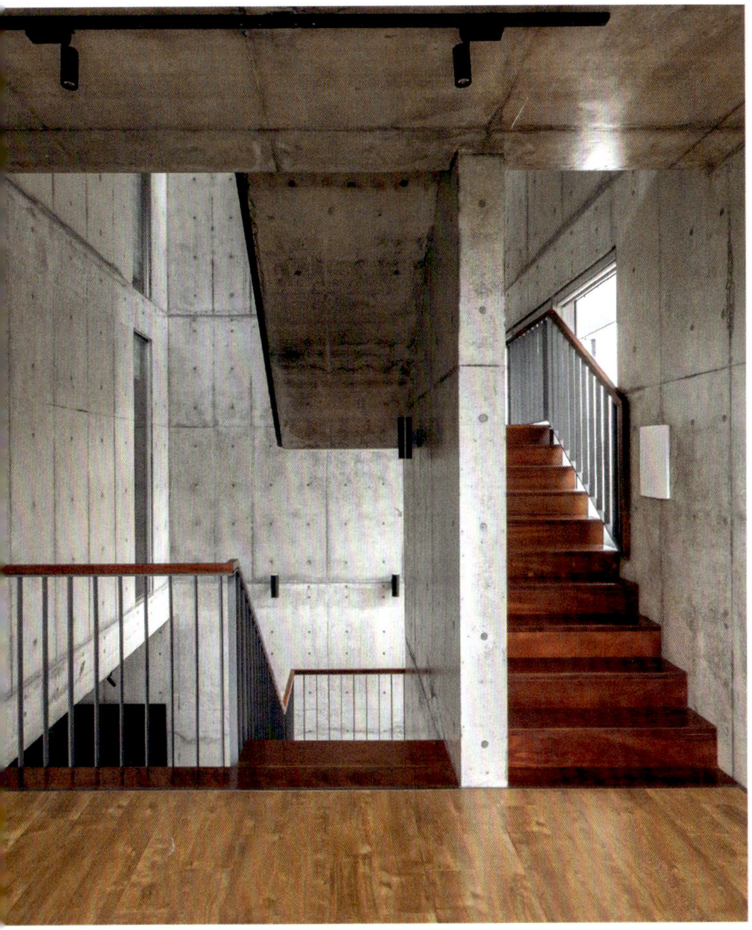

# HO KHUE ARCHITECTS (ALPES Green Design & Build)

**Arch. Ho Khuê**

www.alpes.vn

Ho Khue Architects (ALPES Green Design and Build) is a Vietnamese architecture firm founded in 2014 by Ho Khue. The firm is dedicated to sustainable and green design, and its projects have been recognized for their environmental innovation and social responsibility.

"For more than 10 years pursuing the sustainable and creative style of architects, we always mix up the feeling of joy and anxiety, whenever it is a big resort or a cozy house.
It's full of joy when we have the chance to contribute to the society great works of architecture. It's full of anxiety because we acknowledge that the price will be high if we keep on satisfying with normal design.
A building may become a legacy in the future, and it contains its own story. We always keep these things in mind and let them guide us to move forward."

Architect Ho Khue

Ho Khue Architects (ALPES Green Design and Build) ist ein vietnamesisches Architekturbüro, das 2014 von Ho Khue gegründet wurde. Das Büro hat sich nachhaltigem und grünem Design verschrieben, und seine Projekte wurden für ihre ökologische Innovation und soziale Verantwortung anerkannt.

„Seit mehr als 10 Jahren verfolgen wir als Architekten einen nachhaltigen und kreativen Stil und mischen immer das Gefühl von Freude und Unruhe, egal ob es sich um ein großes Resort oder ein gemütliches Haus handelt.
Es erfüllt uns mit Freude, wenn wir die Möglichkeit haben, der Gesellschaft großartige architektonische Werke zu liefern. Es erfüllt uns mit Sorge, weil wir erkennen, dass der Preis hoch sein wird, wenn wir uns weiterhin mit einem gewöhnlichen Entwurf zufrieden geben.
Ein Gebäude kann in der Zukunft zu einem Vermächtnis werden, und es enthält seine eigene Geschichte. Wir behalten diese Dinge immer im Hinterkopf und lassen uns von ihnen leiten."

Architekt Ho Khue

Ho Khue Architects (ALPES Green Design and Build) est un studio d'architecture vietnamien fondé en 2014 par Ho Khue. Le cabinet se consacre à la conception durable et écologique, et ses projets ont été reconnus pour leur innovation environnementale et leur responsabilité sociale.

« Depuis plus de 10 ans que nous poursuivons le style durable et créatif des architectes, nous mélangeons toujours le sentiment de joie et d'anxiété, qu'il s'agisse d'un grand centre de villégiature ou d'une maison confortable.
La joie nous envahit lorsque nous avons l'occasion d'apporter de grandes œuvres architecturales à la société. L'anxiété nous envahit parce que nous savons que le prix à payer sera élevé si nous continuons à nous satisfaire d'une conception ordinaire.
Un bâtiment peut devenir un héritage dans le futur, et il contient sa propre histoire. Nous gardons toujours ces éléments à l'esprit et les laissons nous guider vers l'avenir ».

Architecte Ho Khue

Ho Khue Architects (ALPES Green Design and Build) es un estudio de arquitectura vietnamita fundado en 2014 por Ho Khue. La firma se dedica al diseño sostenible y ecológico, y sus proyectos han sido reconocidos por su innovación medioambiental y responsabilidad social.

«Durante más de 10 años persiguiendo el estilo sostenible y creativo de los arquitectos, siempre mezclamos el sentimiento de alegría y ansiedad, siempre que se trate de un gran complejo turístico o de una casa acogedora.
Nos llena de alegría cuando tenemos la oportunidad de aportar a la sociedad grandes obras de arquitectura. Está lleno de ansiedad porque reconocemos que el precio será alto si seguimos satisfaciendo con un diseño normal.
Un edificio puede convertirse en un legado en el futuro, y contiene su propia historia. Siempre tenemos estas cosas en mente y dejamos que nos guíen para seguir adelante».

Arquitecto Ho Khue

# THALIA BOUTIQUE HOTEL

**Hoi An City, Quang Nam province, Vietnam**

Photos: © Hiroyuki Oki

In contrast to the many current hotel projects in the area that present a dull and emotionless design, this hotel exhibits a liberal architectural style imbued with a nostalgic feeling of traditional value. Five floors high, the building devotes 50 % of its surface area to creating voids that allow it to "breathe" on its own and achieve a harmonious symphony of nature, architecture and people, where each room is treated as an element that moves randomly and freely. The design reflects the soul of the ancient city of Hoi An through details, materials and colours. The exterior of the building has features of exposed concrete, laterite patches and rustic yin and yang tile roofs. Inside, the use of homogeneous materials such as concrete and small details combine to create a simple and elegant atmosphere and bring an emotional experience to the users.

Im Gegensatz zu den vielen aktuellen Hotelprojekten in der Gegend, die sich durch ein langweiliges und emotionsloses Design auszeichnen, weist dieses Hotel einen liberalen architektonischen Stil auf, der von einem nostalgischen Gefühl traditioneller Werte durchdrungen ist. Das fünfstöckige Gebäude widmet 50 % seiner Grundfläche der Schaffung von Leerräumen, die es ihm ermöglichen, von selbst zu „atmen" und eine harmonische Symphonie aus Natur, Architektur und Menschen zu schaffen, in der jedes Zimmer als ein sich zufällig bewegendes, frei fließendes Element behandelt wird. Das Design spiegelt die Seele der alten Stadt Hoi An durch Details, Materialien und Farben wider. Das Äußere des Gebäudes weist Merkmale von Sichtbeton, Lateritflicken und rustikalen Yin- und Yang-Ziegeldächern auf. Im Inneren schaffen die Verwendung homogener Materialien wie Beton und kleine Details eine schlichte und elegante Atmosphäre und vermitteln den Nutzern ein emotionales Erlebnis.

Contrairement aux nombreux projets hôteliers actuels de la région qui présentent un design terne et sans émotion, cet hôtel affiche un style architectural libéral imprégné d'un sentiment nostalgique de valeur traditionnelle. Haut de cinq étages, le bâtiment consacre 50 % de sa surface à la création d'espaces vides qui lui permettent de « respirer » par lui-même, créant une symphonie harmonieuse entre la nature, l'architecture et les gens, où chaque chambre est traitée comme un élément qui se déplace au hasard et s'écoule librement. La conception reflète l'âme de l'ancienne ville de Hoi An à travers les détails, les matériaux et les couleurs. L'extérieur du bâtiment se caractérise par du béton apparent, des plaques de latérite et des toits rustiques en tuiles yin et yang. À l'intérieur, l'utilisation de matériaux homogènes tels que le béton et les petits détails se combinent pour créer une atmosphère simple et élégante et apporter une expérience émotionnelle aux utilisateurs.

Frente a los múltiples proyectos hoteleros actuales de la zona que presentan un diseño aburrido y sin emoción, este hotel exhibe un estilo arquitectónico liberal imbuido de un sentimiento nostálgico de valor tradicional. Con cinco plantas de altura, el edificio destina el 50 % de su superficie a crear vacíos que le permiten «respirar» por sí mismo y consiguen una armoniosa sinfonía de naturaleza, arquitectura y personas, en la que cada habitación es tratada como un elemento que se desplaza de forma aleatoria y libre. El diseño refleja el alma de la ciudad antigua de Hoi An a través de los detalles, los materiales y los colores. El exterior del edificio tiene rasgos de hormigón visto, parches de laterita y rústicos tejados de tejas yin y yang. En el interior, el uso de materiales homogéneos como el hormigón y los pequeños detalles se combinan para crear una atmósfera sencilla y elegante y aportar una experiencia emocional a los usuarios.

**Awards:**
**VMark Awards 2022 – Gold Prize – Best Hotel Design**

**Project team:**
Ho Khue Architects

**Construction period:**
18 months

**Total built area:**
470 m$^2$

**General contractor:**
PCons

**Consultants:**
Ho Khue Architects

Thalia Boutique Hotel

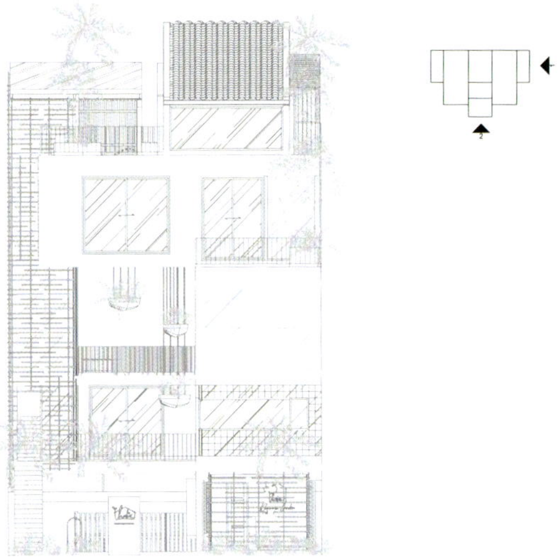

Elevation 1

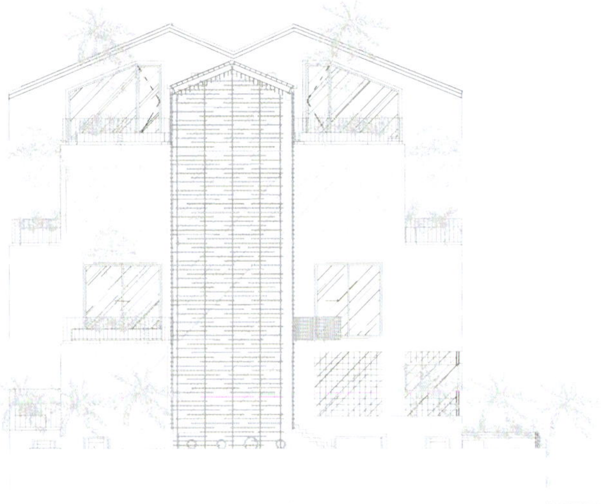

Elevation 2

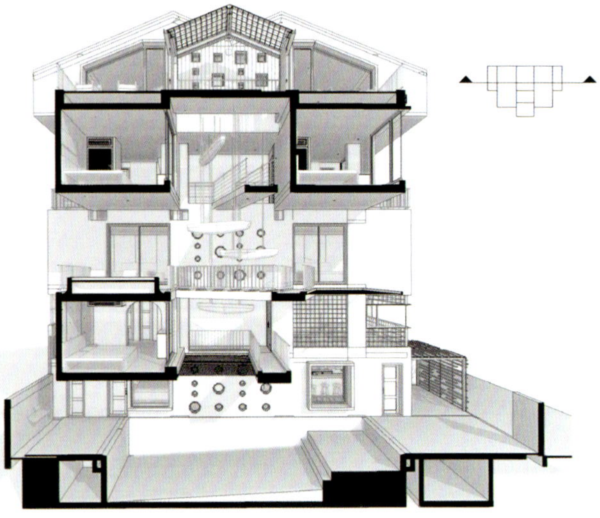

3D section

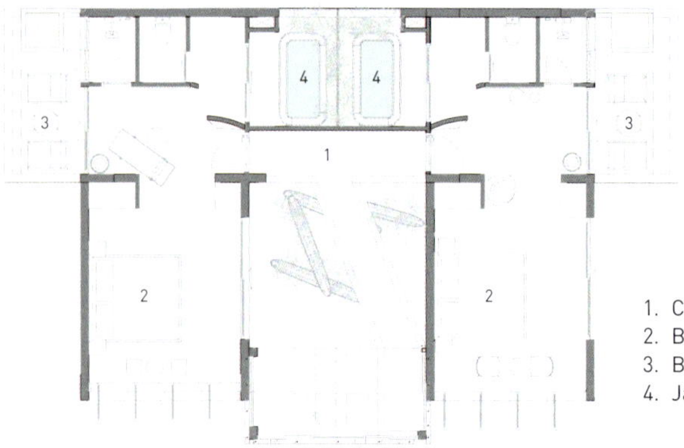

1. Corridor
2. Bedroom
3. Balcony
4. Jacuzzi

Fourth floor plan

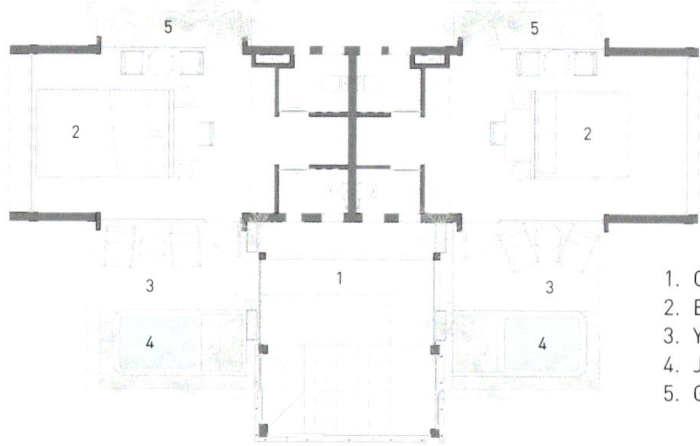

1. Corridor
2. Bedroom
3. Yard
4. Jacuzzi
5. Garden

Attic floor plan

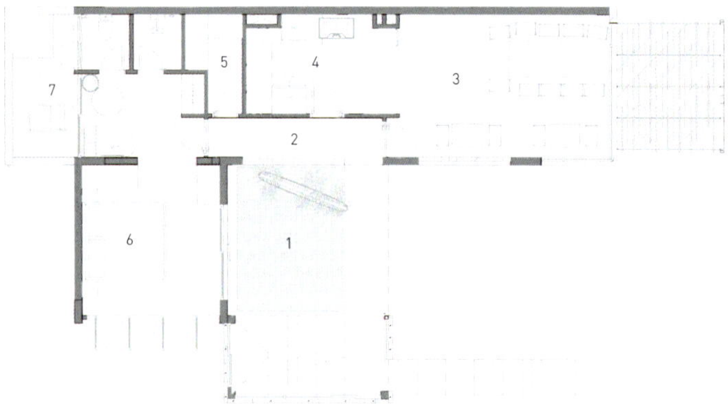

Second floor plan

1. Mesh relaxation
2. Corridor
3. Restaurant
4. Kitchen
5. Storage
6. Bedroom
7. Balcony

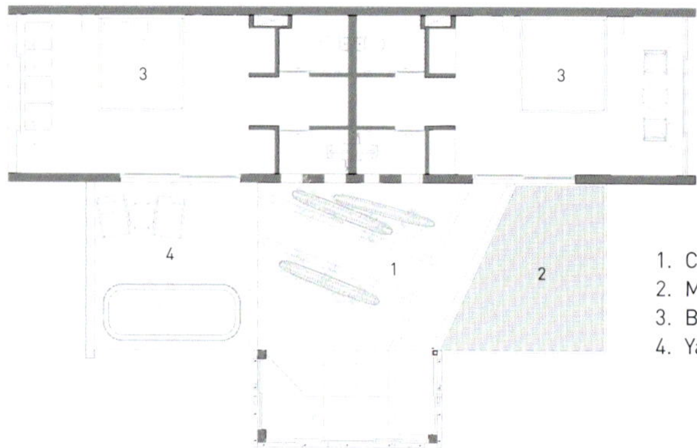

1. Corridor
2. Mesh relaxation
3. Bedroom
4. Yard

Third floor plan

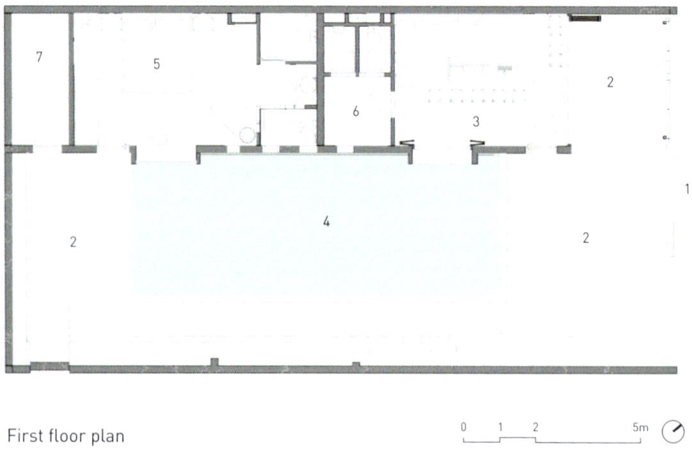

First floor plan

1. Entrance
2. Terrace
3. Bar/reception
4. Pool
5. Bedroom
6. WC
7. Technical room

## JDA Co.

**James Davidson**

www.jdaco.com.au

JDA Co. is a Brisbane-based architecture firm, specialising in the design and adaptation of urban environments to withstand floods, cyclones, bushfires, storm surges and extreme heat. JDA Co. is sought by governments, councils and private enterprise to provide advice on climate responsive architecture solutions, and has authored dozens of landmark climate-resilient design guidelines.

Founded by architect James Davidson, the studio is renowned for its sustainable design strategies to create beautiful new homes and major refurbishments.

JDA Co. is known for its ability to transform cultural, heritage and commercial building stock into contemporary hospitality venues, commercial offices and theatres.

JDA Co. ist ein in Brisbane ansässiges Architekturbüro, das sich auf die Gestaltung und Anpassung von städtischen Umgebungen an Überschwemmungen, Wirbelstürme, Feuer, Stürme und extreme Hitze spezialisiert hat. JDA Co. wird von Regierungen, Stadtverwaltungen und privaten Unternehmen um Ratschläge zu klimaresistenten architektonischen Lösungen und ist Autor von Dutzenden von Richtlinien für klimaresistente Gestaltung.

Das von dem Architekten James Davidson gegründete Unternehmen ist bekannt für seine nachhaltigen Designstrategien für die Gestaltung schöner neuer Häuser und großer Gebäude sowie für umfangreiche Renovierungen.

JDA Co. ist bekannt für seine Fähigkeit, kulturelle, historische und kommerzielle Gebäude in moderne Geschäftsräume und Theater zu verwandeln.

JDA Co. est un cabinet d'architectes basé à Brisbane, spécialisé dans la conception et l'adaptation des environnements urbains pour qu'ils résistent aux inondations, aux cyclones, aux incendies, aux tempêtes et aux chaleurs extrêmes. Les gouvernements, les conseils municipaux et les entreprises privées font appel à JDA Co. pour obtenir des conseils sur des solutions architecturales résistantes au climat. JDA Co. est l'auteur de dizaines de lignes directrices en matière de conception résiliente au climat.

Fondée par l'architecte James Davidson, l'entreprise est réputée pour ses stratégies de conception durable permettant de créer de belles maisons neuves et de grands bâtiments, ainsi que des rénovations majeures.

JDA Co. est connue pour sa capacité à transformer des bâtiments culturels, patrimoniaux et commerciaux en bureaux commerciaux et théâtres contemporains.

JDA Co. es un estudio de arquitectura con sede en Brisbane, especializado en el diseño y adaptación de entornos urbanos para resistir inundaciones, ciclones, incendios, tormentas y calor extremo. JDA Co. es solicitada por gobiernos, ayuntamientos y empresas privadas para asesoramiento sobre soluciones arquitectónicas adaptadas al clima, y es autora de docenas de directrices de diseño resistentes a las condiciones climáticas.

Fundado por el arquitecto James Davidson, el estudio es célebre por sus estrategias de diseño sostenible para crear hermosas casas nuevas y grandes edificios, ademas de reformas importantes.

JDA Co. es conocida por su capacidad de transformar edificios culturales, patrimoniales y comerciales en contemporáneas oficinas comerciales y teatros.

# THE HOUSE AT LIZARD ISLAND

**Lizard Island, Queensland, Australia**

Photos: © Peter Bennetts

Located on the fringe of the Great Barrier Reef, the design of The House is inspired by its connection to its untamed and ruggedly Australian surroundings. Respectful in its placement on the site, it is both an aesthetic and functional structure, adapted to withstand cyclonic winds.
The remote and environmentally sensitive location called for ingenuity when it came to the build. Touching lightly on earth, the design mimics the form of stingrays found meters away from the site, vertical apertures resembling "gills" guide winds though the house allowing it to breathe on hot days. The materials used in the construction of the house are intentionally restrained framing vibrant colors of the spectacular Coral Sea and surrounds. The concrete form is fragmented by rich Rosewood timber and copper accents. The finishes are deliberate and carried from the outside in, the connection to the spectacular location remains intact throughout the house.

Das Haus, das am Rande des Great Barrier Reef liegt, wurde in seinem Design von seiner Verbindung zu seiner wilden und raubeinigen australischen Umgebung inspiriert. Respektvoll in seiner Platzierung auf dem Grundstück, ist es sowohl eine ästhetische als auch funktionale Struktur, die so angepasst ist, dass sie Zyklonwinde standhält.
Die abgelegene und umweltsensible Lage erforderte Einfallsreichtum beim Bau. Das Design berührt leicht die Erde und imitiert die Form von Stachelrochen, die sich Meter entfernt von der Baustelle befinden. Vertikale Öffnungen, die „Kiemen" ähneln, lenken die Winde durch das Haus und ermöglichen es ihm, an heißen Tagen zu atmen. Die beim Bau des Hauses verwendeten Materialien sind bewusst zurückhaltend und rahmen die lebhaften Farben des spektakulären Korallenmeeres und seiner Umgebung ein. Die Betonform wird durch edles Rosewood-Holz und Kupferakzente unterbrochen. Die Oberflächen sind absichtlich gewählt und ziehen sich von außen nach innen, die Verbindung zur spektakulären Lage bleibt im gesamten Haus erhalten.

Située à la périphérie de la Grande Barrière de Corail, la conception de la Maison s'inspire de sa connexion avec son environnement australien sauvage et robuste. Respectueuse de son emplacement sur le site, elle est à la fois une structure esthétique et fonctionnelle, conçue pour résister aux vents cycloniques.
L'emplacement éloigné et sensible sur le plan environnemental a nécessité de la créativité lors de la construction. Touchant légèrement la terre, la conception imite la forme des raies situées à quelques mètres du site, des ouvertures verticales ressemblant à des « branchies » guident les vents à travers la maison, permettant ainsi à celle-ci de respirer les jours de chaleur. Les matériaux utilisés dans la construction de la maison sont délibérément sobres, encadrant les couleurs vives du spectaculaire récif de corail de la mer et de ses environs. La forme en béton est fragmentée par du précieux bois de rose et des accents en cuivre. Les finitions sont délibérées et s'étendent de l'extérieur vers l'intérieur, la connexion avec l'emplacement spectaculaire reste intacte dans toute la maison.

Situada al borde de la Gran Barrera de Coral, el diseño de The House se inspira en su conexión con el indómito y agreste entorno australiano. Respetuosa con su emplazamiento, representa una atractiva y funcional edificación, diseñada para resistir vientos ciclónicos.
Su ubicación remota y sensible desde el punto de vista medioambiental exigió ingenio a la hora de construirla. Tocando ligeramente el terreno, su diseño imita la forma de las rayas que se encuentran a pocos metros; unas aberturas verticales a modo de «branquias» guían el viento a través de la casa, permitiéndole respirar en los días calurosos. La paleta de materiales de la casa es intencionadamente sobria, enmarcando los colores del espectacular Mar del Coral. La forma del hormigón se fragmenta con madera de palisandro y detalles de cobre. La similitud entre los acabados del exterior y del interior mantiene intacta la conexión de la casa con su espectacular ubicación.

**Project team:**
Design team: JDA Co. – James Davidson, Sam Bowstead, Kane Murray, Martin Arroyo, Clive Ba-Pe, Brendan Pointon, Arjan Sandhu.
Interior Styling: Sophie Hart

**Construction period:**
February 2020–May 2022 approximately

**Total built area:**
260 m$^2$

**General contractor:**
Completed by Field Construct

**Consultants:**
Interior styling: Sophie Hart (Sophie Hart Studio)
Interior design: Rowena Cornwell (Coop Creative) with JDA Co.
Landscape consultant: Tanya Basile (Pearl Landscape)
Structural engineer: STP
Mechanical engineer: Sequal
Hydraulic engineer: H2O
Superintendent/project manager: Black & More

Section

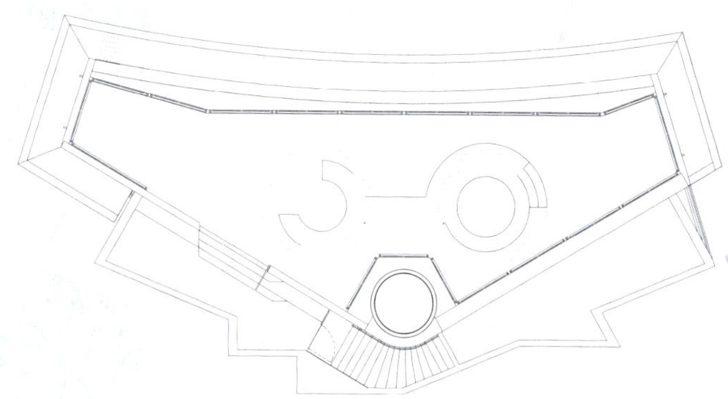

Roof plan

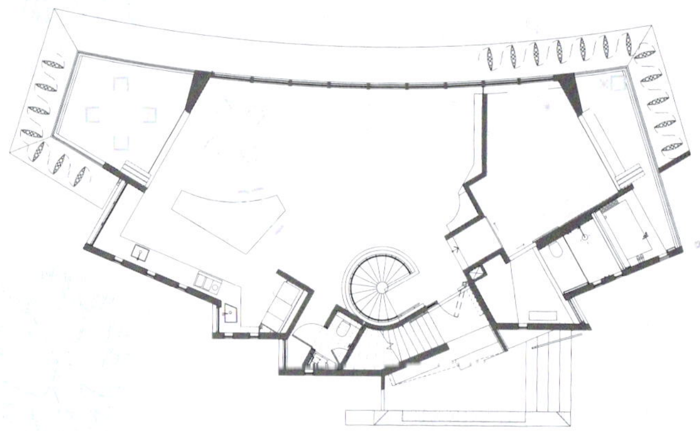

First floor plan

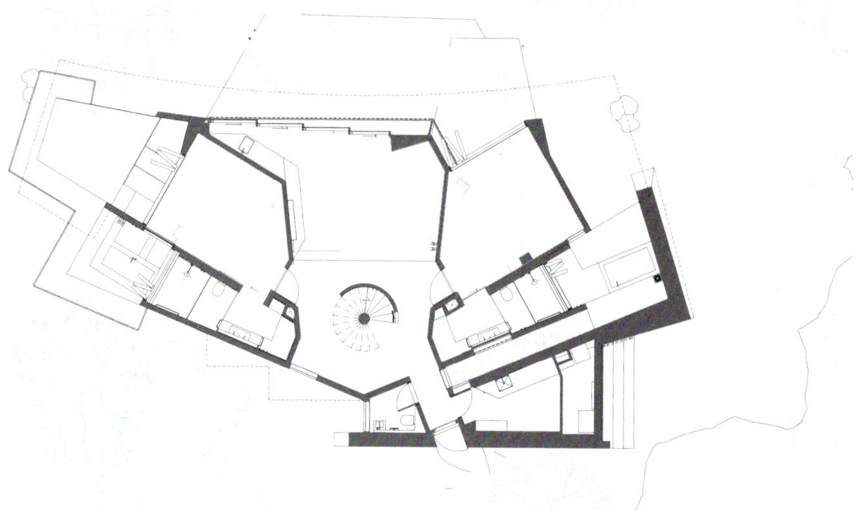

Ground floor plan

## KOHLERSTRAUMANN

**Aaron Kohler, Marc Straumann**

www.kohlerstraumann.com

Architecture is more than just the physical structures that we see and inhabit - it's an art form that can be transformative, transcendent, and deeply meaningful. Our approach to architecture is not just about creating structures that serve a function, but about creating architecture that connect us to the world around. We strive for simplicity and minimalism in our designs.

We use locally sourced, natural materials, paying close attention to every element, and work with the existing environment rather than against it.

We believe that the essence and purpose of architecture lies in its ability to transform live and to create a deeper connection to nature. By prioritizing the feeling of space, details, light and sustainable materials in our designs, and taking a sensitive approach to every project. We aim to create architecture that is both functional and awe-inspiring.

Architektur ist mehr als nur die physischen Strukturen, die wir sehen und bewohnen - sie ist eine Kunstform, die transformativ, transzendent und von tiefer Bedeutung sein kann. Unser Ansatz in der Architektur besteht nicht nur darin, Strukturen zu schaffen, die einer Funktion dienen, sondern auch darin, Architektur zu schaffen, die uns mit der Welt um uns herum verbindet. Wir streben nach Einfachheit und Minimalismus in unseren Entwürfen.

Wir verwenden natürliche Materialien aus der Region, achten auf jedes Element und arbeiten mit der vorhandenen Umgebung, anstatt gegen sie.

Wir glauben, dass das Wesen und der Zweck der Architektur in ihrer Fähigkeit liegt, das Leben zu verändern und eine tiefere Verbindung zur Natur zu schaffen. Indem wir bei unseren Entwürfen dem Raumgefühl, den Details, dem Licht und den nachhaltigen Materialien Vorrang einräumen und bei jedem Projekt einen sensiblen Ansatz verfolgen. Unser Ziel ist es, Architektur zu schaffen, die sowohl funktional als auch beeindruckend ist.

L'architecture est plus qu'une simple structure physique que nous voyons et habitons : c'est une forme d'art qui peut être transformative, transcendantale et profondément significative. Notre approche de l'architecture ne consiste pas seulement à créer des structures qui servent une fonction, mais à créer une architecture qui nous relie au monde qui nous entoure. Nous visons la simplicité et le minimalisme dans nos conceptions.
Nous utilisons des matériaux naturels sourcés localement, en prêtant une attention particulière à chaque élément, et travaillons avec l'environnement existant plutôt que contre lui.
Nous croyons que l'essence et le but de l'architecture résident dans sa capacité à transformer la vie et à créer une connexion plus profonde avec la nature. En privilégiant la sensation d'espace, les détails, la lumière et les matériaux durables dans nos conceptions, et en adoptant une approche sensible à chaque projet, nous visons à créer une architecture à la fois fonctionnelle et inspirante.

La arquitectura es algo más que las estructuras físicas que vemos y habitamos: es una forma de arte que puede ser transformadora, trascendente y profundamente significativa. Nuestro enfoque de la arquitectura no consiste únicamente en crear estructuras que cumplan una función, sino en crear una arquitectura que nos conecte con el mundo que nos rodea. Buscamos la sencillez y el minimalismo en nuestros diseños.
Utilizamos materiales naturales de origen local, prestando especial atención a cada elemento, y trabajamos con el entorno existente en lugar de contra él.
Creemos que la esencia y el propósito de la arquitectura reside en su capacidad para transformar la vida y crear una conexión más profunda con la naturaleza. Damos prioridad a la sensación de espacio, los detalles, la luz y los materiales sostenibles en nuestros diseños, y adoptamos un enfoque sensible en cada proyecto. Nuestro objetivo es crear una arquitectura que sea a la vez funcional e inspiradora.

# HASENRAINSTRASSE APARTMENT COMPLEX

Binningen, Switzerland

Photos: © marismezulis.com

This monolithic yet minimalist apartment building is characterized by its cascading terraces, allowing the seven units it comprises to enjoy panoramic views of the city. Its fragmented and angular layout adapts to the urban context, mostly consisting of single-family houses. Its rigorous facade features a pronounced vertical treatment with exposed in-situ concrete walls, tall windows, and simple details.
The building is organized around a central staircase core with a glass facade, its interior featuring a concrete finish similar to the facades, contrasting with the white walls and stone floors of the apartments. The asymmetrical and varied floor plans of the building ensure that each apartment has a completely distinct layout. Likewise, different orientations and views create a strong sense of privacy in each unit.

**Project team:**
Aaron Kohler, Marc Straumann

**Construction period:**
2019-2021

**Total built area:**
820 $m^2$

Dieses monolithische, aber minimalistische Wohngebäude zeichnet sich durch seine kaskadenförmigen Terrassen aus, von denen aus die sieben Wohnungen einen Panoramablick über die Stadt genießen können. Sein fragmentierter, kantiger Grundriss fügt sich in den städtischen Kontext ein, der überwiegend aus Einfamilienhäusern besteht. Die strenge Fassade weist eine starke vertikale Behandlung mit vor Ort geformten Sichtbetonwänden, hohen Fenstern und einfachen Details auf.
Das Gebäude gruppiert sich um ein zentrales Treppenhaus mit Glasfassade, dessen Innenraum eine ähnliche Betonoberfläche wie die Fassade aufweist, die im Kontrast zu den weißen Wänden und Steinböden der Wohnungen steht. Die asymmetrischen und unterschiedlichen Grundrisse des Gebäudes sorgen dafür, dass jede Wohnung einen völlig anderen Grundriss hat. Außerdem schaffen die unterschiedlichen Ausrichtungen und Ausblicke ein starkes Gefühl von Privatsphäre in jeder Einheit.

Cet immeuble d'appartements monolithique mais minimaliste se caractérise par ses terrasses en cascade, qui permettent aux sept unités de jouir de vues panoramiques sur la ville. Son plan d'étage fragmenté et anguleux s'inscrit dans le contexte urbain, qui se compose principalement de maisons individuelles. Sa façade rigoureuse présente un traitement vertical fort avec des murs en béton apparent formés sur place, de hautes fenêtres et des détails simples.
Le bâtiment est organisé autour d'une cage d'escalier centrale avec une façade vitrée, dont l'intérieur a une finition en béton similaire à celle des façades qui contraste avec les murs blancs et les sols en pierre des appartements. Les plans asymétriques et variés du bâtiment font que chaque appartement a un agencement complètement différent. De plus, les différentes orientations et vues créent un fort sentiment d'intimité dans chaque unité.

Este monolítico pero minimalista edificio de apartamentos se caracteriza por sus terrazas en cascada, que permiten a las siete unidades que lo componen disfrutar de vistas panorámicas sobre la ciudad. Su planta fragmentada y angular se adapta al contexto urbano, constituido en su mayoría por casas unifamiliares. Su rigurosa fachada presenta un marcado tratamiento vertical mediante muros de hormigón visto encofrados in situ, altos ventanales y sencillos detalles.
El edificio se organiza en torno a un núcleo central de escalera con fachada acristalada, cuyo interior presenta un acabado de hormigón similar al de las fachadas que contrasta con las paredes blancas y suelos de piedra de los apartamentos. Los asimétricos y variados planos de planta del edificio garantizan que cada apartamento tenga una distribución completamente distinta. Así mismo, las diferentes orientaciones y vistas crean una fuerte sensación de privacidad en cada unidad.

Northeast elevation

South elevation

Northwest elevation

Southeast elevation

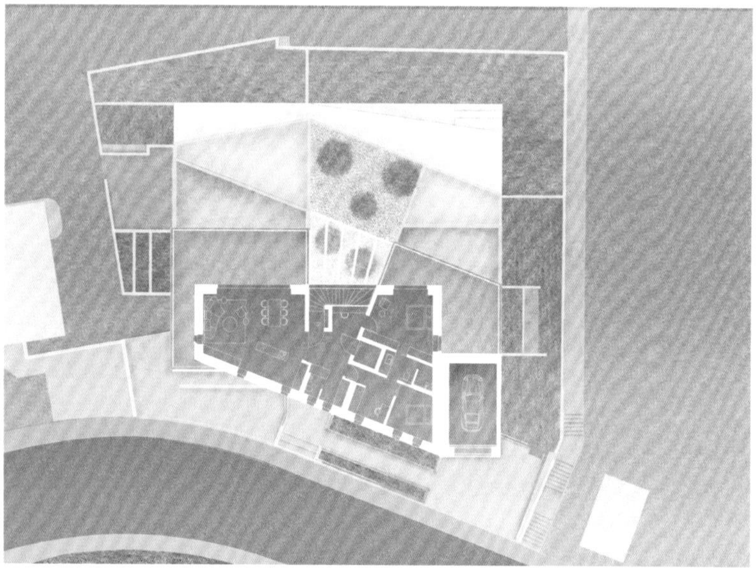

Level +1

Level 0

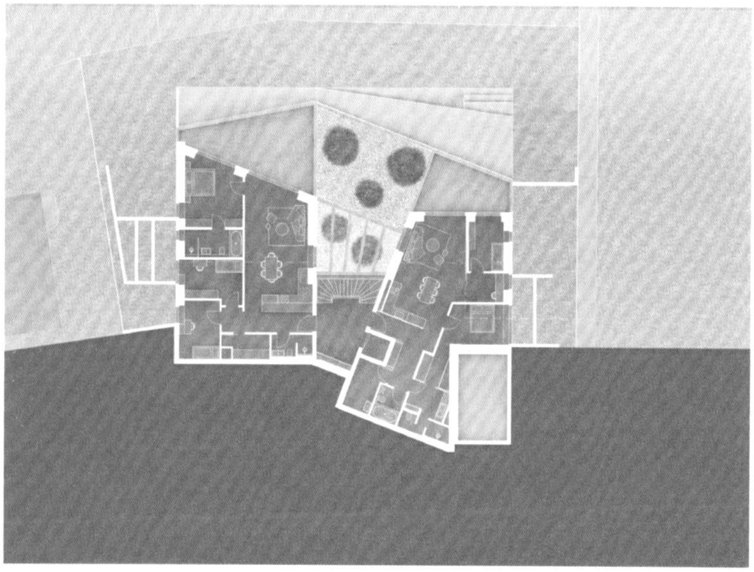

Level -1

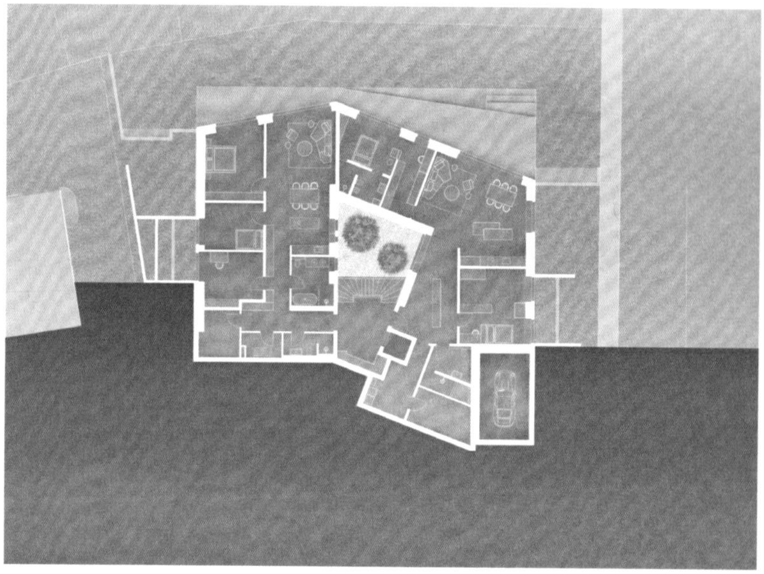

Level -2

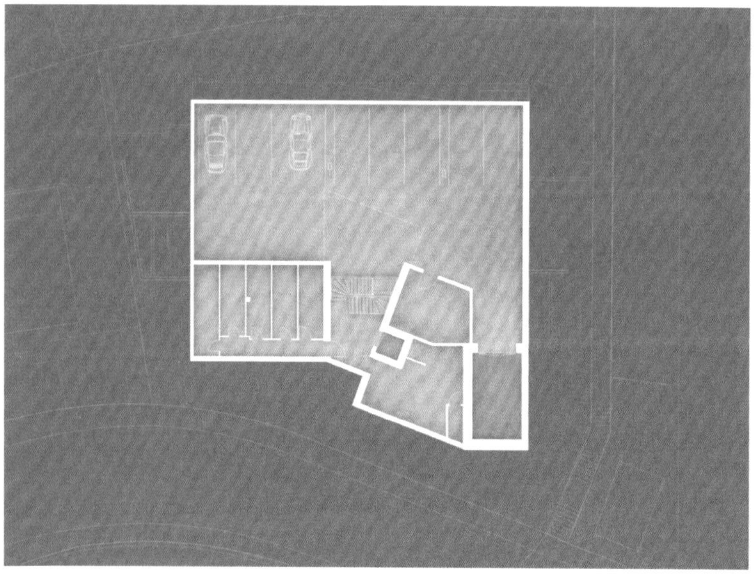

Level -3

Section

## KRIS YAO | ARTECH

**Kris Yao, Hon. FAIA**

www.krisyaoartech.com

KRIS YAO | ARTECH is an Asia-based architectural firm comprised of more than 160 professionals with offices in Taipei and Shanghai. Our projects are mainly located in the Greater China area, but are also found in the United States, Europe and South Asia. Established in 1985 by Kris Yao, Hon. FAIA, the firm is one of the most influential architectural professional practices in Asia, as well as an internationally renowned firm. Using a creative and critical design process supplemented with extensive professional experience, our mission is to deliver high quality projects. Although architecture is at the core of our practice, our involvement in projects often extends to feasibility studies, master planning, and programming. Our firm's portfolio demonstrates years of practice in cultural, corporate, commercial, hotels, performing arts centers, transportation, education, residential, spiritual spaces and urban design.

KRIS YAO | ARTECH ist ein in Asien ansässiges Architekturbüro mit mehr als 160 Mitarbeitern und Büros in Taipeh und Shanghai. Wir arbeiten hauptsächlich an Projekten im Großraum China, aber auch in den Vereinigten Staaten, Europa und Südasien. 1985 von Kris Yao, Hon. FAIA, gegründet, ist das Unternehmen nicht nur eines der einflussreichsten Architekturbüros Asiens, sondern auch ein weltweit renommiertes Unternehmen. Mit unserem kreativen und kritischen Entwurfsprozess, ergänzt durch umfangreiche Berufserfahrung streben wir danach, qualitativ hochwertige Projekte zu liefern. Auch wenn die Architektur im Mittelpunkt unserer Tätigkeit steht, beinhaltet unsere Beteiligung an Projekten oft auch Machbarkeitsstudien, Masterplanung und Programmierung. Das Portfolio unseres Unternehmens belegt unsere jahrelange Erfahrung in den Bereichen Kultur, Unternehmen, Handel, Hotels, Zentren für darstellende Künste, Verkehr, Bildung, Wohnen, spirituelle Räume und Stadtgestaltung.

KRIS YAO | ARTECH est un cabinet d'architectes basé en Asie, comprenant de plus de 160 professionnels avec des bureaux à Taïpei et à Shanghai. Nos projets se situent principalement dans la région de la Grande Chine, mais également aux États-Unis, en Europe et en Asie du Sud. Fondé en 1985 par Kris Yao, Hon. FAIA, c'est l'un des cabinets d'architectes les plus influents d'Asie, ainsi qu'un cabinet de renommée internationale. Grâce à un processus de conception créatif et critique, assorti d'une vaste expérience professionnelle, notre mission est de fournir des projets de haute qualité. Bien que l'architecture soit au cœur de notre pratique, notre implication dans les projets s'étend souvent aux études de faisabilité, à la planification générale et à la programmation. Le portefeuille de notre cabinet témoigne d'années de pratique dans les domaines de la culture, de l'entreprise, du commerce, de l'hôtellerie, des centres des arts de la scène, du transport, de l'éducation, des espaces résidentiels, spirituels et de l'aménagement urbain.

KRIS YAO | ARTECH es un estudio de arquitectura con sede en Asia compuesto por más de 160 profesionales con oficinas en Taipéi y Shanghái. Nuestros proyectos se sitúan principalmente en la Gran China, pero también se encuentran en Estados Unidos, Europa y el sur de Asia. Fundada en 1985 por Kris Yao, Hon, FAIA, la empresa es uno de los estudios profesionales de arquitectura más influyentes de Asia, así como una firma de renombre internacional. Utilizando un proceso de diseño creativo y crítico complementado con una amplia experiencia profesional, nuestra misión es entregar proyectos de alta calidad. Aunque la arquitectura es el núcleo de nuestra práctica, nuestra participación en los proyectos a menudo se extiende a los estudios de viabilidad, la planificación general y la programación. La cartera de nuestra empresa demuestra años de práctica en el ámbito cultural, corporativo, comercial, hotelero, centros de artes escénicas, transporte, educación, residencial, espacios espirituales y diseño urbano.

# HAN PAO-TEH MEMORIAL MUSEUM

Tainan, Taiwan

Photos: © KRIS YAO I ARTECH, Shephotoerd Co.

This building recognizes the figure of architect Han Pao-Teh, mentor to Kris Yao, and his contribution to the arts and architecture of Taiwan. The center integrates exhibition and teaching spaces that facilitate experiential learning. The project is conceived as a cube within another cube, two simple geometric forms materialized in concrete that collide to generate multiple facets. An impressive exhibition space 13.5 m in height welcomes visitors. Above it hovers a two-story cube-shaped auditorium that overlooks the exterior and houses the Permanent Exhibition. The rotation of this cube relative to its envelope creates a gap in the wall that dramatically projects natural light into the dark space below. Views of the green surroundings on the ground floor guide visitors through a theatrical ascent via stairs that enter and exit the building and lead to the Permanent Exhibition.

Dieses Gebäude würdigt die Persönlichkeit des Architekten Han Pao-Teh, des Mentors von Kris Yao, und dessen Beitrag zur Kunst und Architektur Taiwans. Das Zentrum umfasst Ausstellungs- und Unterrichtsräume, die das erfahrungsorientierte Lernen erleichtern. Das Projekt ist als ein Würfel in einem anderen Würfel konzipiert, zwei einfache geometrische Formen, die in Beton materialisiert sind und zusammenstoßen, um mehrere Facetten zu erzeugen. Die Besucher werden von einem beeindruckenden Ausstellungsraum von 13,5 m Höhe empfangen. Darüber schwebt ein zweistöckiges, würfelförmiges Auditorium, das den Außenbereich überblickt und die Dauerausstellung beherbergt. Durch die Drehung dieses Kubus im Verhältnis zu seiner Umhüllung entsteht ein Spalt in der Wand, durch den auf dramatische Weise natürliches Licht in den dunklen Raum darunter fällt. Von einer grünen Umgebung im Erdgeschoss gelang der Besucher durch einen theatralischen Aufstieg über eine Treppe, die das Gebäude erreicht und verlässt und zur Dauerausstellung führt.

Ce bâtiment rend hommage à l'architecte Han Pao-Teh, mentor de Kris Yao, et à sa contribution aux arts et à l'architecture de Taïwan. Le centre intègre des espaces d'exposition et d'enseignement favorisant l'apprentissage par l'expérience. Le projet est conçu comme un cube imbriqué dans un autre cube, deux formes géométriques simples matérialisées dans le béton qui entrent en collision pour générer de multiples facettes. Un impressionnant espace d'exposition de 13,5 m de haut accueille les visiteurs. Il est surplombé par un auditorium cubique de deux étages donnant sur l'extérieur et abritant l'exposition permanente. La rotation de ce cube par rapport à son enveloppe crée une brèche dans le mur qui projette de façon spectaculaire la lumière naturelle dans l'espace sombre situé en dessous. Les vues sur les environs verdoyants du rez-de-chaussée guident les visiteurs à travers une ascension théâtrale par des escaliers qui entrent et sortent du bâtiment et mènent à l'exposition permanente.

Este edificio reconoce la figura del arquitecto Han Pao-Teh, mentor de Kris Yao, y su contribución a las artes y la arquitectura de Taiwán. El centro integra espacios de exposición y enseñanza que facilitan el aprendizaje experimental. El proyecto se plantea como un cubo dentro de otro cubo, dos formas geométricas simples materializadas en hormigón que colisionan para generar múltiples facetas. Un impresionante espacio de exposición de 13,5 metros de altura recibe a los visitantes. Sobre él flota un cubo de dos plantas con forma de auditorio que se asoma al exterior y alberga la Exposición Permanente. El giro de este cubo respecto de su envolvente produce una brecha en el muro que proyecta dramáticamente la luz natural hacia el oscuro espacio inferior. Las vistas del verde exterior en planta baja guían a los visitantes hacia un teatral ascenso a través de escaleras que entran y salen del edificio y que desembocan en la Exposición Permanente.

**Awards:**
**- 2023 DFA Awards - Bronze Award**
**- 2023 LOOP Design Awards - Winner - Cultural**
**- 2023 DNA Paris Design Awards - Honorable Mention - Cultural**
**- 2023 The Plan Award Shortlist - Culture**
**- 2022 Architizer A+ Awards Finalist – Culture**

**Client:**
Joseph ST Han and Karen Han

**Design architect:**
Kris Yao

**Inspection architect:**
Glen Lu

**Design team:**
Albert Liu, Naiwen Cheng, Kai-Chih Chang, Megle Lin, Eden Sung, Yuan-Heng Shih

**Construction inspection team:**
Jui-Hung Lin

**Project advisor supervisor:**
Willy Yu, Jun-Ren Chou

**Consultants:**
Structural: Chuang Wei Structural Engineering Inc.
MEP: Majestic Engineering Consultants Inc.
HVAC: I. S. LIN & Associates Consulting Engineers

**Contractor:**
Shyh Auh Construction Co., Ltd.

**Building structure:**
Reinforced concrete

**Exterior materials:**
Architectural concrete

**Building use:**
Exhibition

**Area:**
Site area: 2,850 $m^2$
Lot coverage area: 238 $m^2$
Gross building floor area: 690 $m^2$

**Construction period:**
Design phase: 2015.08-2016.12
Construction phase: 2018.05-2022.11
Completion: 2022.11

Sketch

漢寶德
紀念館
HAN PAO-TEH
MEMORIAL
MUSEUM

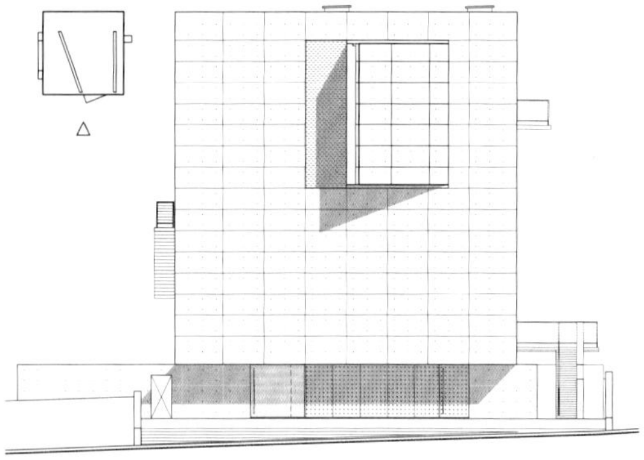

South elevation

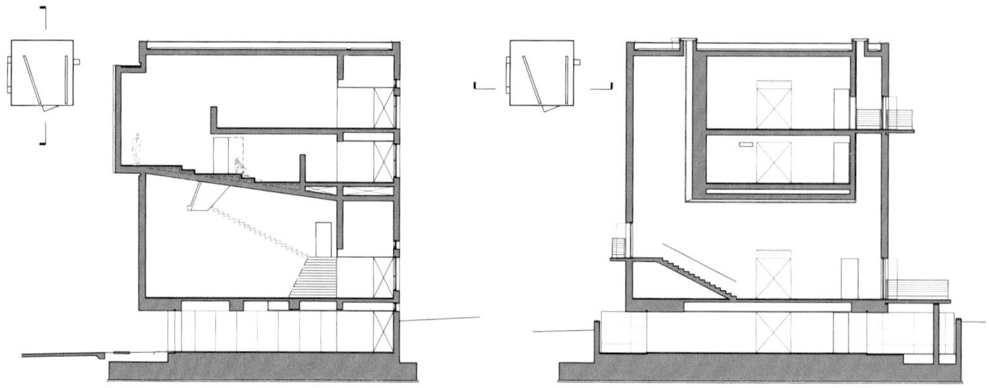

Sections

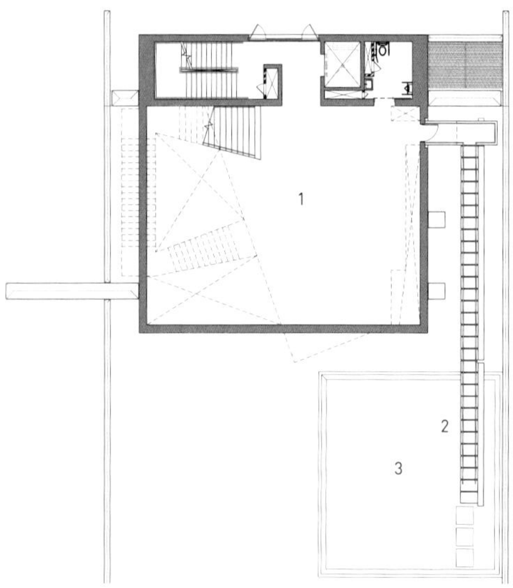


Second floor plan

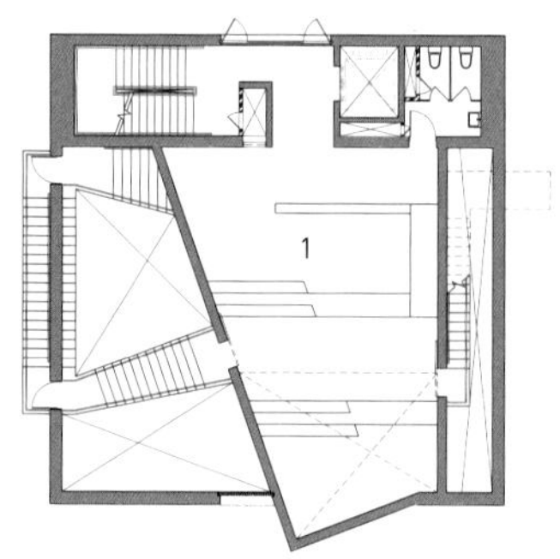


Third floor plan

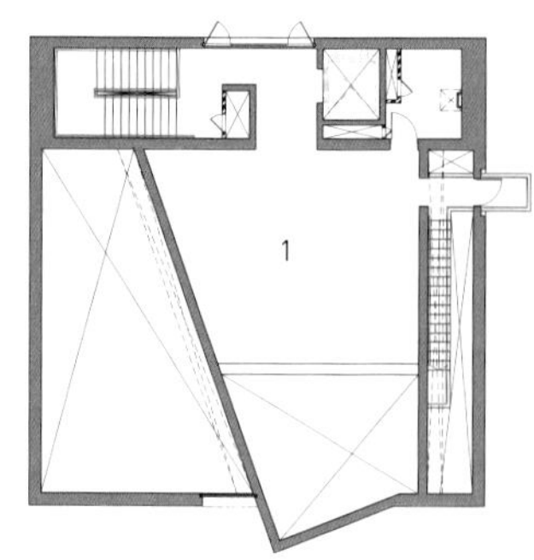


Fourth floor plan

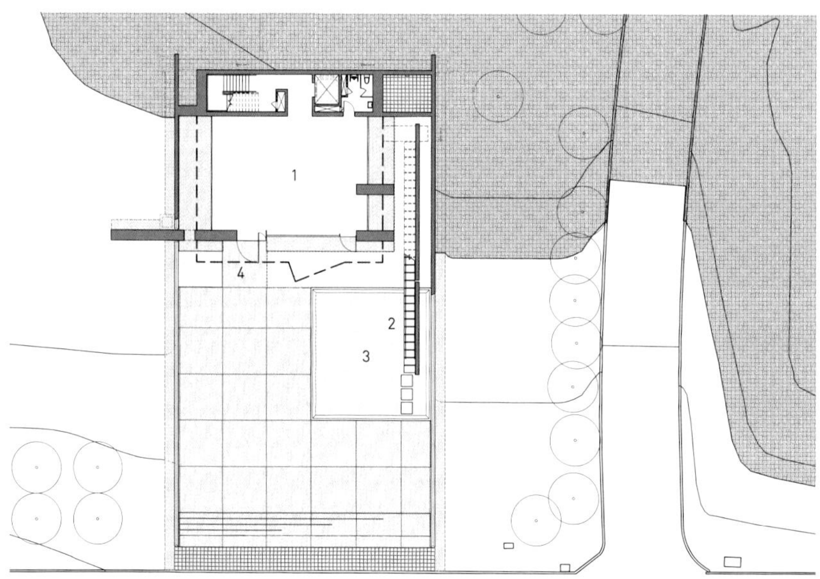


First floor plan

0 200 500 1000
CM

1. Exhibition
2. Stairs
3. Reflecting pool
4. Entrance

# HOTEL RESONANCE TAIPEI

**Taipei, Taiwan**

Photos: © Dean Cheng, Shawn Liu Studio

The building occupies a corner lot dominated by a slender volume of rooms. Its design exhibits an architectural language with multiple interpretations. The program is organized in a logical progression that leads visitors from public to private spaces. The first floor houses generous public spaces, the second floor has hotel services for guests, and the upper floors feature 175 compact and economical rooms. The long facades have vertical openings of varying widths. On the short facades, large square windows are situated, the most prominent of which extends over the entrance to the building. The hotel represents an oasis of tranquility in a busy district populated by educational and administrative institutions. Despite being located in a degraded residential area, its unexpected elegance comfortably fits in with its neighbors.

Das Gebäude befindet sich auf einem Eckgrundstück und wird von einer schmalen Raumfolge dominiert. Sein Design zeigt eine architektonische Sprache mit verschiedenen Interpretationen. Das Programm ist in einer logischen Abfolge organisiert, durch die die Besucher von den öffentlichen zu den privaten Räumen gelangen. Im ersten Stockwerk befinden sich großzügige öffentliche Räume, im zweiten Stockwerk die Hoteldienstleistungen für die Gäste und in den oberen Stockwerken 175 kompakte und wirtschaftliche Zimmer. Die langen Fassaden haben vertikale Öffnungen von unterschiedlicher Breite. An den kurzen Fassaden befinden sich große quadratische Fenster, wobei sich das auffälligste über dem Eingang des Gebäudes befindet. Das Hotel ist eine Oase der Ruhe in einem geschäftigen, von Bildungs- und Verwaltungseinrichtungen geprägten Viertel. Obwohl es in einem heruntergekommenen Wohngebiet liegt, fügt es sich mit seiner unerwarteten Eleganz gut in die Nachbarschaft ein.

Le bâtiment occupe un terrain en angle dominé par un volume élancé de chambres. Sa conception présente un langage architectural aux interprétations multiples. Le programme est organisé selon une progression logique qui conduit les visiteurs des espaces publics aux espaces privés. Le rez-de-chaussée abrite des espaces publics généreux, le premier étage des services hôteliers pour les clients, et les étages supérieurs 175 chambres compactes et économiques. Les longues façades présentent des ouvertures verticales de différentes largeurs. Sur les façades courtes sont disposées de grandes fenêtres carrées, dont la plus saillante s'étend au-dessus de l'entrée du bâtiment. L'hôtel évoque une oasis de tranquillité dans un quartier animé, peuplé d'institutions éducatives et administratives. Bien que situé dans une zone résidentielle dégradée, son élégance inattendue s'intègre harmonieusement à son environnement.

El edificio ocupa una parcela en esquina presidida por un esbelto volumen de habitaciones. Su diseño exhibe un lenguaje arquitectónico con múltiples interpretaciones. El programa se organiza en una progresión lógica que conduce a los visitantes de lo público a lo privado. La primera planta alberga generosos espacios públicos, la segunda planta los servicios del hotel para huéspedes y los pisos superiores 175 habitaciones compactas y económicas. Las fachadas largas presentan aberturas en forma de hendiduras verticales de diferentes anchuras. En las fachadas cortas se sitúan ventanales cuadrados de gran tamaño, el más prominente de los cuales vuela sobre la entrada al edificio. El hotel supone un oasis de tranquilidad dentro de un distrito con tráfico intenso y poblado por instituciones educativas y administrativas. A pesar de ubicarse en una zona residencial degradada, su inesperada elegancia se asienta cómodamente junto a sus vecinos.

**Awards:**
- 2023 DNA Paris Design Awards - Winner - Hospitality
- 2021 Eurasian Prize - Gold Diploma - HoReCa
- 2021 The Plan Award Finalist - Hospitality

**Client:**
Fubon Life Insurance Co., Ltd.

**Design architect:**
Kris Yao

**Project principal:**
Albert Liu

**Design team:**
Yen-Hsun Li, Yi-Lung Sung, Pei-Ying Jiang, Kai-Wei Weng, Roy Sung, Megle Lin, Ray Chen, Yuan-Heng Shih, Alan Cheng, Shih-Chieh Lin

**Construction inspection team:**
Jun-Ren Chou, Alex Liu, Jun-Shun Wang

**Consultants:**
Structural: Chuang Wei Structural Engineering Inc.
Plumbing, electrical & fire protection: Heng Kai Engineering Consultants, Inc.
HVAC: I. S. LIN & Associates Consulting Engineers
Landscape: The SWA Group (SD), CNHW Planning & design consultants (CD)
Lighting: Chroma33 Architectural Lighting Design

**Contractor:**
Dehwa Construction Co., Ltd.

**Building structure:**
Reinforced concrete

**Exterior materials:**
Precast architectural concrete panel, laminated heat strengthened glass, aluminum panel

**Building use:**
Hotel

**Area:**
Site area: 3,616 $m^2$
Lot coverage area: 1,233 $m^2$
Gross building floor Area: 18,711 $m^2$

**Construction period:**
Design phase: 2013-2017.07
Construction phase: 2017.07-2019.12
Completion: 2019.12

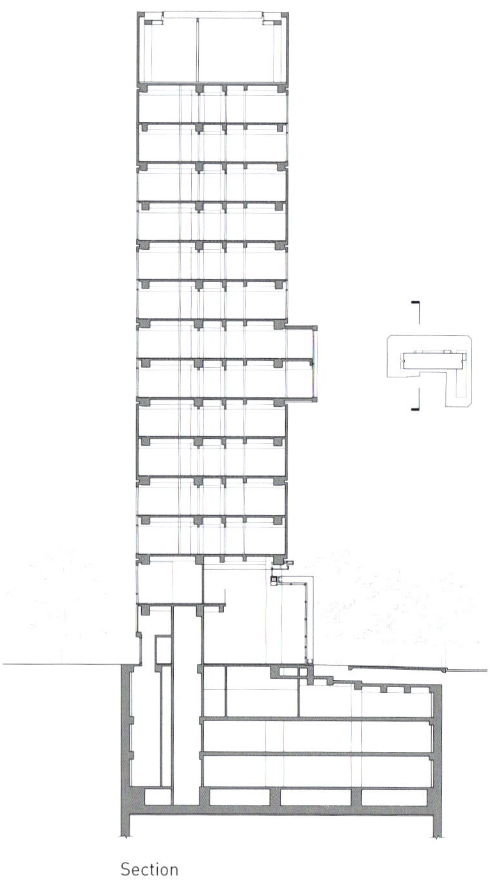

Section

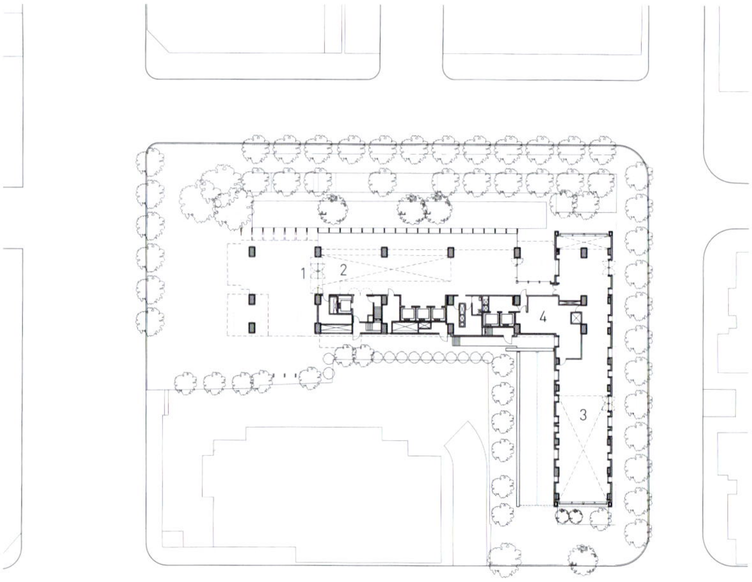


First floor plan

1. Entrance
2. Lobby
3. Cafe
4. Kitchen

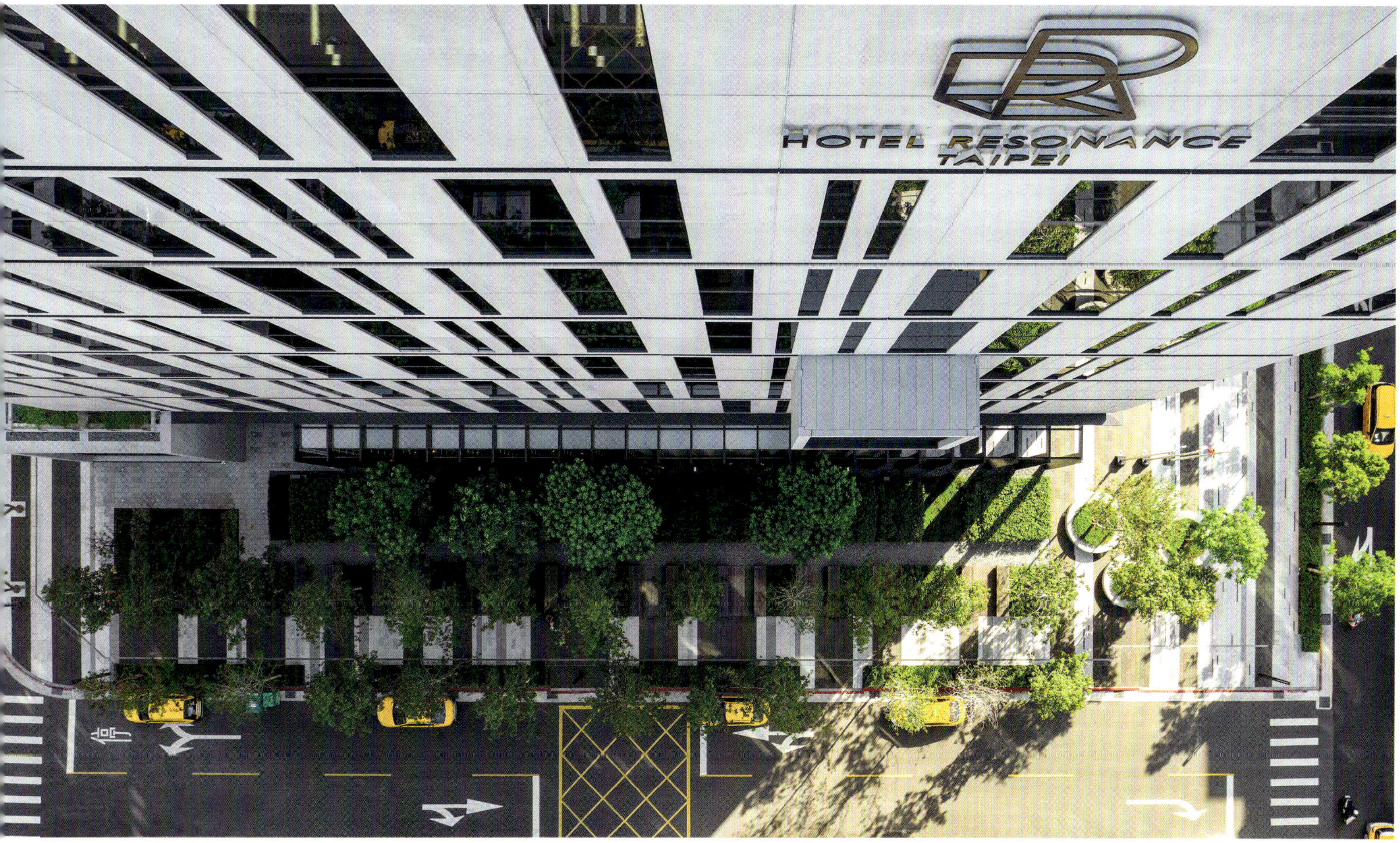
HOTEL RESONANCE
TAIPEI

# MATHEW AND GHOSH Architects

**Nisha Mathew Ghosh, Soumitro Ghosh**

www.mathewghosh.com

MGA is an architectural office founded in 1995 in Bangalore, India, by architects Soumitro Ghosh and Nisha Mathew Ghosh. MGA's works has been widely recognised nationally and internationally.

The thinking and practice of MGA centres, among other things, of an architecture investigating the present as a threshold of time gone and aspired futures; exploring contextual conditions; suggestion of sensation, perception and understanding desire; engagement in the process of making; natural light, its emancipatory promise and an opportunity of spatial structuring; material and its hapticity; the pragmatism of paucity and frugality; resource skill and technique; connecting space, time, and nature in the moment; empathy of landscapes and the conversation within and without; cognitive organisation; precision, the poetry of geometry and deviations; durability, resource and detail.

MGA ist ein Architekturbüro, das 1995 in Bangalore, Indien, von den Architekten Soumitro Ghosh und Nisha Mathew Ghosh gegründet wurde. Die Arbeiten von MGA haben auf nationaler und internationaler Ebene große Anerkennung gefunden.

Im Zentrum des Denkens und der Praxis von MGA steht unter anderem eine Architektur, die die Gegenwart als Schwelle zu vergangenen Zeiten und angestrebten Zukünften untersucht; das Erforschen kontextueller Bedingungen; die Suggestion von Empfindung, Wahrnehmung und Verstehenswünschen; das Engagement im Prozess des Machens; natürliches Licht, sein emanzipatorisches Versprechen und als Möglichkeit der räumlichen Strukturierung; Material und seine Haptik; der Pragmatismus der Knappheit und Genügsamkeit; Ressourcenkenntnis und Technik; die Verbindung von Raum, Zeit und Natur im Moment; die Empathie von Landschaften und die Konversation innerhalb und außerhalb; kognitive Organisation; Präzision, die Poesie der Geometrie und Abweichungen; Haltbarkeit, Ressourcen und Details.

MGA est un bureau d'architecture fondé en 1995 à Bangalore, en Inde, par les architectes Soumitro Ghosh et Nisha Mathew Ghosh. Les travaux de MGA ont été largement reconnus au niveau national et international.

La pensée et la pratique de MGA se concentrent, entre autres, sur une architecture qui étudie le présent comme un seuil du temps passé et des futurs aspirés ; l'exploration des conditions contextuelles ; la suggestion de la sensation, la perception et la compréhension du désir ; l'engagement dans le processus de fabrication ; la lumière naturelle, sa promesse d'émancipation et comme opportunité de structuration spatiale ; le matériau et son hapticité ; le pragmatisme de la pauvreté et de la frugalité ; la compétence et la technique des ressources ; la connexion de l'espace, du temps et de la nature dans l'instant ; l'empathie des paysages et la conversation à l'intérieur et à l'extérieur ; l'organisation cognitive ; la précision, la poésie de la géométrie et des déviations ; la durabilité, la ressource et le détail.

MGA es un estudio de arquitectura fundado en 1995 en Bangalore (India) por los arquitectos Soumitro Ghosh y Nisha Mathew Ghosh. Los trabajos de MGA han sido ampliamente reconocidos a nivel nacional e internacional.

El pensamiento y la práctica de MGA se centran, entre otras cosas, en una arquitectura que investiga el presente como umbral del tiempo pasado y de futuros a los que se aspira; la exploración de las condiciones contextuales; la sugerencia de la sensación, la percepción y el deseo de comprensión; el compromiso en el proceso de creación; la luz natural, su promesa emancipadora y como oportunidad de estructuración espacial; el material y su tactilidad; el pragmatismo de la escasez y la frugalidad; la habilidad y la técnica de los recursos; la conexión del espacio, el tiempo y la naturaleza en el momento; la empatía de los paisajes y la conversación dentro y fuera; la organización cognitiva; la precisión, la poesía de la geometría y las desviaciones; la durabilidad, los recursos y el detalle.

# HOUSE OF STORIES

**Epsilon layout, Bengaluru, India**

Photos: © Pallon Daruwala

The project began with the challenge of designing for a former architect turned writer. Similar to a literary process, this house gradually reveals itself through modulated darkness, guiding the journey inward and hiding interior spaces that change from various perspectives offered by the design.
Upon entering the entrance gate, the visitor encounters a concrete spinal and structural threshold with high walls that leads to the living room, the public heart of the house. Sloping walls and skylights articulate spaces mapping the natural light that penetrates the house. The metal staircase and bridge insert another narration, leading to the upper levels where wood and zinc cladding define the most intimate spaces within the envelope of the building.

Das Projekt begann mit der Herausforderung, für einen ehemaligen Architekten zu entwerfen, der zum Schriftsteller wurde. Ähnlich wie ein literarischer Prozess enthüllt sich dieses Haus allmählich durch modulierte Dunkelheit, die den Weg nach innen leitet und Innenräume verbirgt, die sich aus verschiedenen Perspektiven, die das Design bietet, verändern.
Beim Betreten der Eingangspforte stößt der Besucher auf eine Schwelle aus Beton mit hohen Mauern, die in das Wohnzimmer, das öffentliche Herz des Hauses, führt. Schräge Wände und Oberlichter gliedern Räume, die das natürliche Licht, das in das Haus eindringt, abbilden. Die Metalltreppe und die Brücke fügen eine weitere Erzählung ein, die in die oberen Stockwerke führt, wo Holz- und Zinkverkleidungen die intimsten Räume innerhalb der Hülle des Gebäudes definieren.

Le projet a débuté avec le défi de concevoir pour un ancien architecte devenu écrivain. Semblable à un processus littéraire, cette maison se dévoile progressivement à travers une obscurité modulée, guidant le voyage vers l'intérieur et cachant des espaces intérieurs qui changent selon les différentes perspectives offertes par le design.
En franchissant le portail d'entrée, le visiteur rencontre une colonne vertébrale en béton et un seuil structurel avec de hauts murs qui mènent au salon, le cœur public de la maison. Les murs inclinés et les puits de lumière articulent des espaces qui reflètent la lumière naturelle qui pénètre dans la maison. L'escalier et le pont en métal insèrent une autre narration, menant aux niveaux supérieurs où le bardage en bois et en zinc définit les espaces les plus intimes à l'intérieur de l'enveloppe du bâtiment.

El proyecto comenzó con el reto de diseñar para un antiguo arquitecto reconvertido en escritor. Similar a un proceso literario, esta casa se revela gradualmente a través de una oscuridad modulada, guiando el viaje hacia el interior y ocultando espacios interiores que cambian desde las diversas perspectivas que ofrece el diseño.
Al cruzar la puerta de entrada, el visitante se encuentra con un umbral estructural y espinal de hormigón con altos muros que conduce al salón, el corazón público de la casa. Paredes inclinadas y claraboyas articulan los espacios mapeando la luz natural que penetra en la casa. La escalera y el puente metálicos insertan otra narración, que conduce a los niveles superiores, donde los revestimientos de madera y zinc definen los espacios más íntimos dentro de la envolvente del edificio.

**Awards:**
**- EDIDA 2017 – Elle Decor Light Design**
**- THE PLAN AWARD 2020 (shortlisted)**
**- INDIA'S BEST DESIGN AWARDS 2021**
**- IDA 2022 (Honourable mention)**

**Designers (architecture, interiors, lighting & landscape design):**
Nisha Mathew Ghosh + Soumitro Ghosh (Mathew & Ghosh Architects, Bangalore)

**Project team:**
Sahana, Joby , Arjun, Upasana, Micky, Asha, Raksha, Saikat, Aishwarya, Jincy, Esha, Justin, Khusboo and others.

**Construction period:**
2013-2017

**Total built area:**
6,000 sq ft

**General contractor:**
Anantharamu HK

**Consultants:**
Cruthi Consultants

Model images

Sequential section

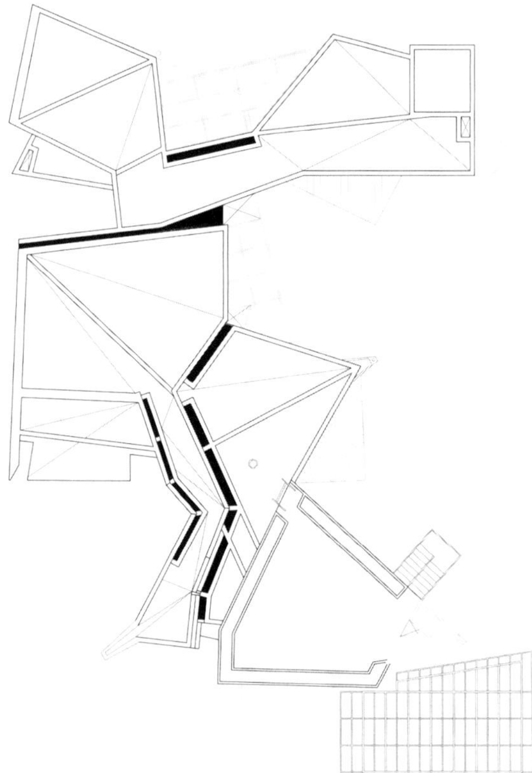

Roof plan

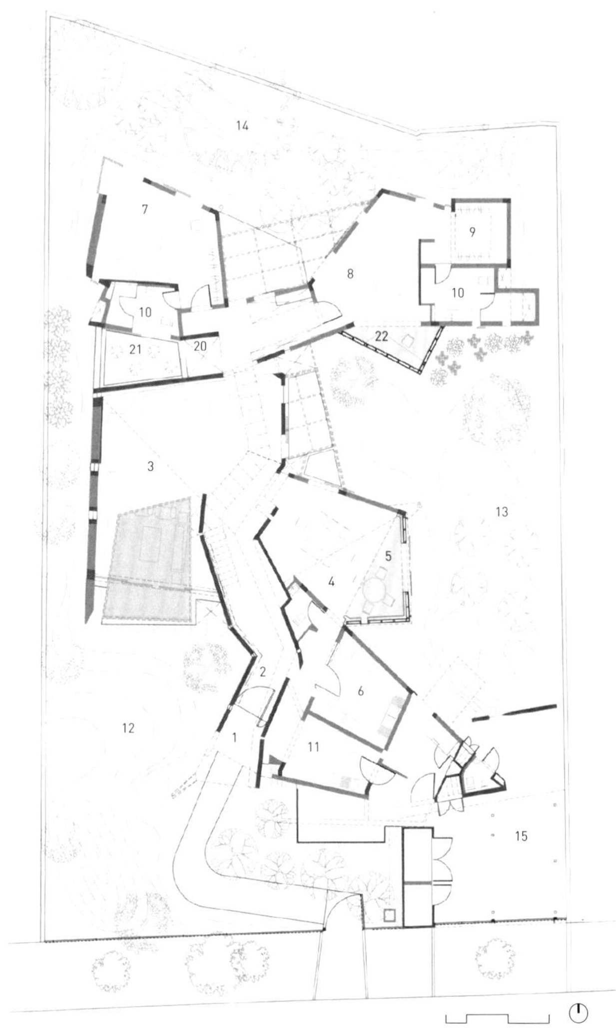

Ground floor plan

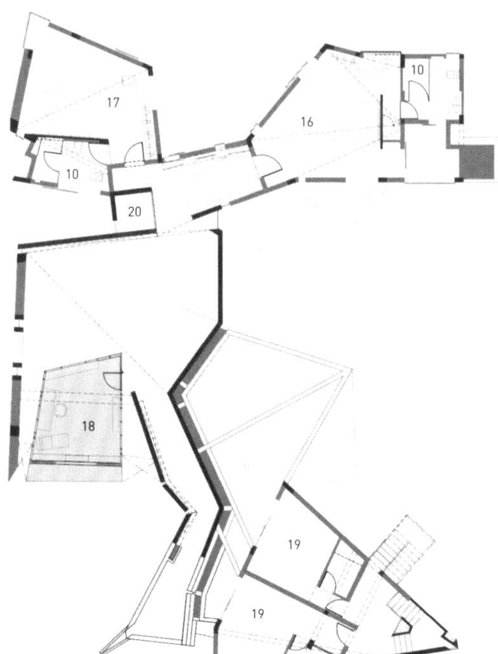

First floor plan

1. Entry
2. Concrete cavern
3. Living room
4. Dining room
5. Breakfast alcove
6. Kitchen
7. Bedroom
8. Master bedroom
9. Walk-in closet
10. Toilet
11. Service area
12. Fore-court
13. East court
14. North court
15. Parking
16. Bedroom
17. Bedroom
18. Study room
19. Domestic help room
20. Elevator
21. Lotus pond
22. Study niche

# mf+arquitetos

**Filipi Oliveira, Mariana Oliveira**

www.mfmaisarquitetos.com

Mariana Garcia Oliveira and Filipi Oliveira, both graduates in architecture and urban planning, met in their first year of university. After graduating in 2009, they got married and founded MF arquitetos. In 2015, the office was restructured and became known as mf+arquitetos.
Located in the city of Franca, in the interior of the state of São Paulo, the office works on residential, commercial, industrial, and interior design projects. Their work stands out for its contemporary style, always proposing a design concept that seeks to integrate the interior with the exterior, combined with formal purity, straight lines, and the use of native materials from Brazil, instilling a new concept of living.

Mariana Garcia Oliveira und Filipi Oliveira, beide Absolventen der Architektur und des Städtebaus, lernten sich im ersten Studienjahr kennen. Nach ihrem Abschluss im Jahr 2009 heirateten sie und gründeten MF Arquitetos. Im Jahr 2015 wurde das Büro restrukturiert und in mf+arquitetos umbenannt.
Das Büro befindet sich in Franca, einer Stadt im Landesinneren des Bundesstaates São Paulo, und arbeitet an Wohn-, Gewerbe-, Industrie- und Innenarchitekturprojekten. Ihre Arbeiten zeichnen sich durch einen zeitgenössischen Stil aus, der immer ein Designkonzept verfolgt, das die Verbindung von Innen- und Außenräumen anstrebt und dabei auf klare Formen und die Verwendung einheimischer Materialien aus Brasilien setzt, was ein neues Konzept des Wohnens vermittelt.

Mariana Garcia Oliveira et Filipi Oliveira, tous deux diplômés en architecture et urbanisme, se sont rencontrés lors de leur première année d'université. Après leur diplôme en 2009, ils se sont mariés et ont fondé MF arquitetos. En 2015, le cabinet a été restructuré et est devenu mf+arquitetos.

Basé dans la ville de Franca, dans l'intérieur de l'État de São Paulo, le cabinet travaille sur des projets résidentiels, commerciaux, industriels et d'aménagement intérieur. Leurs travaux se distinguent par leur style contemporain, avec une recherche constante d'une intégration entre intérieur et extérieur, caractérisée par la pureté des formes, des lignes droites et l'utilisation de matériaux locaux du Brésil, créant ainsi un nouveau concept d'habitat.

Mariana Garcia Oliveira y Filipi Oliveira, ambos licenciados en arquitectura y urbanismo, se conocieron en su primer año de universidad. Tras graduarse en 2009, se casaron y fundaron MF arquitetos. En 2015, la oficina se reestructuró y pasó a llamarse mf+arquitetos.

Ubicado en la ciudad de Franca, en el interior del estado de São Paulo, la oficina trabaja en proyectos residenciales, comerciales, industriales y de interiorismo. Sus trabajos destacan por su estilo contemporáneo, proponiendo siempre un concepto de diseño que busca integrar el interior con el exterior, combinado con la pureza formal, las líneas rectas y el uso de materiales autóctonos de Brasil, que inculcan un nuevo concepto de habitar.

# LAKE HOUSE

**Uberlândia, Minas Gerais, Brazil**

Photos: © Felipe Araújo

Upon entering the plot, the visitor to this house sees a pool set on the shores of a lake and a rectangular block with pure lines measuring 36.5 m in length. The subtle sensation of not touching the ground gives an elegant lightness to the brutality of this concrete block, with its 2.60 m of clear height providing a human scale that allows the architecture to frame the surrounding nature.
The entrance to the house is via a walkway over a pond located between two stone-clad volumes. Openings oriented on both sides of the plot allow nature to enter the house's large living room. The soft palette of natural materials in the living room, including stone floors and walls, a concrete ceiling, and wood panels, contrasts with the textures of leather and linen furniture. Rope sunshades add beauty and dynamism to the facade, helping to protect from the sun and provide privacy.

Wenn man das Grundstück betritt, sieht der Besucher dieses Hauses einen Pool am Ufer eines Sees und einen rechteckigen Block mit klaren Linien von 36,5 Metern Länge. Das subtile Gefühl, den Boden nicht zu berühren, verleiht der Brutalität dieses Betonblocks eine elegante Leichtigkeit, wobei eine freie Höhe von 2,60 Metern eine menschliche Maßstäblichkeit ermöglicht, die es der Architektur ermöglicht, die umgebende Natur einzufassen.
Der Zugang zum Haus erfolgt über eine Gehweg über einem Teich zwischen zwei steinverkleideten Volumina. Öffnungen auf beiden Seiten des Grundstücks ermöglichen es der Natur, in das große Wohnzimmer des Hauses einzutreten. Die sanfte Materialpalette des Wohnzimmers, einschließlich Steinböden und -wände, einer Betondecke und Holzpaneelen, steht im Kontrast zu den Texturen von Leder- und Leinenmöbeln. Seilsonnenschirme verleihen der Fassade Schönheit und Dynamik und schützen vor der Sonne und gewähren Privatsphäre.

En entrant sur la parcelle, le visiteur de cette maison découvre une piscine bordée d'un lac et un bloc rectangulaire aux lignes pures de 36,5 mètres de longueur. La sensation subtile de ne pas toucher le sol confère une élégance légère à la brutalité de ce bloc de béton, avec une hauteur libre de 2,60 mètres qui permet une échelle humaine pour encadrer la nature environnante.
L'entrée de la maison se fait par une passerelle sur un étang situé entre deux volumes revêtus de pierre. Des ouvertures orientées des deux côtés de la parcelle permettent à la nature de pénétrer dans le grand salon de la maison. La palette de matériaux doux du salon, comprenant des sols et des murs en pierre, un plafond en béton et des panneaux en bois, contraste avec les textures des meubles en cuir et en lin. Les brise-soleil en corde ajoutent beauté et dynamisme à la façade, protégeant du soleil et offrant de l'intimité.

Al entrar en la parcela, el visitante de esta casa divisa una piscina insertada a orillas de un lago y un bloque rectangular de líneas puras de 36,5 m de longitud. La sutil sensación de no tocar el suelo otorga una elegante ligereza a la brutalidad de este bloque de hormigón, cuyos 2,60 m de altura libre otorgan una escala humana que permite a la arquitectura enmarcar la naturaleza circundante.
La entrada a la casa se produce a a través de una pasarela sobre un estanque situado entre dos volúmenes revestidos de piedra. Las aberturas orientadas hacia ambos lados de la parcela permiten que la naturaleza penetre en el gran salón de la casa. La suave paleta de materiales naturales del salón: suelo y paredes de piedra, techo de hormigón y paneles de madera, contrasta con las texturas de cuero y lino de los muebles. Los brise-soleil de cuerda confieren belleza y dinamismo a la fachada, ayudando a proteger del sol y aportando intimidad.

**Awards:**
**AZ awards 2023**

**Project team:**
Filipi Oliveira, Mariana Oliveira, Luis Fernando, Luis Felipe, Lucas Ferrari, Talita Faciroli, Guilherme Takahashi, Renato Ubiali, Dionésio Júnior

**Location:**
Uberlândia, MG Brazil

**Construction period:**
2019-2022

**Total built area:**
557 $m^2$

**Consultants:**
Structural project: Sergio Azara

Sketch

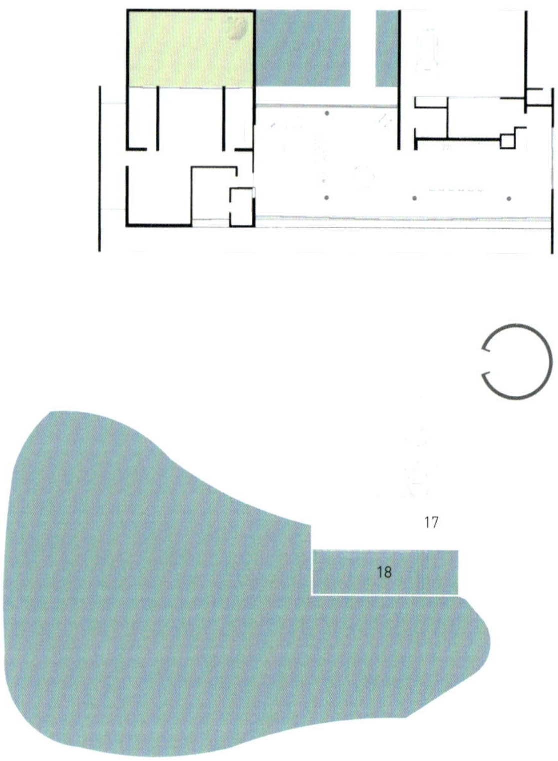


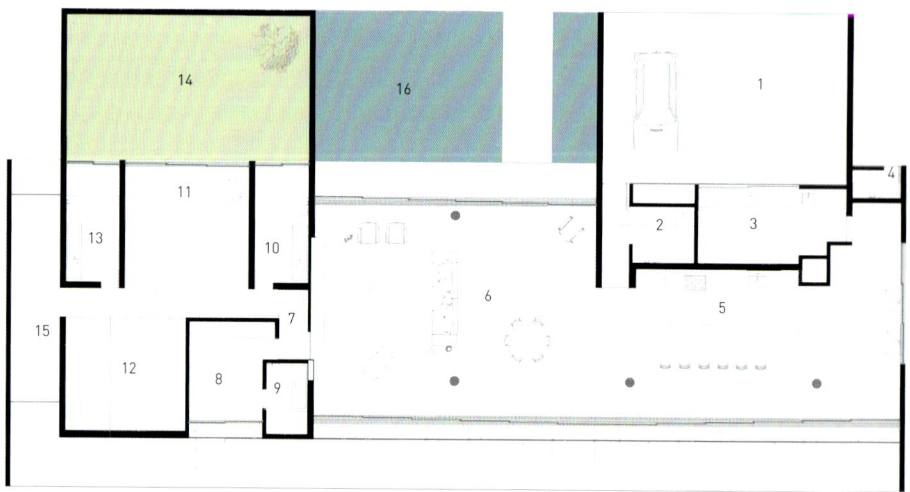


Floor plan

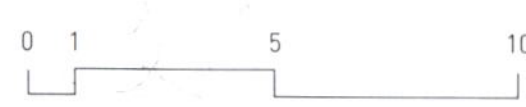


1. Garage
2. Toilet
3. Laundry
4. Service bathroom
5. Gourmet area
6. Living
7. Intimate hall
8. Bedroom
9. Bathroom
10. Bathroom
11. Bedroom
12. Closet
13. Bathroom
14. Private garden
15. Office
16. Reflecting pool
17. Deck
18. Pool

Site plan

## MICHELE ARNABOLDI Architetti

**Michele Arnaboldi, Carlo Barra, Enzo Rombolà, Anja Ureta**

www.ma-a.ch

The office of Michele Arnaboldi Architetti was founded in Locarno in 1985. Michele Arnaboldi is one of the most important representatives of the "second generation" of the "Ticino School". Through the deepening and refinement of rational approaches and the close relationship to the landscape, he has developed his own architectural language.

The geometrically clear buildings, often executed in exposed concrete, emerge as true "places to live" and are developed and built in close relation to the landscape. The pre-Alpine topography and the Mediterranean climate influence the design of the buildings: steep entrances, terraces, logias... In the interiors, views and the incidence of light play a design role, while structures are emphasised in the constructive layout. The programme of functions is translated into orderly, partly flowing spaces and materials are deliberately used in a reduced way.

Das Büro Michele Arnaboldi Architetti wurde 1985 in Locarno gegründet. Michele Arnaboldi ist einer der wichtigsten Vertreter der „zweiten Generation" der „Tessiner Schule". Durch die Vertiefung und Verfeinerung der rationalen Ansätze und den engen Bezug zur Landschaft hat er eine eigene architektonischen Sprache entwickelt.

Die häufig in Sichtbeton ausgeführten, geometrisch klaren Bauten entstehen als wahre „Orte des Wohnens" und werden in enger Beziehung zur Landschaft entwickelt und gebaut. Die voralpine Topografie und das mediterrane Klima beeinflussen die Ausprägung der Gebäude: steile Zugänge, Terrassen, Loggien. In den Innenräumen spielen Ausblicke und der Lichteinfall eine gestalterische Rolle, während im konstruktiven Layout die Strukturen betont werden. Das Programm der Funktionen wird in geordnete, teilweise fließende Räume übertragen und die Materialien werden bewusst reduziert eingesetzt.

Le cabinet Michele Arnaboldi Architetti a été fondé à Locarno en 1985. Michele Arnaboldi est l'un des représentants les plus importants de la « deuxième génération » de l'« École du Tessin ». En approfondissant et en affinant les approches rationnelles et en entretenant des relations étroites avec le paysage, il a développé son propre langage architectural.
Les bâtiments géométriquement clairs, souvent réalisés en béton apparent, se présentent comme de véritables « lieux de vie » et sont conçus et construits en relation étroite avec le paysage. La topographie préalpine et le climat méditerranéen influencent la conception des bâtiments : entrées abruptes, terrasses, loggias... À l'intérieur, les vues et l'incidence de la lumière jouent un rôle dans la conception, tandis que les structures sont mises en valeur dans la disposition constructive. Le programme des fonctions est traduit en espaces ordonnés, en partie fluides, et les matériaux sont délibérément utilisés de manière réduite.

El estudio Michele Arnaboldi Architetti se fundó en Locarno en 1985. Michele Arnaboldi es uno de los representantes más importantes de la «segunda generación» de la «Escuela del Tesino». Mediante la profundización y el refinamiento de planteamientos racionales y la estrecha relación con el paisaje, ha desarrollado un lenguaje arquitectónico propio.
Los edificios geométricamente claros, a menudo ejecutados en hormigón visto, surgen como verdaderos «lugares para vivir» y se desarrollan y construyen en estrecha relación con el paisaje. La topografía pre-alpina y el clima mediterráneo influyen en el diseño de los edificios: entradas empinadas, terrazas, logias... En los interiores, las vistas y la incidencia de la luz desempeñan un papel de diseño, mientras que las estructuras se acentúan en la disposición constructiva. El programa de funciones se traduce en espacios ordenados, en parte fluidos, y los materiales se utilizan deliberadamente de forma reducida.

# REMORINO 16

## Minusio, Switzerland

Photos: © Nicola Roman Walbeck

The residential and commercial building Remorino 16 is located in a residential area with low building quality. With the arrival of the new Tilo regional train stop, the neighbourhood will undergo a slow transformation over the next few years. The project proposes a development that is able to find a new urban identity by incorporating the Remorino stream, the bridge and the public park behind it. The building, which was constructed on a particularly difficult terrain due to its topographical conditions, offers differentiated residential typologies on the upper floors and workspaces on the first two levels under the bridge, which open onto the Remorino stream. The building with a concrete structure is characterised by the presence of sliding panels with vertical wooden slats, which guarantee the appropriate intimacy to the large loggias overlooking the surrounding green spaces.

Das Wohn-und Geschäftshaus Remorino 16 befindet sich in einer Wohngegend mit geringer Bauqualität. Mit der Ankunft der neuen Haltestelle des Regionalzuges Tilo wird das Viertel in den nächsten Jahren eine langsame Transformation erfahren. Das Projekt schlägt eine Bebauung vor, welche durch die Einbeziehung des Baches Remorino, der Brücke und dem dahinter liegenden öffentlichen Park in der Lage ist, eine neue städtische Identität zu finden.Der Bau, welcher aufgrund seiner topographischen Gegebenheiten auf einem besonders schwierigen Gelände errichtet wurde, bietet differenzierte Wohntypologien in den oberen Geschossen und Arbeitsräume in den ersten beiden Etagen unter der Brücke, welche sich zum Bach Remorino öffnen. Das Gebäude mit Betonstruktur zeichnet sich durch die Präsenz von Schiebepaneelen mit vertikalen Holzlamellen aus, welche den großen Loggien mit Blick auf die umliegenden Grünflächen die passende Intimität garantieren.

Le bâtiment résidentiel et commercial Remorino 16 est situé dans une zone résidentielle de faible qualité de construction. Avec l'arrivée du nouveau train régional Tilo, le quartier connaîtra une transformation lente au cours des prochaines années. Le projet propose un développement capable de trouver une nouvelle identité urbaine en incorporant le ruisseau Remorino, le pont et le parc public derrière lui. Le bâtiment, construit sur un terrain particulièrement difficile en raison de ses conditions topographiques, offre des typologies résidentielles différenciées aux étages supérieurs et des espaces de travail aux deux premiers niveaux sous le pont, qui s'ouvrent sur le ruisseau Remorino. Le bâtiment, avec une structure en béton, se caractérise par la présence de panneaux coulissants avec des lames de bois verticales, garantissant l'intimité appropriée aux grandes loggias donnant sur les espaces verts environnants.

El edificio residencial y comercial Remorino 16 se ubica en una zona residencial de baja calidad constructiva. Con la llegada de la nueva parada del tren regional de la compañía Tilo, el barrio experimentará una lenta transformación en los próximos años. El proyecto propone una intervención capaz de encontrar una nueva identidad urbana mediante la incorporación del arroyo Remorino, el puente y el parque público situados en la parte posterior. El edificio, construido en un terreno especialmente difícil por sus condiciones topográficas, ofrece tipologías residenciales diferenciadas en las plantas superiores y espacios de trabajo en las dos primeras plantas bajo el nivel de acceso, que se abren hacia el arroyo. El edificio de estructura de hormigón se caracteriza por la presencia de paneles correderos con lamas verticales de madera, que garantizan la privacidad adecuada a las amplias logias con vistas a los espacios verdes circundantes.

**Awards:**
**Die 50 besten Wohnbauten - AdW 2021, nominiert**

**Project team:**
Michele Arnaboldi, Enzo Rombolà, Anja Ureta, Nicola Castelletti, Andrea Macchi

**Construction period:**
2016-2019

**Total built area:**
1,750 $m^2$

**General contractor:**
Ugo Bassi SA, Via Arbostra 35, CH-6963 Pregassona Lugano

Before construction

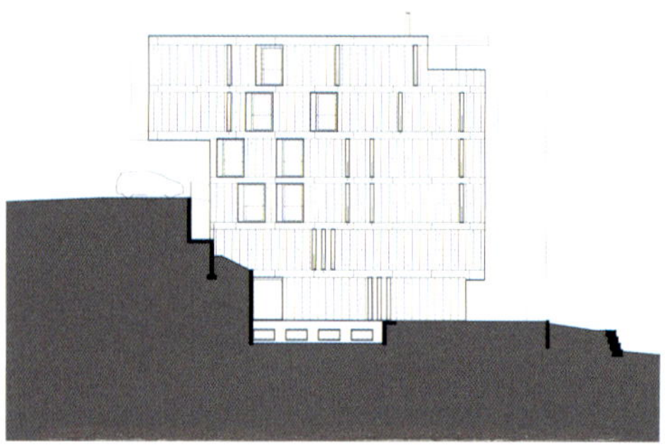

North elevation

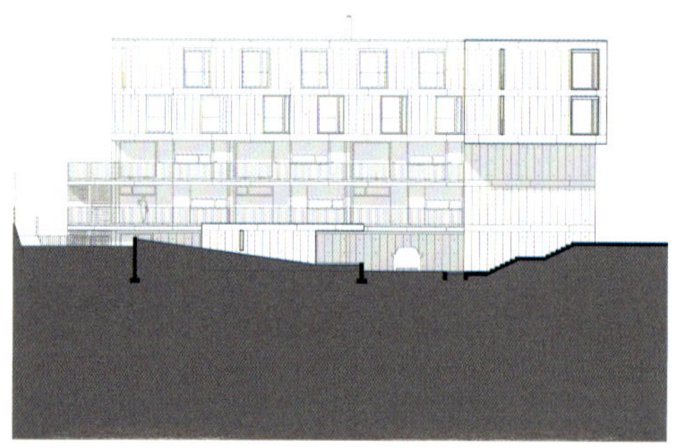

East elevation

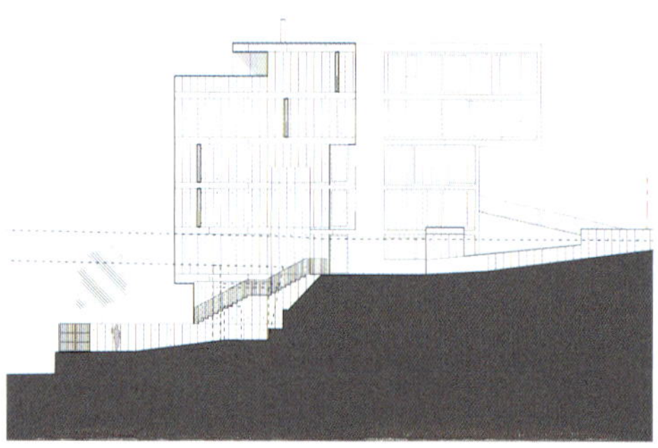

South elevation

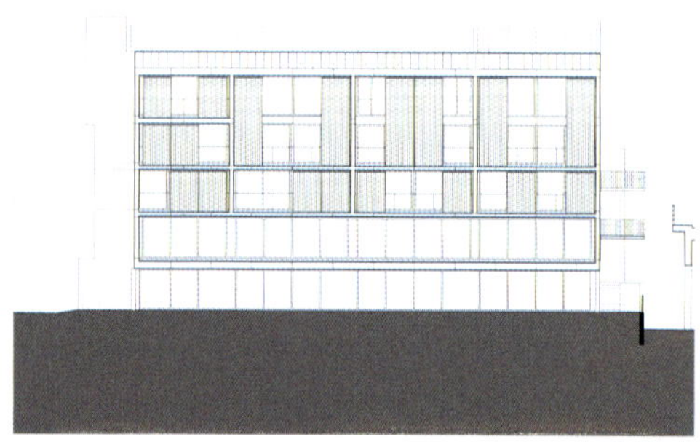

West elevation

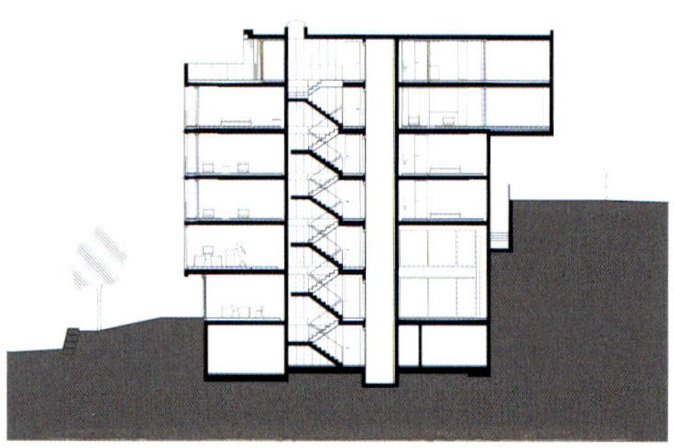

Main staircase section

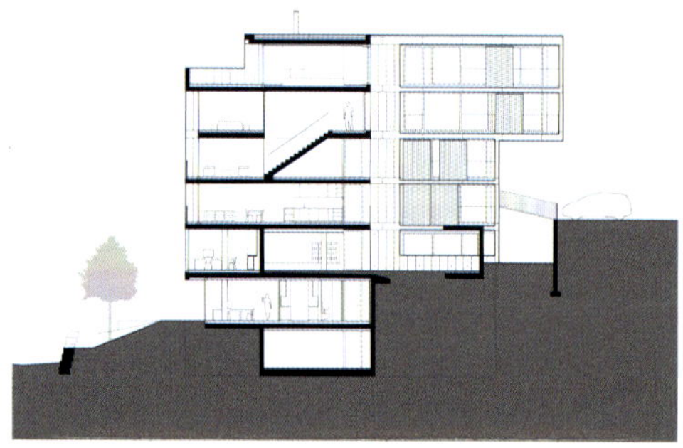

Section

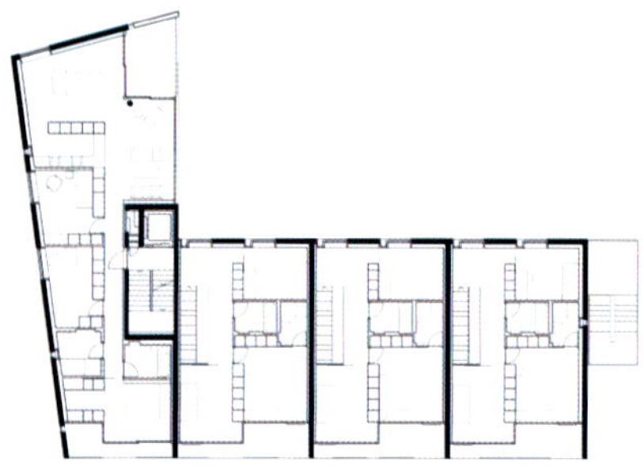

Second floor plan

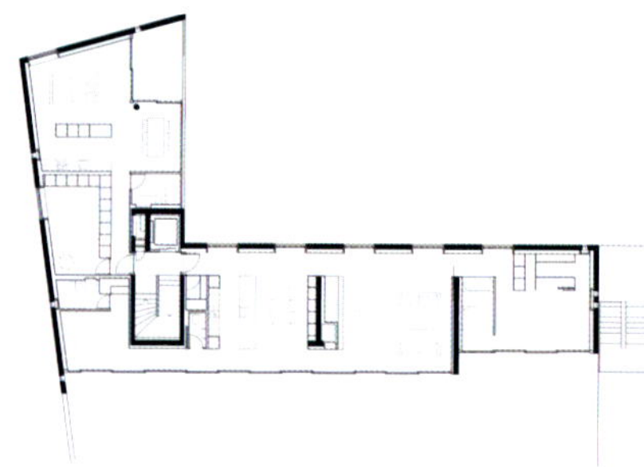

Third floor plan

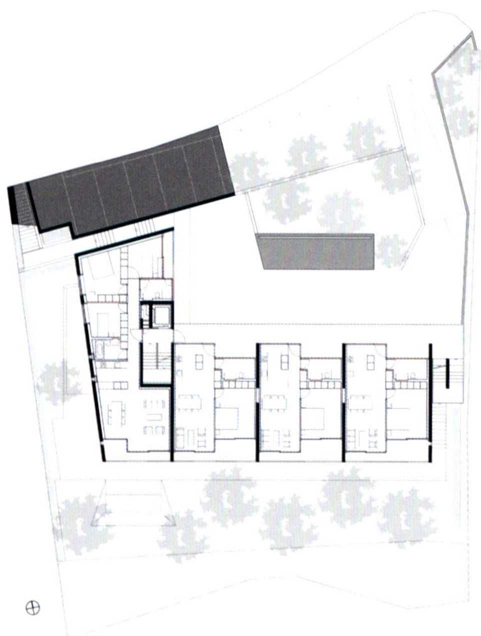

Ground floor plan

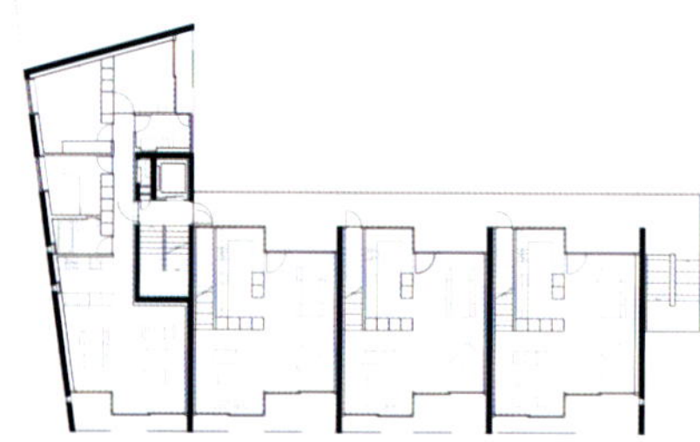

First floor plan

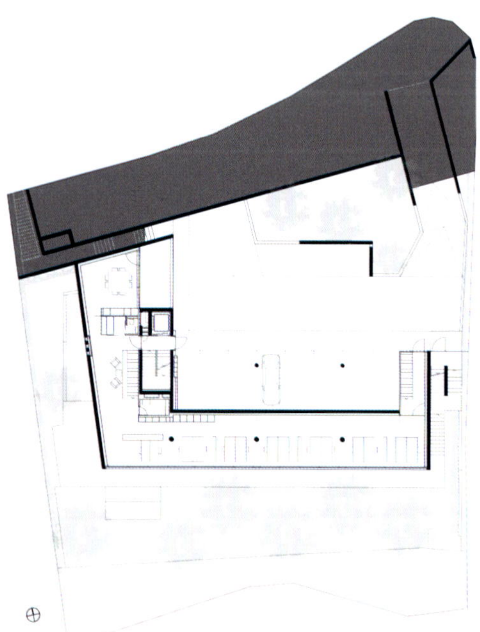

Basement plan 1

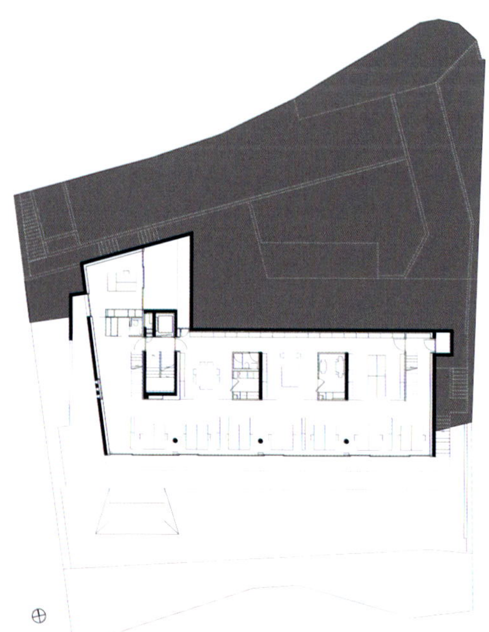

Basement plan 2

0 2 12m

# MONTEMURRO AGUIAR Architects

**Arch. Cristiano Aguiar, Arch. Tiziana Montemurro**

www.montemurroaguiar.ch

Montemurro Aguiar is an architecture atelier founded in 2008. Our architecture is distinguished by a dialogue with the place. Buildings respond to context and extend it by developing existing structures further. Every Montemurro Aguiar project develops its own identity. This also applies to the smaller residential buildings. These works are an area of experimentation: exploring the suspenseful relation between intimacy and opening of the facade, while incorporating the needs of the client in the design.

What unites the architecture created is the method or approach to building. This includes conceptual work on spatial programmes, clearly articulated craftsmanship and a conscious implementation of materiality. The quest for honesty with regard to material often leads to utilisation of concrete, which creates a feeling of security through its atmospheric density and intensity.

Montemurro Aguiar ist ein im Jahr 2008 gegründetes Architekturbüro. Unsere Architektur zeichnet sich durch einen Dialog mit dem Ort aus. Die Gebäude reagieren auf den Kontext und erweitern ihn, indem sie bestehende Strukturen weiterentwickeln. Jedes Projekt von Montemurro Aguiar entwickelt seine eigene Identität. Das gilt auch für die kleineren Wohngebäude. Diese Arbeiten sind ein Experimentierfeld: Sie erforschen das Spannungsverhältnis zwischen Intimität und Öffnung der Fassade und beziehen gleichzeitig die Bedürfnisse des Bauherrn in die Gestaltung mit ein.

Was die entstandene Architektur eint, ist die Methode oder der Ansatz beim Bauen. Dazu gehören die konzeptionelle Arbeit an Raumprogrammen, eine klar artikulierte handwerkliche Ausführung und ein bewusster Umgang mit der Materialität. Das Streben nach Ehrlichkeit in Bezug auf das Material führt oft zur Verwendung von Beton, der durch seine atmosphärische Dichte und Intensität ein Gefühl der Geborgenheit vermittelt.

Montemurro Aguiar est un atelier d'architecture fondé en 2008. Notre architecture se distingue par un dialogue avec le lieu. Les bâtiments répondent au contexte et l'étendent en développant davantage les structures existantes. Chaque projet de Montemurro Aguiar développe sa propre identité. Cela s'applique également aux petits bâtiments résidentiels. Ces travaux sont une zone d'expérimentation : exploration de la relation tendue entre l'intimité et l'ouverture de la façade, tout en intégrant les besoins du client dans la conception.

Ce qui unit l'architecture créée, c'est la méthode ou l'approche de la construction. Cela inclut le travail conceptuel sur les programmes spatiaux, l'artisanat clairement articulé et une mise en œuvre consciente de la matérialité. La quête de l'honnêteté envers le matériau conduit souvent à l'utilisation du béton, qui crée un sentiment de sécurité par sa densité atmosphérique et son intensité.

Montemurro Aguiar es un estudio de arquitectura fundado en 2008. Nuestra arquitectura se distingue por el diálogo con el lugar. Los edificios responden al contexto y lo amplían desarrollando aún más las estructuras existentes. Cada proyecto de Montemurro Aguiar desarrolla su propia identidad. Esto también se aplica a los edificios residenciales más pequeños. Estas obras son un área de experimentación: explorar la relación suspensiva entre intimidad y apertura de la fachada, al tiempo que se incorporan las necesidades del cliente en el diseño.

Lo que une a la arquitectura creada es el método o enfoque de la construcción. Esto incluye un trabajo conceptual sobre programas espaciales, una artesanía claramente articulada y una aplicación consciente de la materialidad. La búsqueda de la honestidad con respecto al material lleva a menudo a la utilización del hormigón, que crea una sensación de seguridad por su densidad e intensidad atmosféricas.

# CASA IN COLLINA

Lugano, Switzerland

Photos: © Giorgio Marafioti

The house is located in an area of single-family homes surrounded by vegetation and vineyards. The project proposes a two-story building characterized by an articulated interplay of volumes that adapts with respect to the location and does not disturb the view of the neighboring house.
The entrance to the building constitutes a double-height space that integrates the staircase, bathed in natural light from the northeast. The upper floor houses bedrooms, a study, and storage areas. On the ground floor, the large windows of the southeast-oriented living room allow for a connection with the valley and the mountains. On the north facade, lacking openings, the garage doors and main entrance integrate into a wood-clad surface that contrasts with the characteristic exposed concrete of the building. All interior and exterior carpentry is made of oak wood with an essence oak finish, as well as all the fixed interior furniture design.

**Project team:**
Montemurro Aguiar Architects

**Construction period:**
July 2020-October 2021

**Total built area:**
296 $m^2$

**Consultants:**
Arch. Piero Conconi,
Ing. Marcionelli & Winkler

Das Haus befindet sich in einem Einfamilienhausgebiet, das von Grünflächen und Weinbergen umgeben ist. Das Projekt sieht ein zweigeschossiges Gebäude vor, das sich durch ein artikuliertes Spiel der Volumina auszeichnet, das sich respektvoll an den Standort anpasst und die Aussicht auf das Nachbarhaus nicht stört.
Der Eingang des Gebäudes ist ein Raum mit doppelter Höhe, in den das Treppenhaus integriert ist und der von Nordosten her mit natürlichem Licht durchflutet wird. Im Obergeschoss befinden sich die Schlafzimmer, ein Arbeitszimmer und Lagerräume. Im Erdgeschoss geben die großen Fenster des nach Südosten ausgerichteten Wohnzimmers den Blick auf das Tal und die Berge frei. An der Nordfassade, die keine Öffnungen aufweist, sind die Garage und die Haupteingangstür in eine mit Holz verkleidete Fläche integriert, die einen Kontrast zum charakteristischen Sichtbeton des Gebäudes bildet. Die gesamte Innen- und Außenverschalung ist aus Eichenholz gefertigt, ebenso wie die gesamte Gestaltung der festen Inneneinrichtung.

La maison est située dans une zone de maisons individuelles entourées de verdure et de vignobles. Le projet propose un bâtiment de deux étages caractérisé par un jeu articulé de volumes qui s'adapte respectueusement au site et ne perturbe pas la vue de la maison voisine.
L'entrée du bâtiment est un espace à double hauteur intégrant l'escalier, baigné de lumière naturelle depuis le nord-est. L'étage supérieur abrite des chambres, un bureau et des espaces de rangement. Au rez-de-chaussée, les grandes baies vitrées du séjour, orientées au sud-est, offrent une vue sur la vallée et les montagnes. Sur la façade nord, dépourvue d'ouvertures, les portes du garage et de l'entrée principale sont intégrées dans un revêtement en bois qui contraste avec le béton apparent caractéristique du bâtiment. Toutes les menuiseries intérieures et extérieures sont en essence de chêne, de même que l'ensemble du mobilier fixe intérieur.

La casa se sitúa en una zona de viviendas unifamiliares rodeadas de vegetación y viñedos. El proyecto plantea un edificio de dos niveles caracterizado por un juego articulado de volúmenes que se adapta con respeto al emplazamiento y no perturba la vista de la vivienda vecina.
La entrada al edificio constituye un espacio a doble altura que integra la escalera, bañado con luz natural del noreste. La planta superior alberga dormitorios, un estudio y zonas de almacenaje. En la planta baja, los grandes ventanales de la sala de estar orientada al sureste permiten la relación con el valle y las montañas. En la fachada norte, carente de aberturas, las puertas del garage y del acceso principal se integran en una superficie revestida de madera que contrasta con el hormigón visto característico del edificio. Toda la carpintería interior y exterior es de madera de roble acabado essence oak, así como todo el diseño del mobiliario fijo interior.

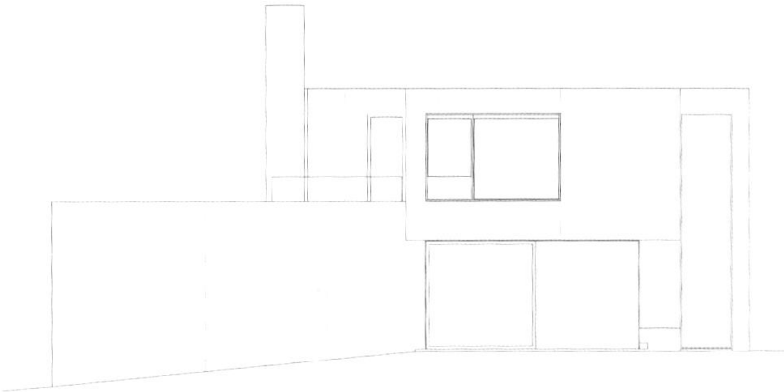

Northeast elevation

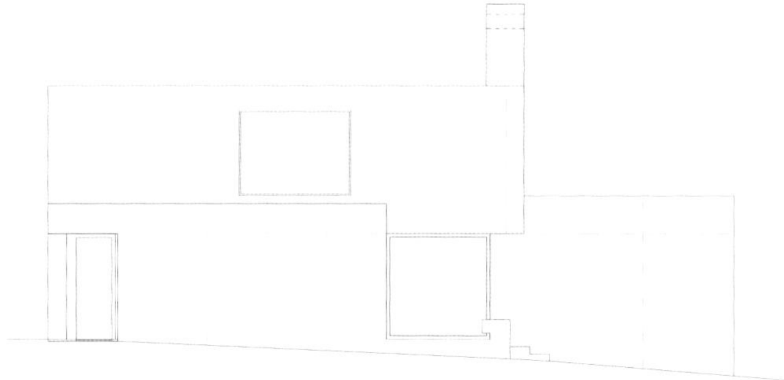

Southwest elevation

Northwest elevation

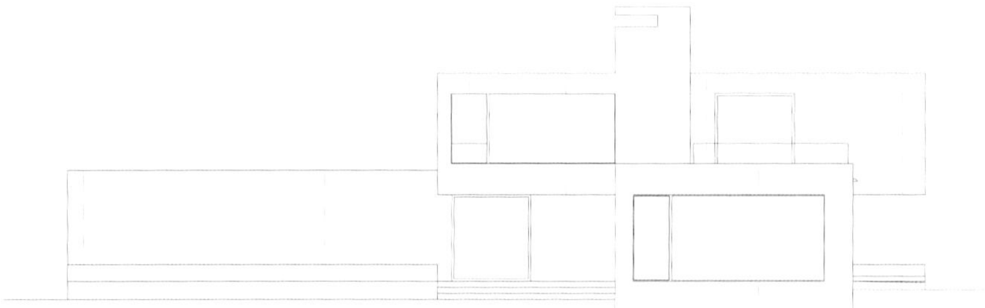

Southeast elevation

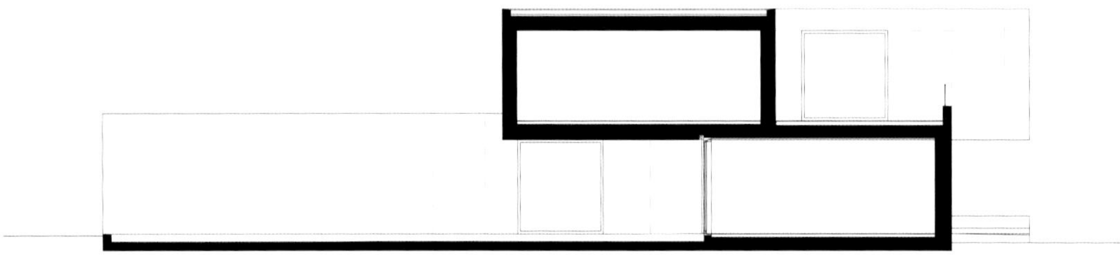

Longitudinal section

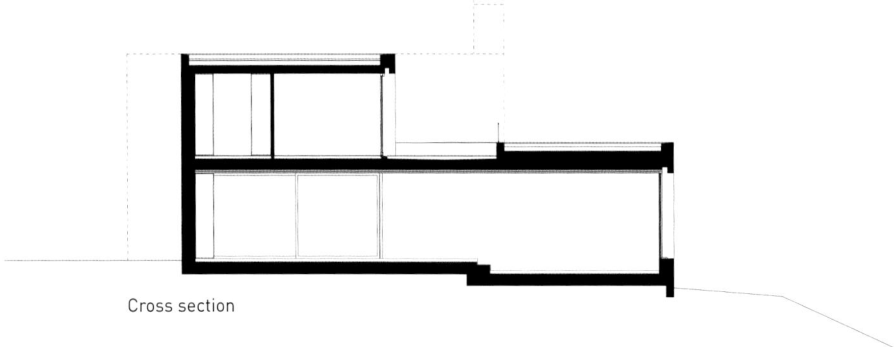

Cross section

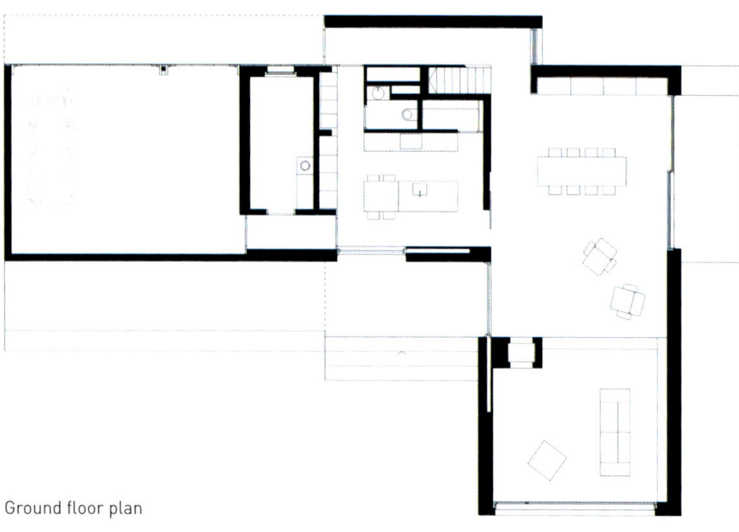

Ground floor plan

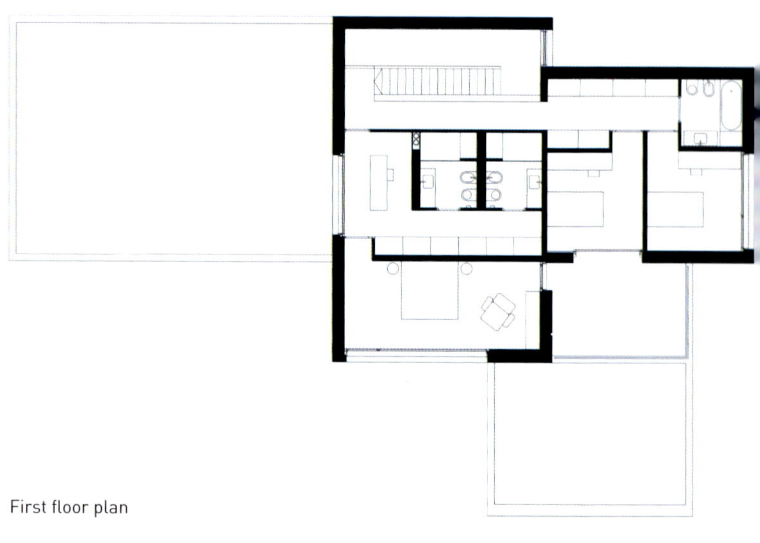

First floor plan

## OAX arquitectos

Arch. José García Toledo

www.oaxarquitectos.com

We believe in architecture as a craft extension to create spaces that reflect the identity of our users.
We continuously work on finding new construction solutions, value economy, sustainability, and interdisciplinary collaboration, developing each work as a unique piece with social value while respecting the environment.
Our commitment is to choose and develop the best contemporary architectural projects.

Wir glauben an die Architektur als eine Erweiterung des Handwerks, um Räume zu schaffen, die die Identität unserer Nutzer widerspiegeln.
Wir sind ständig auf der Suche nach neuen konstruktiven Lösungen, legen Wert auf Wirtschaftlichkeit, Nachhaltigkeit und interdisziplinäre Zusammenarbeit und entwickeln jedes Werk als Einzelstück, mit sozialem Wert und unter Berücksichtigung der Umwelt.
Unser Ziel ist es, die besten zeitgenössischen Architekturprojekte auszuwählen und zu entwickeln.

Nous pensons que l'architecture est une extension de l'artisanat pour créer des espaces qui reflètent l'identité de nos utilisateurs.
Nous travaillons constamment à la recherche de nouvelles solutions constructives, nous valorisons l'économie, la durabilité et la collaboration interdisciplinaire, en développant chaque œuvre comme une pièce unique, avec une valeur sociale et en respectant l'environnement.
Notre engagement est de choisir et de développer les meilleurs projets d'architecture contemporaine.

Creemos en la arquitectura como una extensión artesanal para crear espacios que reflejen la identidad de nuestros usuarios.
Trabajamos constantemente en la búsqueda de nuevas soluciones constructivas, valoramos la economía, la sustentabilidad y la colaboración interdisciplinaria, desarrollando cada obra como pieza única, con valor social y respetando el medio ambiente.
Nuestro compromiso es elegir y desarrollar los mejores proyectos de arquitectura contemporánea.

# CASA MAJALCA

**Parque Nacional Majalca, Chihuahua, México**

Photos: © Arch. Francisco Álvarez

Conceived as a sustainable restful building equipped for short stays, this self-sufficient house is located in a privileged location with excellent views. Its program focuses on the distribution of several rooms with bathrooms suitable for accommodating a complete family, a spacious social area with terraces, storage area, and motorcycle parking.
The building is designed as a series of staggered volumes ascending towards the center of the property, arranged in a zigzag pattern to open up to the views and preserve existing trees. Its construction design aims to achieve maximum sustainability and thermal efficiency. Its exterior appearance, dominated by the concrete finish of the walls, reflects a commitment to a concept of imperfection that gives the house a rustic and brutalist character, blending in with the characteristic rock formations of the area.

Dieses als nachhaltiges Erholungsgebäude für Kurzaufenthalte konzipierte Selbstversorgerhaus befindet sich in einer privilegierten Lage mit ausgezeichneter Aussicht. Im Mittelpunkt des Programms steht die Aufteilung mehrerer Zimmer mit Badezimmern, die für eine ganze Familie geeignet sind, ein großer Gemeinschaftsbereich mit Terrassen, ein Abstellraum und ein Parkplatz für Motorräder.
Das Gebäude ist als eine Reihe von Volumen konzipiert, die zur Mitte des Grundstücks hin gestaffelt und im Zickzack angeordnet sind, um die Aussicht zu öffnen und den vorhandenen Baumbestand zu erhalten. Seine konstruktive Gestaltung zielt auf maximale Nachhaltigkeit und thermische Effizienz ab. Sein äußeres Erscheinungsbild, das von der Betonoberfläche der Wände dominiert wird, entspricht dem Konzept der Unvollkommenheit, das dem Haus einen rustikalen und brutalistischen Charakter verleiht, dessen Farbe und Morphologie die für die Gegend charakteristischen Felsformationen nachahmen.

Conçue comme un bâtiment de repos durable équipé pour des séjours de courte durée, cette maison autosuffisante est située dans un endroit privilégié avec d'excellentes vues. Son programme se concentre sur la distribution de plusieurs chambres avec salles de bains adaptées à une famille entière, un grand espace social avec des terrasses, un espace de stockage et un parking pour les motos.
Le bâtiment est conçu comme une série de volumes échelonnés vers le centre de la propriété, disposés en zigzag pour ouvrir la vue et préserver les arbres existants. Sa conception constructive vise à atteindre une durabilité et une efficacité thermique maximales. Son image extérieure, dominée par la finition en béton des murs, répond à l'engagement en faveur d'un concept d'imperfection qui confère à la maison un caractère rustique et brutaliste, dont la couleur et la morphologie imitent les formations rocheuses caractéristiques de la région.

Concebida como una edificación sustentable de descanso equipada para cortas estancias, esta casa autosuficiente se sitúa en una ubicación privilegiada con excelentes vistas. Su programa se centra en la distribución de varias estancias con baño aptas para recibir a una familia completa, amplia área social con terrazas, zona de almacenamiento y aparcamiento para motocicletas.
El edificio se plantea como una serie de volúmenes escalonados de forma ascendente hacia el centro de la propiedad, dispuestos en forma de zigzag para abrirse hacia las vistas y preservar los árboles existentes. Su diseño constructivo se orienta a conseguir la máxima sostenibilidad y eficiencia térmica. Su imagen exterior, dominada por el acabado de hormigón de los muros, responde a la apuesta por un concepto de imperfección que otorga a la casa un carácter rústico y brutalista, cuyo color y morfología se mimetizan con las formaciones rocosas características de la zona.

**Awards:**
**Primer Premio, Vivienda unifamiliar hasta 500 m$^2$ XXI Bienal de Arquitectura del CANL, 2021**

**Project team:**
Oaxarquitectos
Arch. José García Toledo
Arch. Fernanda Roiz Silva
LDI. Luis Carlos Rodríguez González

**Construction period:**
Start date: 9 june 2017
Date of conclusion: 12 july 2021

**Total built area:**
300 m$^2$

**General contractor:**
Arch. Aileen García

**Consultants:**
Structural engineering: Ing. Manuel Jezzini
Energy efficiency: Arch. Carlos Estrada Zubía
Interior design: Arch. Aileen García

Facade detail

Section detail

1. Corrugated sheet Kr=18
2. Fomular insulation
3. Wooden ceiling
4. 1" metal lattice
5. Concrete slab
6. 9 mm glass window
7. Mezzanine/concrete slab
8. Laundry room
9. Reinforced double grill vs 1/2".
10. Finished concrete based on formwork
11. Compacted backfilled bench
12. Apparent concrete

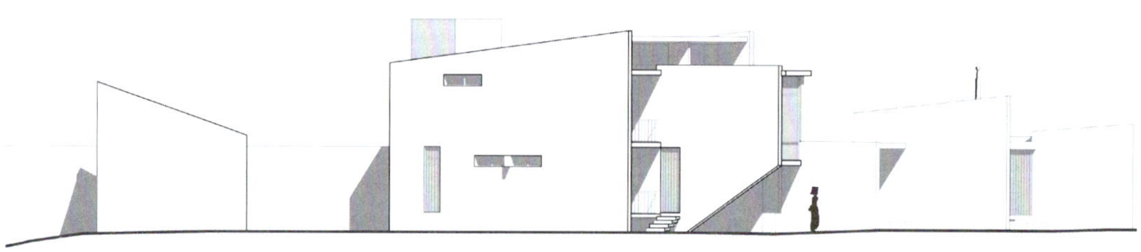

West elevation

South elevation

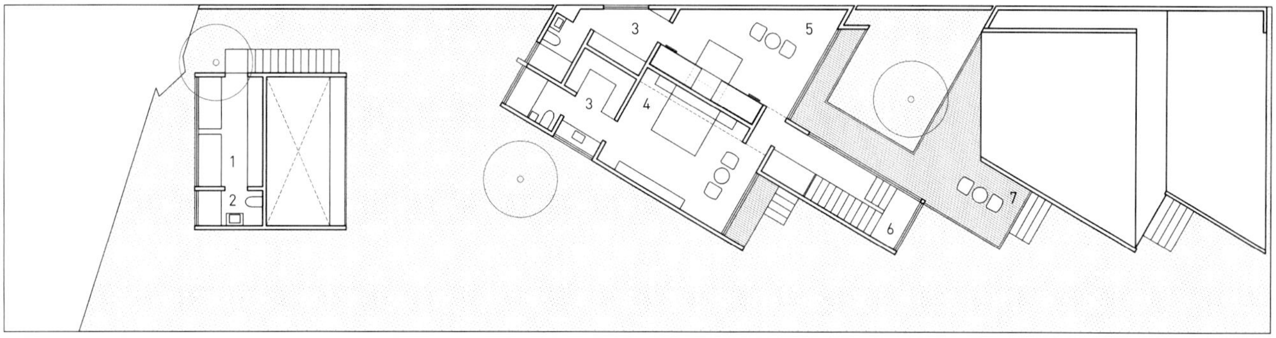

First floor plan

1. Service room
2. Bathroom
3. Bathroom/dressing room
4. Master bedroom
5. Bedroom 3
6. Staircase
7. Terrace

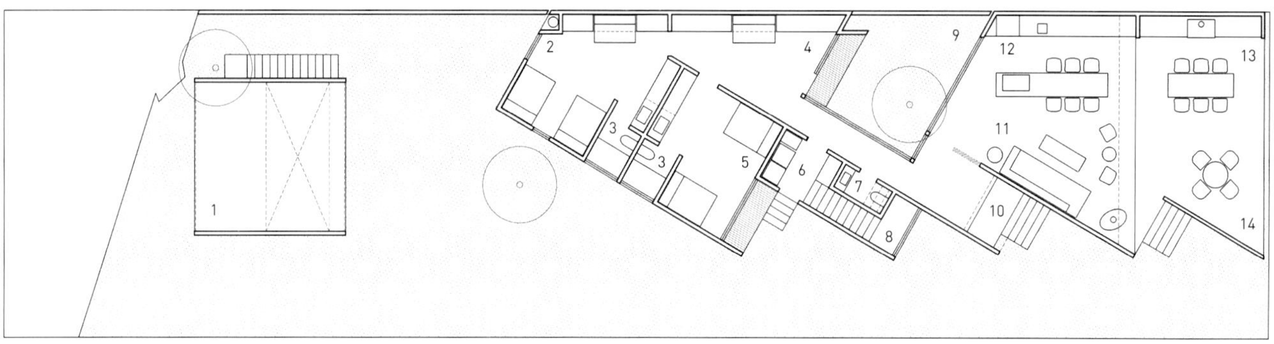

Ground

0 2 4m

| | |
|---|---|
| 1. Garage | 8. Staircase |
| 2. Bedroom 1 | 9. Inner courtyard |
| 3. Bathroom | 10. Entrance hall |
| 4. Living room | 11. Living room |
| 5. Bedroom 2 | 12. Kitchen |
| 6. Laundry room | 13. Bar |
| 7. Half bathroom | 14. Terrace |

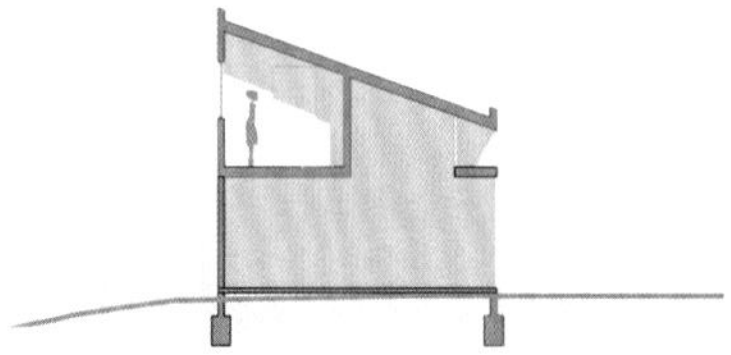

Cross section

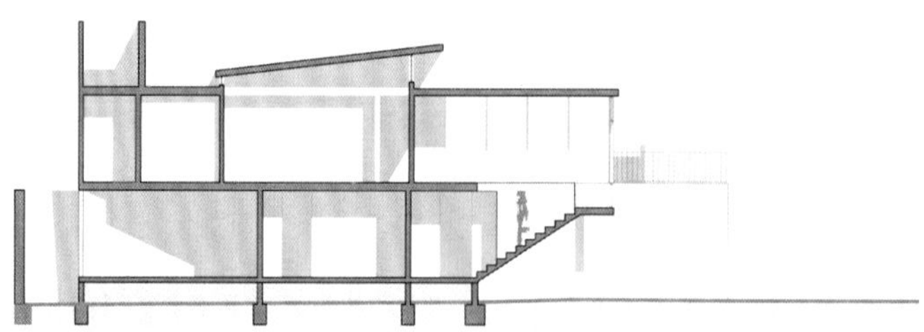

Longitudinal section

0 2 4m

# PABLO SENMARTIN Arquitectos

**Pablo Senmartin**

www.pablosenmartinarquitectos.com

Pablo Senmartín is an architect graduated from the National University of Cordoba, Argentina (2005) and Master in Sustainable Design and Bioclimatic Architecture from the University of Barcelona, Spain. He has been a professor at the Istanbul Technical University and is an assistant professor at the Faculty of Architecture, Urbanism and Design of the UNC.
Founder and director of Pablo Senmartín Arquitectos, he has accumulated architectural experience in the residential and hotel sector, as well as in individual and social housing projects. He is interested in developing architectural designs that are functional, safe and economical (LEED certification) and is truly motivated to be part of a team that creates buildings that can last for decades and have a positive impact on people's lives and the environment.

Pablo Senmartín ist Architekt mit einem Abschluss der Nationalen Universität von Córdoba, Argentinien (2005) und einem Master in nachhaltigem Design und bioklimatischer Architektur der Universität von Barcelona, Spanien. Er war Professor an der Technischen Universität Istanbul und ist Assistenzprofessor an der Fakultät für Architektur, Städtebau und Design der UNC.
Als Gründer und Direktor von Pablo Senmartín Arquitectos hat er architektonische Erfahrungen im Wohn- und Hotelsektor sowie im individuellen und sozialen Wohnungsbau gesammelt. Er interessiert sich für die Entwicklung architektonischer Entwürfe, die funktional, sicher und wirtschaftlich sind (LEED-Zertifizierung), und ist sehr motiviert, Teil eines Teams zu sein, das Gebäude schafft, die jahrzehntelang halten und einen positiven Einfluss auf das Leben der Menschen und die Umwelt haben.

Pablo Senmartín est un architecte diplômé de l'Université nationale de Córdoba, Argentine (2005) et titulaire d'un Master en conception durable et architecture bioclimatique de l'Université de Barcelone, Espagne. Il a enseigné à l'Université technique d'Istanbul et est professeur assistant à la Faculté d'architecture, d'urbanisme et de design de l'UNC.

Fondateur et directeur de Pablo Senmartín Arquitectos, il a accumulé une expérience architecturale dans le secteur résidentiel et hôtelier, ainsi que dans des projets de logements individuels et sociaux. Il s'intéresse au développement de conceptions architecturales fonctionnelles, sûres et économiques (certification LEED) et est réellement motivé pour faire partie d'une équipe qui crée des bâtiments pouvant durer des décennies et avoir un impact positif sur la vie des gens et sur l'environnement.

Pablo Senmartín es arquitecto graduado por la Universidad Nacional de Córdoba, Argentina (2005) y Máster en Diseño Sostenible y Arquitectura Bioclimática por la Universidad de Barcelona, España. Ha sido profesor en la Istambul Technical University y es profesor asistente en la Facultad de Arquitectura, Urbanismo y Diseño de la UNC.

Fundador y director de Pablo Senmartín Arquitectos, acumula experiencia arquitectónica en el sector residencial y hotelero, así como en proyectos de vivienda individual y social. Se muestra interesado en elaborar diseños arquitectónicos que sean funcionales, seguros y económicos (certificación LEED) y realmente motivado para ser parte de un equipo que cree edificios que pueden durar décadas y que tengan un impacto positivo en la vida de las personas y el medio ambiente.

# CASA EN EL RODEO

**La Calera, Córdoba, Argentina**

Photos: © Andrés Domínguez

This house is located in a suburban area in contact with nature and with views over the city. The building sits in the centre of a steeply sloping plot, aiming to minimise its visual and environmental impact. The project develops a pure, solid concrete volume which, through the action of movement and displacement, mutates into two superimposed blocks with different layouts. This superimposition produces intermediate spaces that protect the fronts of the facades and enhance the interaction between inside and outside, generating galleries, terraces, balconies, etc. In the interior, fluid and integrating spaces of different heights are generated. The choice of concrete as a material responds to the tradition of lime and cement production for construction in the area. The material conditions of the house together with the passive design measures aimed at optimising its thermal performance consolidate a natural and unique atmosphere.

Dieses Haus befindet sich in einem Vorstadtviertel in Kontakt mit der Natur und mit Blick auf die Stadt. Das Gebäude befindet sich in der Mitte eines steil abfallenden Grundstücks, um seine visuellen und ökologischen Auswirkungen zu minimieren.
Das Projekt entwickelt ein reines, massives Betonvolumen, das sich durch Bewegung und Verschiebung in zwei übereinander liegende Blöcke mit unterschiedlichen Programmen verwandelt. Durch diese Überlagerung entstehen Zwischenräume, die die Fassadenfronten schützen und die Interaktion zwischen Innen und Außen verstärken, indem Galerien, Terrassen, Balkone usw. entstehen. Im Inneren entstehen fließende und integrierende Räume mit unterschiedlichen Höhen. Die Wahl von Beton als Material ist eine Antwort auf die Tradition der Kalk- und Zementherstellung für den Bau in diesem Gebiet. Die materielle Beschaffenheit des Hauses in Verbindung mit den passiven Konstruktionsmaßnahmen zur Optimierung der thermischen Leistung sorgen für eine natürliche und einzigartige Atmosphäre.

Cette maison est située dans un quartier suburbain en contact avec la nature et avec une vue sur la ville. Le bâtiment se trouve au centre d'un terrain en pente raide et vise à minimiser son impact visuel et environnemental.
Le projet développe un volume pur et solide en béton qui, par l'action du mouvement et du déplacement, se transforme en deux blocs superposés avec des programmes différents. Cette superposition produit des espaces intermédiaires qui protègent les façades et renforcent l'interaction entre l'intérieur et l'extérieur, générant des galeries, des terrasses, des balcons, etc. À l'intérieur, des espaces fluides et intégrateurs de différentes hauteurs sont générés. Le choix du béton comme matériau répond à la tradition de production de chaux et de ciment pour la construction dans la région. Les conditions matérielles de la maison ainsi que les mesures de conception passive visant à optimiser sa performance thermique consolident une atmosphère naturelle et unique.

Esta vivienda se sitúa en un barrio suburbano en contacto con la naturaleza y con vistas sobre la ciudad. El edificio se asienta en el centro de una parcela con fuerte pendiente, aspirando a minimizar su impacto visual y ambiental.
El proyecto desarrolla un volumen puro y macizo de hormigón que, mediante la acción de movimiento y desfase, muta a 2 bloques superpuestos con diferente programa. Esta superposición produce espacios intermedios que protegen los frentes de las fachadas y potencian la interacción interior-exterior, generando galerías, terrazas, balcones, etc. En el interior se generan espacios fluidos e integradores de diferentes alturas. La elección del hormigón como material responde a la tradición de producción de cal y cemento para la construcción de la zona. Las condiciones materiales de la casa junto a las medidas de diseño pasivo destinadas a optimizar su rendimiento térmico consolidan una atmósfera natural y única.

**Project team:**
Giovanna Rimoldi, Suyay Baigorri, Valentin Vodanovic, Alfaro Guadalupe, Giordano Agostina, Mansilla Ariana, Nieva Florencia, Oviedo Macarena.

**Construction period:**
2022

**Total built area:**
450 m$^2$

**Consultants:**
Structural engineering consultant:
Ing. Andrés Mole

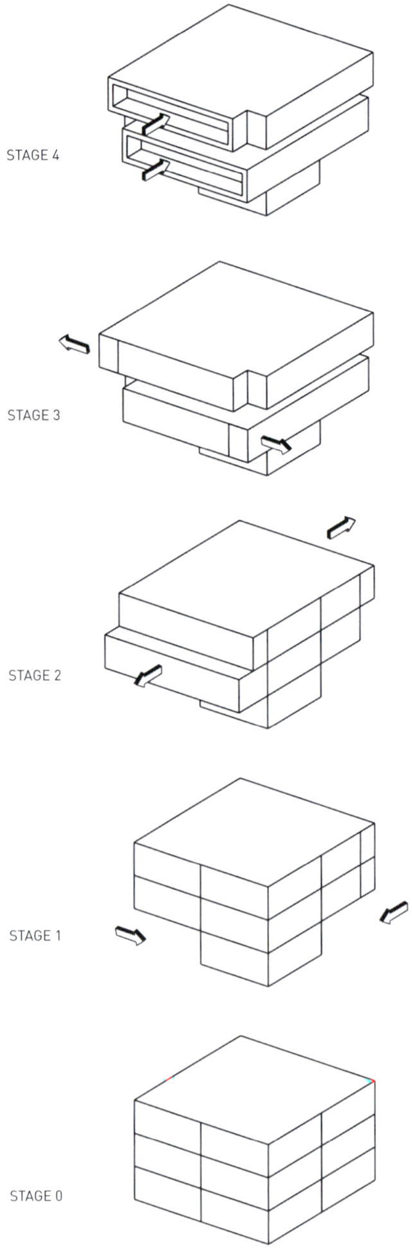

Design process

Axonometric

AC 908 LV

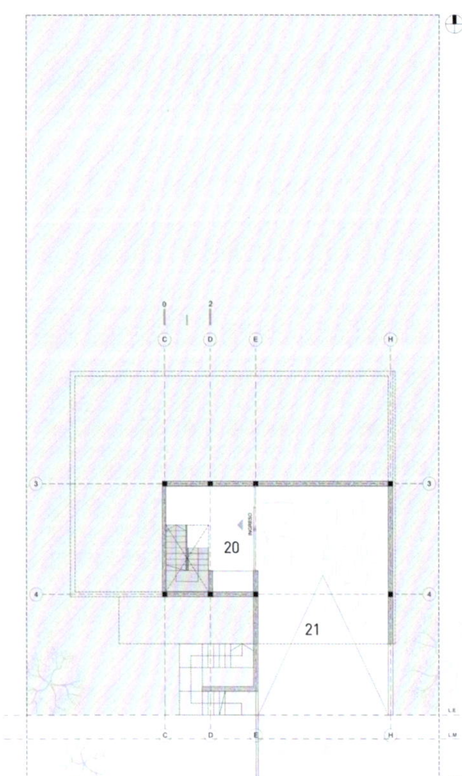


Basement plan

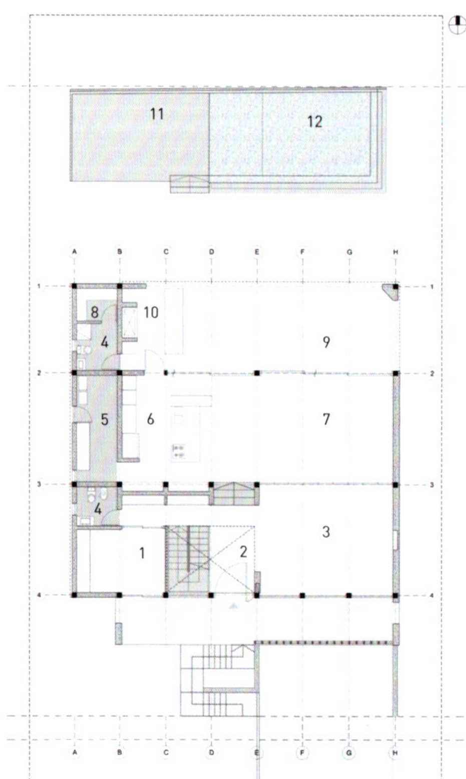


First floor plan

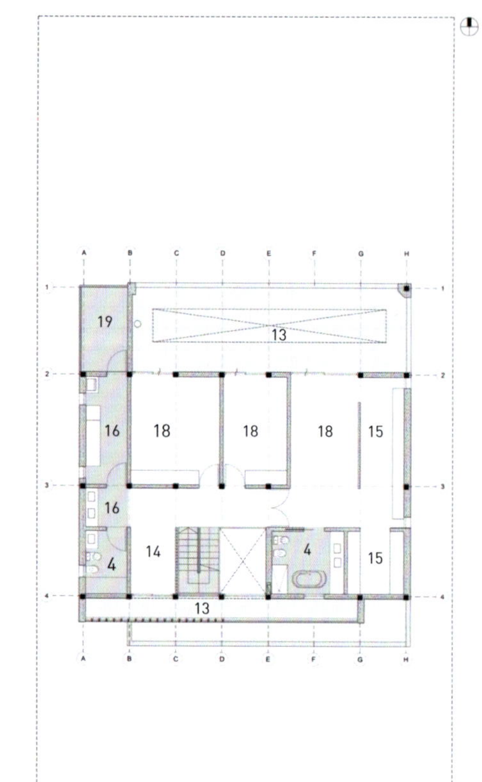


Second floor plan

1. Study
2. Hall
3. Living room
4. Bathroom
5. Pantry
6. Kitchen
7. Dining room
8. Dry sauna
9. Gallery
10. Grill
11. Deck
12. Pool
13. Terrace
14. Play room
15. Dressing room
16. Bathroom
17. Laundry
18. Bedroom
19. Tender
20. Cellar
21. Garage

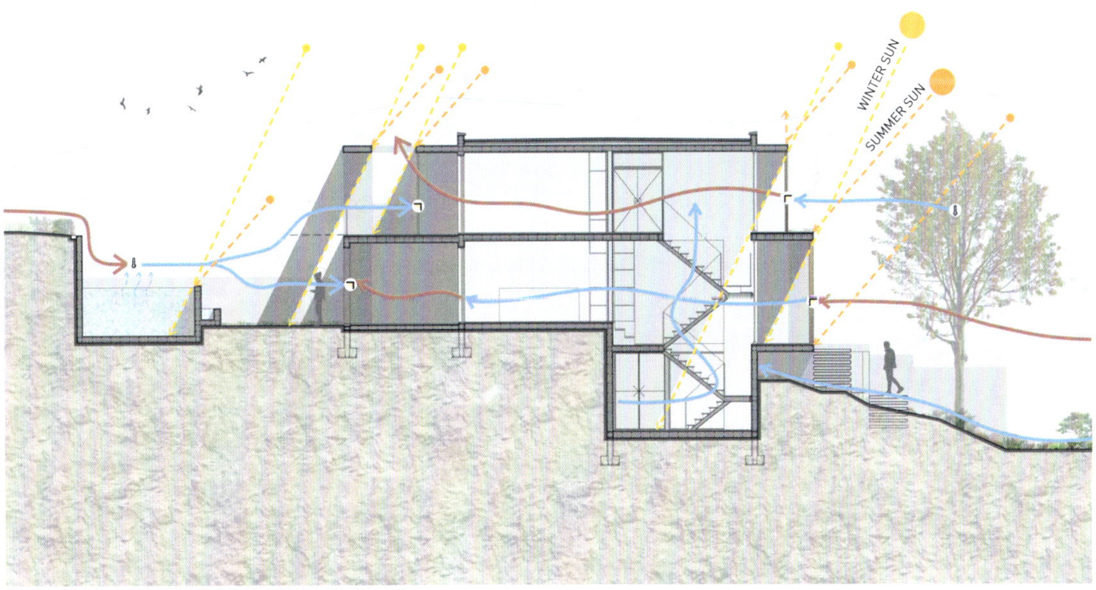


Bioclimatic diagram

- The pool and vegetation's location allows air cooling through humidification.
- Permanent convective air flow on the ground floor allows for cross ventilation.
- The northeast gallery prevents the passage of solar radiation in summer and allows its entry during the winter.
- Climate control is achieved through the use of solar filters.

## PEDEVILLA Architects

**Armin Pedevilla, Alexander Pedevilla**

www.pedevilla.info

For Pedevilla Architects, building means dealing with the social, cultural, economic and ecological components of everyday life. In this context, the matter of consistency becomes an important factor in planning decisions.
Armin and Alexander Pedevilla studied architecture at the Technical University of Graz. After graduation, they both founded their own studios in Austria. Driven by the desire to build in the mountains, the brothers returned to South Tyrol in 2005 to jointly found Pedevilla Architects. Since then, the studio has made a name for itself in the national and international architectural scene – Pedevilla Architects is today one of the renowned firms in Europe. Their work has received many awards, has been published internationally and been exhibited in numerous architecture exhibitions.

Für Pedevilla Architekten bedeutet das Bauen den bewussten Umgang mit sozialen, kulturellen, ökonomischen und ökologischen Komponenten des alltäglichen Lebens. In diesem Zusammenhang wird das Thema der Konsistenz zum wichtigen Faktor bei planerischen Entscheidungen.
Armin und Alexander Pedevilla studierten Architektur an der Technischen Universität in Graz. Beide gründeten unabhängig voneinander nach dem Studium ein eigenes Büro in Österreich. Vom Verlangen nach alpinem Bauen getrieben kehrten die Brüder 2005 nach Südtirol zurück, um dort gemeinsam das Büro pedevilla architekten zu gründen. Seither haben sich pedevilla architekten einen Namen in der nationalen und internationalen Architekturszene gemacht und zählen mittlerweile zu den renommierten Büros im gesamten europäischen Raum. Ihre Arbeiten wurden vielfach ausgezeichnet, publiziert und waren in zahlreichen Architekturausstellungen zu sehen.

Pour Pedevilla Architects, construire signifie traiter les composantes sociales, culturelles, économiques et écologiques de la vie quotidienne. Dans ce contexte, la question de la cohérence devient un facteur important dans les décisions de planification.
Armin et Alexander Pedevilla ont étudié l'architecture à l'université technique de Graz. Après avoir obtenu leur diplôme, ils ont tous deux fondé leur propre studio en Autriche. Poussés par le désir de construire dans les montagnes, les frères sont retournés dans le Tyrol du Sud en 2005 pour fonder ensemble Pedevilla Architects. Depuis, le studio s'est fait un nom sur la scène architecturale nationale et internationale - Pedevilla Architects est aujourd'hui l'un des cabinets les plus renommés d'Europe. Leur travail a reçu de nombreux prix, a été publié au niveau international et a fait l'objet de nombreuses expositions d'architecture.

Para Pedevilla Architects, construir significa ocuparse de los componentes sociales, culturales, económicos y ecológicos de la vida cotidiana. En este contexto, la cuestión de la coherencia se convierte en un factor importante en las decisiones de planificación.
Armin y Alexander Pedevilla estudiaron arquitectura en la Universidad Técnica de Graz. Tras graduarse, ambos fundaron sus propios estudios en Austria. Impulsados por el deseo de construir en las montañas, los hermanos volvieron al Tirol del Sur en 2005 para fundar conjuntamente Pedevilla Architects. Desde entonces, el estudio se ha hecho un nombre en la escena arquitectónica nacional e internacional. Pedevilla Architects es hoy uno de los estudios de renombre en Europa. Su trabajo ha recibido numerosos premios, se ha publicado internacionalmente y se ha expuesto en numerosas exposiciones de arquitectura.

# BETON EISACK

Chiusa, Italy

Photos: © Gustav Willeit

"From grey to green" is the motto that applies to the conversion of the Beton Eisack HQ. The original office building dated back to 2002. With an increasing focus on research and development then came adapted needs. The aim of the conversion project therefore was to create a functionally efficient, atmospheric and pleasant working environment while providing an appropriate stage for the concrete that is being developed and produced by the company. Fundamentally new is a space for seminars and other events. Inner courtyards and cupola-like skylights improve the daylight situation and sound insulation. The existing grey concrete shell remained untouched due to its established brand message. Characteristic for the interior is the predominant use of green-pigmented AeroBeton®, a special lightweight development by the company itself, used with a variety of surface structures and complemented by elements in black steel and glass.

Von „grau zu grün" war das Motto hinter dem Umbau des Firmensitzes von Beton Eisack. Das ursprüngliche Bürogebäude stammt aus dem Jahr 2002. Mit der zunehmenden Fokussierung auf Forschung und Entwicklung haben sich auch die räumlichen Bedürfnisse des Unternehmens weiterentwickelt. Ziel des aktuellen Projekts war es daher – 20 Jahre später – im Bestand ein funktional effizientes, atmosphärisches und angenehmes Arbeitsumfeld zu schaffen und dem Beton, der im Unternehmen entwickelt und produziert wird, eine angemessene Bühne zu geben. Grundlegend neu ist ein Raum für Seminare und andere Veranstaltungen. Innenhöfe und kuppelartige Oberlichter verbessern die Tageslichtsituation und den Schallschutz. Die bestehende graue Betonhülle blieb aufgrund ihrer etablierten Markenbotschaft unverändert. Charakteristisch für den Innenraum ist die überwiegende Verwendung von grün pigmentiertem AeroBeton®, einer speziellen Leichtbeton-Eigenentwicklung, die mit unterschiedlichen Oberflächenstrukturen eingesetzt und durch Elemente aus schwarzem Stahl und Glas ergänzt wird.

« Du gris au vert » est la devise qui s'applique à la conversion du siège social de Beton Eisack. L'immeuble de bureaux d'origine date de 2002. L'importance croissante accordée à la recherche et au développement s'est traduite par des besoins adaptés. L'objectif du projet de conversion était donc de créer un environnement de travail fonctionnel, efficace, atmosphérique et agréable, tout en fournissant une scène appropriée pour le béton développé et produit par l'entreprise. La nouveauté fondamentale est un espace pour les séminaires et autres événements. Des cours intérieures et des puits de lumière en forme de coupole améliorent l'éclairage naturel et l'isolation phonique. L'enveloppe existante en béton gris est restée intacte en raison du message de la marque. L'intérieur est caractérisé par l'utilisation prédominante d'AeroBeton® pigmenté en vert, un produit léger spécialement développé par la société elle-même, utilisé avec une variété de structures de surface et complété par des éléments en acier noir et en verre.

«Del gris al verde» es el lema aplicado a la reconversión de la sede central de Beton Eisack, edificio de oficinas construido en 2002. El proyecto refleja la creciente focalización de la empresa hacia la investigación y el desarrollo. Esto motivó la adaptación del edificio para crear un entorno de trabajo funcionalmente eficiente y acogedor, a la vez que un escenario adecuado para el hormigón que desarrolla y produce la empresa. Dentro de la reforma destacan los espacio para seminarios y otros eventos. Los patios interiores y las claraboyas en forma de cúpula mejoran la iluminación natural y el aislamiento acústico. El armazón de hormigón gris existente se mantuvo intacto debido a su imagen corporativa. Característico del interior es el uso predominante de AeroBeton® pigmentado en verde, un material ligero especial de la propia empresa, utilizado con diversos acabados superficiales y complementado con elementos de vidrio y de acero negro.

**Project team:**
Alexander Pedevilla, Armin Pedevilla, Lisa Hempfer, Giorgio Larcher, Michael Rollmann

**Construction period:**
2020-2022

**Total built area:**
1,500 m$^2$

**General contractor:**
Oberegger Bau

**Consultants:**
Concrete: Beton Eisack
Structural engineering: Ingenieurteam Bergmeister
Fire protection: Studio Kontakt
HVAC: TKON
Electrics: Georg Oberlechner
Lighting: Lichtstudio Eisenkeil
Acoustics: NiRA Consulting

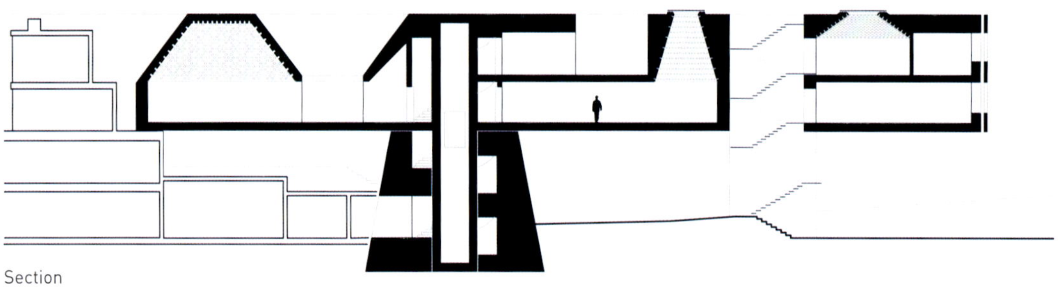

Section

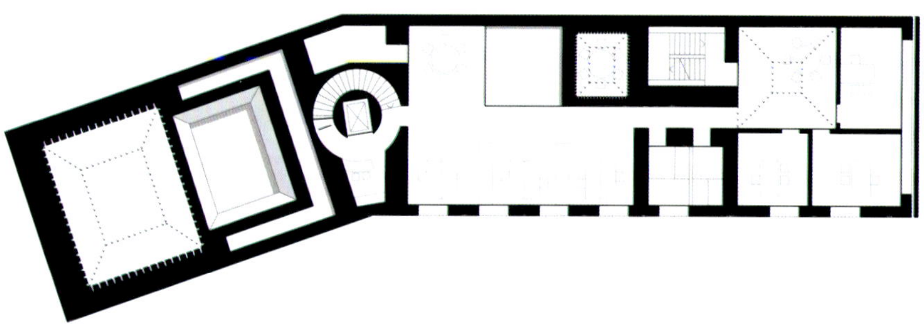

Second level plan

First level plan

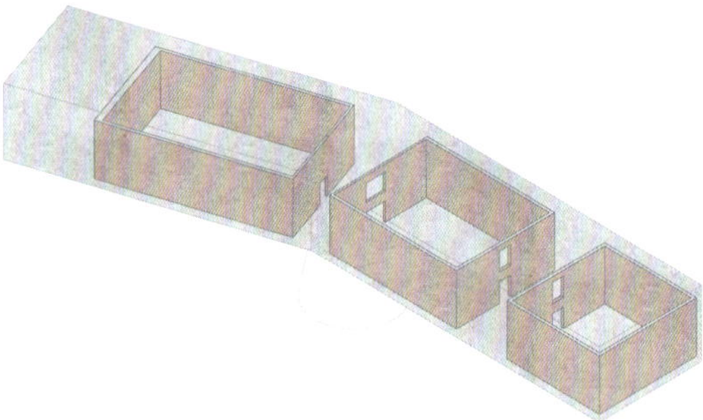

New inner mantle from concrete

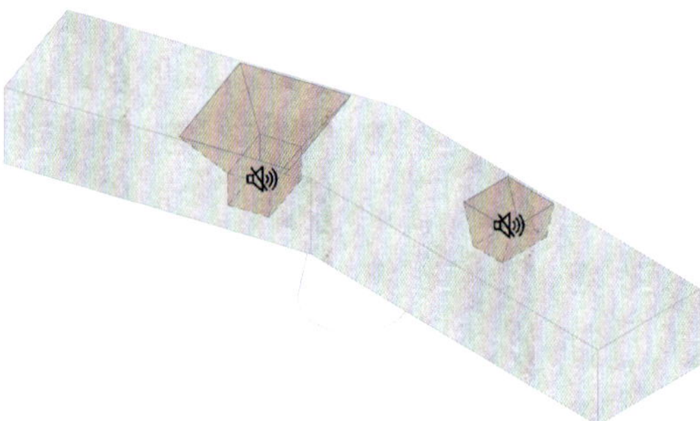

Noise protected outdoor spaces

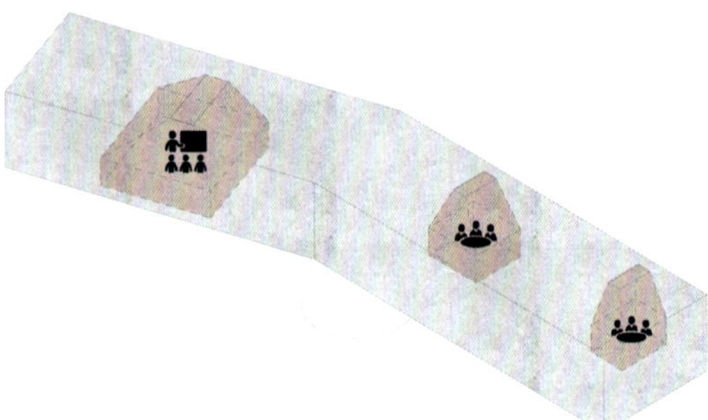

Atmospheric, focused areas for meetings

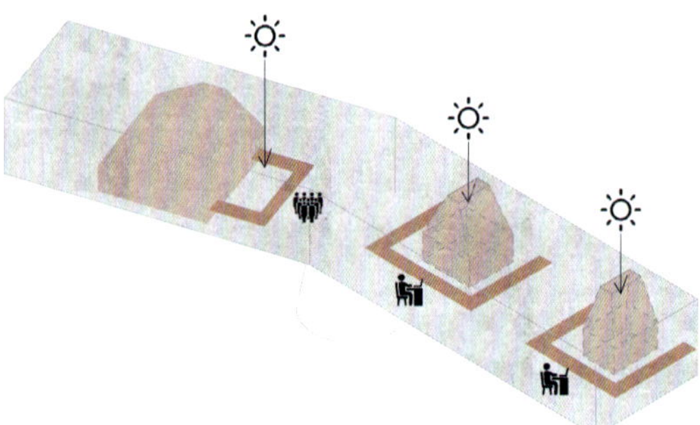

Employees and visitors experiencing and using the outdoor areas

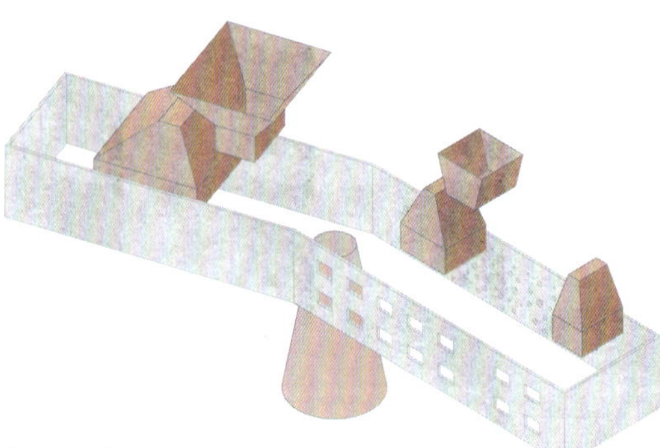

Keeping the outer shell, inserting the new elements

Concept diagrams

Construction process

PROARH

**Davor Matekovic**

www.proarh.hr

Proarh is an architectural office founded in 1992 in Zagreb, Croatia, under the management of its founder and principal architect Davor Matekovic, the firm has evolved into a multidisciplinary workshop, creating different projects of various functions, typologies, as well as programmatic and spatial dimensions.
Architecture is approached as a diversely complex topic, where all its individual elements are formative and the design process is all encompassing.
Proarh's works have been nominated and awarded with a wide variety of international architectural prizes (World Architecture Festival Award, Plan award, Architizer award, The Architecture MasterPrize, BIG SEE Grand Prix architecture award, International CEMEX Building Award, A & D Trophy Award, A'design Award, CEMEX Building Award) presented in many exhibitions and published in renown domestic and international profession related publications.

Proarh ist ein Architekturbüro, das 1992 in Zagreb, Kroatien, gegründet wurde. Unter der Leitung seines Gründers und Hauptarchitekten Davor Matekovic hat sich das Büro zu einer multidisziplinären Werkstatt entwickelt, die verschiedene Projekte mit unterschiedlichen Funktionen, Typologien sowie programmatischen und räumlichen Dimensionen realisiert.
Architektur wird als ein vielschichtiges, komplexes Thema betrachtet, bei dem alle einzelnen Elemente prägend sind und der Entwurfsprozess allumfassend ist.
Proarhs Arbeiten wurden für zahlreiche internationale Architekturpreise nominiert und ausgezeichnet (World Architecture Festival Award, Plan Award, Architizer Award, The Architecture MasterPrize, BIG SEE Grand Prix architecture award, International CEMEX Building Award, A & D Trophy Award, A'design Award, CEMEX Building Award), in zahlreichen Ausstellungen präsentiert und in renommierten nationalen und internationalen Fachpublikationen veröffentlicht.

Proarh est un cabinet d'architecture fondé en 1992 à Zagreb, en Croatie, sous la direction de son fondateur et principal architecte Davor Matekovic, le cabinet est devenu un atelier multidisciplinaire, créant différents projets de diverses fonctions, typologies, ainsi que des dimensions programmatiques et spatiales.

L'architecture est abordée comme un sujet diversifié et complexe, où tous ses éléments individuels sont formatifs et où le processus de conception est global.

Les travaux de Proarh ont été nominés et récompensés par une grande variété de prix architecturaux internationaux (World Architecture Festival Award, Plan Award, Architizer Award, The Architecture MasterPrize, BIG SEE Grand Prix architecture award, International CEMEX Building Award, A & D Trophy Award, A'design Award, CEMEX Building Award) présentés dans de nombreuses expositions et publiés dans des publications professionnelles nationales et internationales renommées.

Proarh es un estudio de arquitectura fundado en 1992 en Zagreb, Croacia. Bajo la dirección de su fundador y arquitecto principal Davor Matekovic, el estudio ha evolucionado hasta convertirse en un taller multidisciplinar, creando diferentes proyectos de diversas funciones, tipologías, así como dimensiones programáticas y espaciales.

La arquitectura se enfoca como un tema diversamente complejo, donde todos sus elementos individuales son formativos y el proceso de diseño lo abarca todo.

Las obras de Proarh han sido nominadas y galardonadas con una amplia variedad de premios internacionales de arquitectura (World Architecture Festival Award, Plan award, Architizer award, The Architecture MasterPrize, BIG SEE Grand Prix architecture award, International CEMEX Building Award, A & D Trophy Award, A'design Award, CEMEX Building Award) presentados en numerosas exposiciones y publicados en publicaciones nacionales e internacionales de renombre relacionadas con la profesión.

# CONCRETE HOUSES

Lukovo Šugarje, Croatia

Photos: © Damir Fabijanić, Miljenko Bernfest

**Awards:**
- Grand Prix / BIG SEE Grand Prix architecture award 2021
- Main Award/Architecture Category, 22nd Salon Of Architecture In Novi Sad

**Project team:**
Davor Matekovic, Oskar Rajko, Tina Havranek

**Construction period:**
2016-2019

**Total built area:**
490.0 m$^2$

Concrete houses are a minimalist architectural gesture on the Adriatic coast. The houses are exposed to the harsh weather conditions, characteristic of the area, conceived as a residential unit made of 3 individual houses, shaped into distorted concrete cubes. The design is based on a traditional coastal house, compact floor plan, strict differentiation of space vertically. Each floor has its own function - sleeping area, living area, kitchen, courtyard/pool terrace. The clear, minimalist character of the space dictates the form of the houses and materializes in natural concrete, with rough textures obtained using fine board formwork, treating the wall and the roof equally.
The aesthetics of the buildings are based on the complete deprivation of the redundant - the construction is also the façade. Gray concrete remains visible as a mirroring of the gray stone in the environment and the grayness of island Pag's bareness in the distance.

Die Betonhäuser sind eine minimalistische architektonische Geste an der Adriaküste. Die Häuser sind den rauen Witterungsbedingungen ausgesetzt, die für die Region charakteristisch sind. Sie sind als eine Wohneinheit konzipiert, die aus drei einzelnen Häusern besteht, die zu verzerrten Betonwürfeln geformt sind. Der Entwurf basiert auf einem traditionellen Küstenhaus, einem kompakten Grundriss und einer strengen vertikalen Differenzierung des Raums. Jede Etage hat ihre eigene Funktion - Schlafbereich, Wohnbereich, Küche, Innenhof/Poolterrasse. Der klare, minimalistische Charakter des Raumes diktiert die Form der Häuser und materialisiert sich in natürlichem Beton, mit rauen Strukturen, die durch eine feine Brettschalung erzielt werden, die Wand und Dach gleichermaßen behandelt.
Die Ästhetik der Gebäude basiert auf dem vollständigen Entzug des Überflüssigen - die Konstruktion ist zugleich die Fassade. Der graue Beton bleibt sichtbar als Spiegelung des grauen Steins in der Umgebung und der grauen Kargheit der Insel Pag in der Ferne.

Les maisons en béton sont un geste architectural minimaliste sur la côte adriatique. Les maisons sont exposées aux conditions météorologiques difficiles caractéristiques de la région, conçues comme une unité résidentielle composée de 3 maisons individuelles, façonnées en cubes en béton déformés. Le design est basé sur une maison côtière traditionnelle, un plan compact, une différenciation stricte de l'espace verticalement. Chaque étage a sa propre fonction - zone de couchage, zone de vie, cuisine, cour/terrasse avec piscine. Le caractère clair et minimaliste de l'espace dicte la forme des maisons et se matérialise en béton naturel, avec des textures rugueuses obtenues grâce à un coffrage en planches fines, traitant le mur et le toit de la même manière.
L'esthétique des bâtiments repose sur la privation complète du superflu - la construction est également la façade. Le béton gris reste visible comme un reflet de la pierre grise de l'environnement et de la nudité de l'île de Pag au loin.

Estas casas de hormigón representan un gesto arquitectónico minimalista en la costa adriática. Expuestas a las duras condiciones climáticas de la zona, se plantean como una unidad residencial formada por 3 casas con forma de cubos de hormigón distorsionados. Su diseño se basa en una casa costera tradicional, de planta compacta y estricta diferenciación vertical del espacio. Cada planta tiene su propia función: zona de dormitorio, zona de estar, cocina y patio/terraza con piscina. El carácter claro y minimalista del proyecto dicta la forma de las casas y se materializa en el hormigón natural con texturas rugosas, obtenidas con un encofrado de tablas finas, y en el tratamiento unitario de muros y cubierta.
La estética de los edificios se basa en la privación total de lo superfluo: la construcción es también la fachada. El hormigón gris se manifiesta como reflejo de la piedra gris del entorno y de la grisura de la isla de Pag en la distancia.

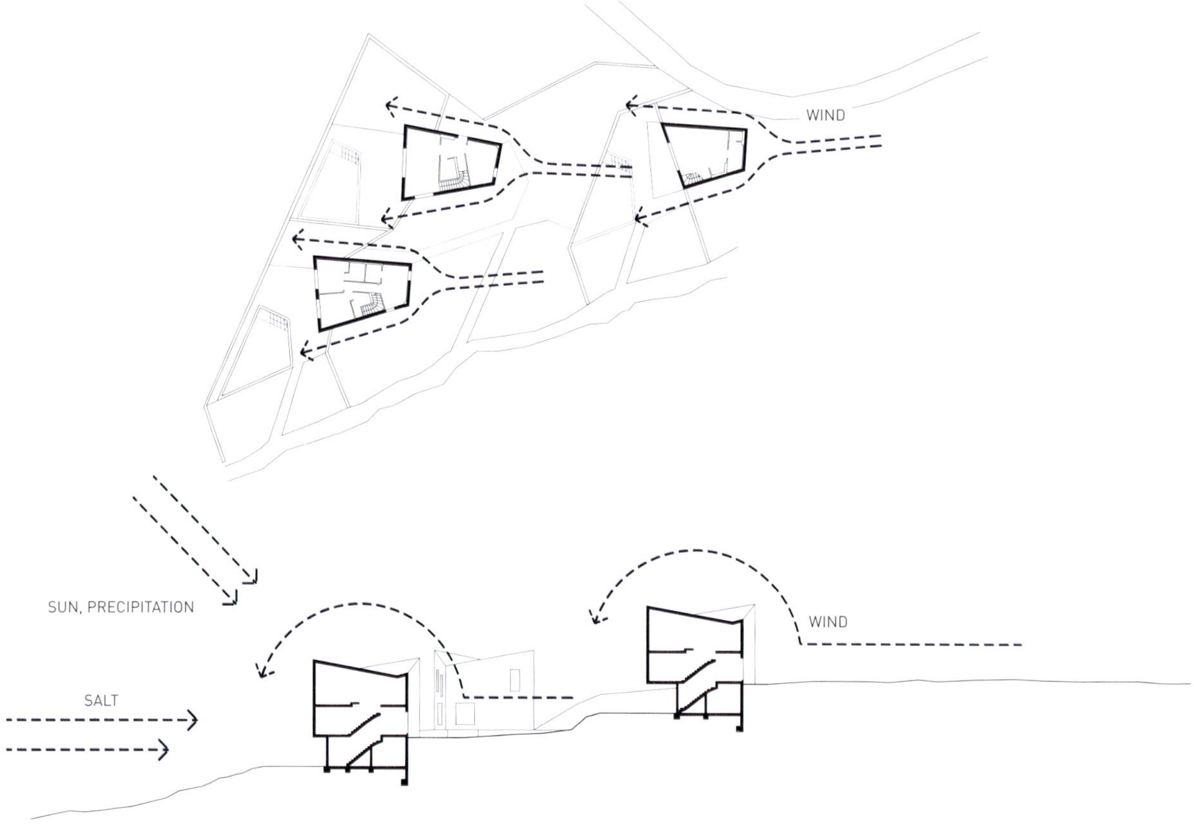


Concept diagram

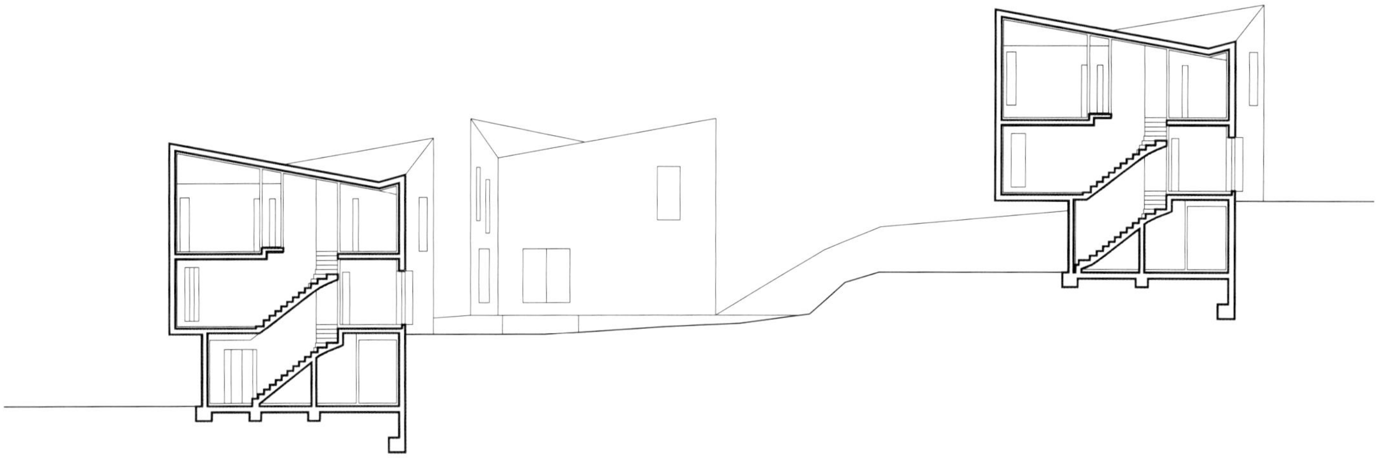

Section

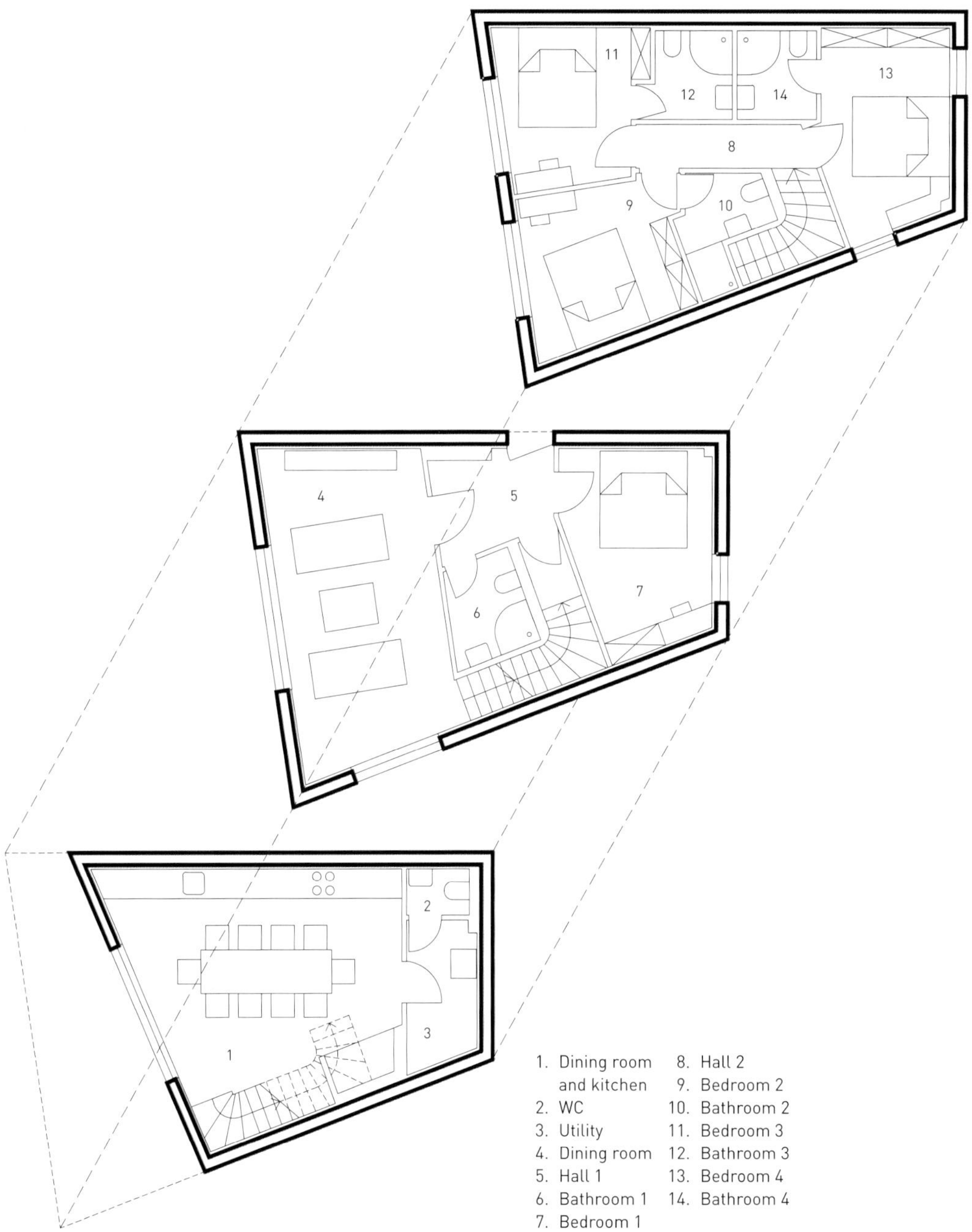

1. Dining room and kitchen
2. WC
3. Utility
4. Dining room
5. Hall 1
6. Bathroom 1
7. Bedroom 1
8. Hall 2
9. Bedroom 2
10. Bathroom 2
11. Bedroom 3
12. Bathroom 3
13. Bedroom 4
14. Bathroom 4

Floor plans

# RACHCOFF VELLA Architecture

**Tony Vella, Stephen Rachcoff, Wade Stephens**

www.rachcoffvella.com.au

Rachcoff Vella Architecture is a boutique design based practice established in 2007 by principals Tony Vella and Stephen Rachcoff. Our work includes single houses, medium density residential developments, commercial and retail projects.

We aspire to produce distinctive, high quality architectural designs that: meet the needs of clients, and showcase our creative skills as architects. We have a holistic approach to our work that can be witnessed in the enjoyment of the end users and long term value of the built products.

Rachcoff Vella Architecture is committed to developing long term relationships with its clients with integrity and honesty towards their projects. This is strongly reflected in our efforts to develop innovative, contemporary design solutions that inspire all involved in the journey.

Rachcoff Vella Architecture ist ein Boutique-Designbüro, das 2007 von den Geschäftsführern Tony Vella und Stephen Rachcoff gegründet wurde. Unsere Arbeit umfasst Einzelhäuser, Wohnanlagen mittlerer Dichte sowie Gewerbe- und Einzelhandelsprojekte.

Wir streben danach, herausragende, hochwertige architektonische Designs zu produzieren, die die Bedürfnisse der Kunden erfüllen und unsere kreativen Fähigkeiten als Architekten zeigen. Wir haben einen ganzheitlichen Ansatz für unsere Arbeit, der sich in der Zufriedenheit der Endnutzer und in den dauerhaften Qualitäten unserer Entwürfe zeigt.

Rachcoff Vella Architecture ist bestrebt, mit Integrität und Ehrlichkeit langfristige Beziehungen zu seinen Kunden aufzubauen. Dies spiegelt sich in unserem Bestreben wider, innovative, zeitgemäße Designlösungen zu entwickeln, die alle Beteiligten auf ihrem Weg inspirieren.

Rachcoff Vella Architecture est un cabinet de conception de boutiques créé en 2007 par les directeurs Tony Vella et Stephen Rachcoff. Notre travail comprend des maisons individuelles, des développements résidentiels de moyenne densité, des projets commerciaux et de vente au détail.

Nous aspirons à produire des conceptions architecturales distinctives et de haute qualité qui répondent aux besoins des clients et mettent en valeur nos compétences créatives en tant qu'architectes. Nous avons une approche holistique de notre travail qui se manifeste dans la satisfaction des utilisateurs finaux et dans les qualités durables de nos conceptions.

Rachcoff Vella Architecture s'engage à développer des relations à long terme avec ses clients en faisant preuve d'intégrité et d'honnêteté à l'égard de leurs projets. Cela se reflète fortement dans nos efforts pour développer des solutions de conception innovantes et contemporaines qui inspirent toutes les personnes impliquées dans le voyage.

Rachcoff Vella Architecture es un estudio de diseño boutique fundado en 2007 por los directores Tony Vella y Stephen Rachcoff. Nuestro trabajo incluye viviendas unifamiliares, desarrollos residenciales de densidad media y proyectos comerciales.

Aspiramos a producir diseños arquitectónicos distintivos y de alta calidad que satisfagan las necesidades de los clientes y muestren nuestras habilidades creativas como arquitectos. Tenemos un enfoque holístico de nuestro trabajo que se hace evidente en la satisfacción de los usuarios finales y las cualidades duraderas de nuestros diseños.

Rachcoff Vella Architecture se compromete a desarrollar relaciones a largo plazo con sus clientes con integridad y honestidad hacia sus proyectos. Esto se refleja en nuestros esfuerzos por desarrollar soluciones de diseño innovadoras y contemporáneas que inspiren a todos los involucrados en el viaje.

# SILVER LININGS

Black Rock, Melbourne, Victoria, Australia

Photos: © Tatjana Plitt

This house presents itself as a robust and heavy mass, dragged from the beach and settled on top of an elevation. Under a textured concrete volume, a deep void in the main facade reveals the dark entrance that initiates a sequence of spaces clad in silver. The particular commission demanded the use of a restricted but robust and raw material palette, with every project challenge resolved through custom and artisanal design, leaving nothing to chance. The controlled material palette consisting of gray and silver cladding boards, raw concrete, brass hardware, and white oak carpentry conveys warmth and protection in the darker and more intimate spaces and the warmth and radiance of the sun in the bright and open spaces. The result is meticulously crafted architecture that conveys a refined and authentic minimalist design.

Dieses Haus präsentiert sich als eine robuste und schwere Masse, die vom Strand gezogen und auf einem Hügel platziert wurde. Unter einem texturierten Betonvolumen offenbart eine tiefe Leere in der Hauptfassade den dunklen Eingang, der eine Abfolge von Räumen zeigt, die in Silber verkleidet sind. Der besondere Auftrag erforderte die Verwendung einer begrenzten, aber robusten und rohen Materialpalette, wobei alle Projektherausforderungen durch maßgeschneidertes und handwerkliches Design gelöst wurden, bei dem nichts dem Zufall überlassen wurde. Die kontrollierte Materialpalette, bestehend aus grauen und silbernen Verkleidungsbrettern, rohem Beton, Messingbeschlägen und weißer Eichenschreinerei, vermittelt Wärme und Schutz in den dunkleren und intimeren Räumen sowie die Wärme und das Strahlen der Sonne in den hellen und offenen Räumen. Das Ergebnis ist eine sorgfältig gestaltete Architektur, die ein raffiniertes und authentisches minimalistisches Design vermittelt.

Cette maison se présente comme une masse robuste et lourde, tirée de la plage et posée sur une colline. Sous un volume de béton texturé, un vide profond dans la façade principale révèle l'entrée sombre, inaugurant une séquence d'espaces revêtus d'argent. La commande particulière a exigé l'utilisation d'une palette de matériaux limitée mais robuste et brute, avec tous les défis du projet résolus par une conception sur mesure et artisanale, où rien n'est laissé au hasard. La palette de matériaux contrôlée, composée de panneaux de revêtement gris et argentés, de béton brut, de ferrures en laiton et de menuiseries en chêne blanc, transmet de la chaleur et de la protection dans les espaces sombres et intimes, ainsi que la chaleur et la luminosité du soleil dans les espaces clairs et ouverts. Le résultat est une architecture méticuleusement conçue qui véhicule un design minimaliste raffiné et authentique.

Esta casa se presenta como una masa robusta y pesada, arrastrada desde la playa y asentada en lo alto de una elevación. Bajo un volumen de hormigón texturizado, un profundo vacío en la fachada principal revela la oscura entrada que inicia una secuencia de espacios revestidos en plata.
El particular encargo exigió la utilización de una paleta de materiales restringida pero robusta y cruda, así como la resolución de todos los desafíos del proyecto mediante un diseño y unos detalles artesanales y a medida que no dejan nada al azar. La controlada paleta de materiales formada por tableros de revestimiento gris y plateado, hormigón en bruto, herrajes de latón y carpintería de roble blanco transmite calidez y protección en los espacios más oscuros e íntimos y el calor y el resplandor del sol en los espacios luminosos y abiertos. El resultado es una arquitectura meticulosamente elaborada que transmite un diseño minimalista refinado y auténtico.

**Awards:**
- Grand Designs - House of the year 2023/23 Interiors Winner
- Design Matters – Building of the year 2021, Best use of concrete.
- Dezeen Awards 2020 – Shortlisted
- Houses Awards 2020 – New House Shortlisted

**Project team:**
Tony Vella, Wade Stephens, Stephen Rachcoff

**Construction period:**
20 Months

**Total built area:**
750 m$^2$

**Consultants:**
Keith Patrick (Structural engineer)

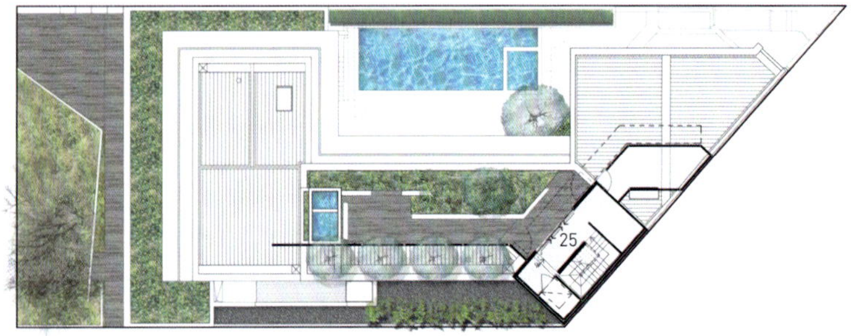

Roof terrace plan

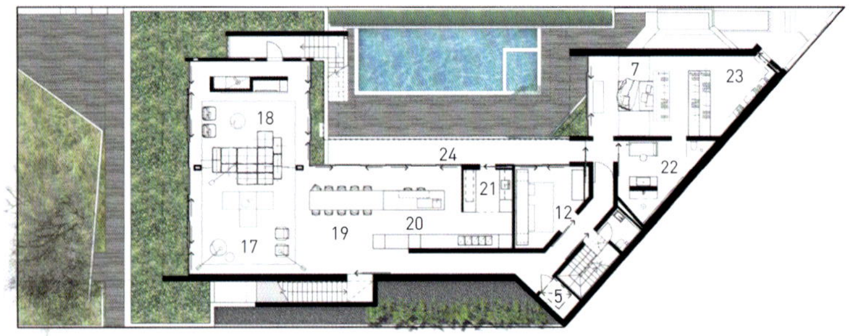

First floor plan

Ground floor plan

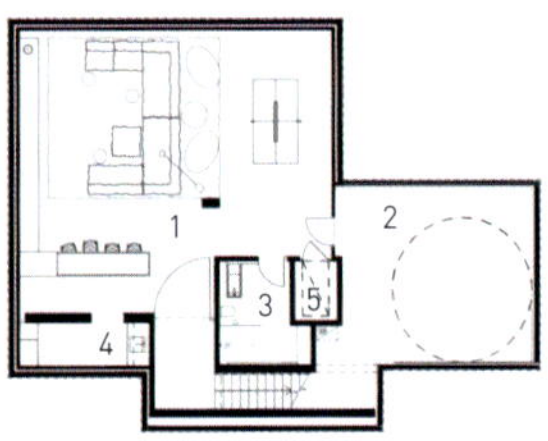

Basement floor plan

1. Multipurpose room
2. Water tank storage
3. WC
4. Kitchenette
5. Lift
6. Entry
7. Bedroom
8. Bathroom
9. Cabana
10. Laundry
11. Drop off
12. Study
13. Store
14. Garage
15. Store/services
16. Cloak
17. Living room
18. Sitting room
19. Dining room
20. Kitchen
21. Pantry
22. Ensuite
23. Dressing room
24. Balcony
25. Lobby

# ROB DUBOIS arquitecte

**Rob Dubois**

www.rob-dubois.com

Rob Dubois was born and raised in The Hague (The Netherlands). After completing his architectural studies at the Delft University, he established his office in Barcelona. He has completed more than 150 projects located between Barcelona and Girona and collaborates regularly with the 'DKHH' group (Dubois Kobari Hidalgo and Hartmann), mainly on cultural building projects.

His continuous search for concrete and balanced geometric and volumetric compositions tries to respond to the complex demands of the commissions. The material and cultural context is always taken into account in order to properly integrate the projects into their surroundings. His proposals avoid standard solutions, but small homages to his masters are often hidden in the details of his projects. Although he has lived in Barcelona for decades, his (modern) Dutch roots are always present in his work.

Rob Dubois ist in Den Haag (Niederlande) geboren und aufgewachsen. Nach dem Abschluss seines Architekturstudiums an der Delft Universität, gründete er sein Büro in Barcelona. Er hat mehr als 150 Projekte zwischen Barcelona und Girona realisiert und arbeitet regelmäßig mit der Gruppe „DKHH" (Dubois Kobari Hidalgo und Hartmann) zusammen, vor allem bei kulturellen Bauprojekten.

Seine ständige Suche nach konkreten und ausgewogenen geometrischen und volumetrischen Kompositionen versucht, auf die komplexen Anforderungen der Aufträge zu reagieren. Der materielle und kulturelle Kontext wird stets berücksichtigt, um die Projekte angemessen in ihre Umgebung zu integrieren. Seine Vorschläge vermeiden Standardlösungen, aber kleine Hommagen an seine Vorbilder sind oft in den Details seiner Projekte versteckt. Obwohl er seit Jahrzehnten in Barcelona lebt, sind seine (modernen) niederländischen Wurzeln in seiner Arbeit stets präsent.

Rob Dubois est né et a grandi à La Haye (Pays-Bas). Après avoir terminé ses études d'architecture à l'université de Delft, il a établi son bureau à Barcelone. Il a réalisé plus de 150 projets entre Barcelone et Gérone et collabore régulièrement avec le groupe DKHH (Dubois Kobari Hidalgo et Hartmann), principalement sur des projets de bâtiments culturels.
Sa recherche constante de compositions géométriques et volumétriques concrètes et équilibrées tente de répondre aux exigences complexes des commandes. Le contexte matériel et culturel est toujours pris en compte afin d'intégrer correctement les projets dans leur environnement. Ses propositions évitent les solutions standard, mais de petits hommages à ses maîtres se cachent souvent dans les détails de ses projets. Bien qu'il vive à Barcelone depuis des décennies, ses racines néerlandaises (modernes) sont toujours présentes dans son travail.

Rob Dubois nació y creció en La Haya (Países Bajos). Tras finalizar sus estudios de arquitectura en la Universidad de Delft, estableció su despacho en Barcelona. Ha realizado más de 150 proyectos ubicados entre Barcelona y Girona y colabora habitualmente con el grupo 'DKHH' (Dubois Koba ri Hidalgo y Hartmann), principalmente en proyectos de edificios culturales.
Su continua búsqueda de composiciones geométricas y volumétricas concretas y equilibradas intenta responder a las complejas exigencias de los encargos. El contexto material y cultural es tenido siempre en cuenta para integrar adecuadamente los proyectos en su entorno. Sus propuestas evitan las soluciones estándar, pero los pequeños homenajes a sus maestros se esconden a menudo en los detalles de sus proyectos. Aunque vive desde hace décadas en Barcelona, sus raíces holandesas (modernas) están siempre presentes en su trabajo.

# CASA BIELMANN - RIOS

## Santa Maria de Palautordera, Barcelona, Spain

Photos: © Jordi Miralles

This house responds to the highest demands of sustainability with a modest budget and without compromising its image. Its layout is distributed over three levels with a rectangular floor plan. The basement contains a gymnasium, garage and other facilities. The ground floor is conceived as an extension of the garden thanks to its glass façades and constitutes a single space housing the living, dining and kitchen areas. The upper floor contains the more private areas of the house. The exterior image of the building stands out for the exposed concrete slab that surrounds it and includes generous overhangs that protect it from the sun in summer and allow it to enter in winter. An installation based on geothermal energy and a heat pump heats the house through underfloor heating in winter and provides passive cooling in summer. In addition, photovoltaic panels on the roof make the house virtually independent of energy networks.

Dieses Haus erfüllt die höchsten Anforderungen an die Nachhaltigkeit mit einem bescheidenen Budget und ohne sein Image zu beeinträchtigen. Sein Programm verteilt sich auf drei Ebenen mit einem rechteckigen Grundriss. Das Untergeschoss beherbergt eine Turnhalle, eine Garage und Einrichtungen. Das Erdgeschoss ist dank seiner Glasfassaden als Erweiterung des Gartens konzipiert und bildet einen einzigen Raum, in dem sich die Wohn-, Ess- und Küchenbereiche befinden. Im Obergeschoss befinden sich die privateren Bereiche des Hauses.
Das äußere Erscheinungsbild des Gebäudes zeichnet sich durch eine Sichtbetonplatte aus, die es umgibt und großzügige Überhänge aufweist, die es im Sommer vor der Sonne schützen und im Winter einfallen lassen. Eine auf Erdwärme und einer Wärmepumpe basierende Anlage heizt das Haus im Winter über eine Fußbodenheizung und sorgt im Sommer für passive Kühlung. Darüber hinaus machen die Photovoltaikmodule auf dem Dach das Haus praktisch unabhängig von den Energienetzen.

Cette maison répond aux exigences les plus élevées en matière de durabilité avec un budget modeste et sans compromettre son image. Son programme est réparti sur trois niveaux avec un plan rectangulaire. Le sous-sol contient un gymnase, un garage et des installations. Le rez-de-chaussée est conçu comme une extension du jardin grâce à ses façades en verre et constitue un espace unique abritant les espaces de vie, de repas et de cuisine. L'étage supérieur contient les zones plus privées de la maison.
L'image extérieure du bâtiment se distingue par la dalle de béton apparent qui l'entoure et comprend de généreux débords qui le protègent du soleil en été et le laissent entrer en hiver. Une installation basée sur la géothermie et une pompe à chaleur permet de chauffer la maison par le sol en hiver et de la rafraîchir passivement en été. De plus, des panneaux photovoltaïques sur le toit rendent la maison pratiquement indépendante des réseaux d'énergie.

Esta vivienda responde a las más altas exigencias de sostenibilidad con un presupuesto modesto y sin comprometer su imagen. Su programa se distribuye entre tres niveles de planta rectangular. El sótano contiene un gimnasio, garage e instalaciones. La planta baja se concibe como una prolongación del jardín gracias a sus fachadas de vidrio y constituye un único espacio que alberga estar, comedor y cocina. La planta superior contiene las zonas más privadas de la vivienda.
La imagen exterior del edificio destaca por la losa de hormigón visto que lo envuelve y que incluye generosos voladizos que protegen del sol en verano y permiten su entrada en invierno. Una instalación basada en energía geotérmica y una bomba de calor calienta la casa a través del suelo radiante en invierno y proporciona frío pasivo en verano. Por otro lado, los paneles fotovoltaicos de la cubierta hacen que la casa sea prácticamente independiente de las redes energéticas.

**Project team:**
Architect: Rob Dubois
Supervisor execution: Jordi Fontanella

**Construction period:**
2017-2018

**Total built area:**
Basement + ground floor + first floor: 279.8 $m^2$

**General contractor:**
Damià Tejera

**Consultants:**
Structural engineer: Agustí Cullell

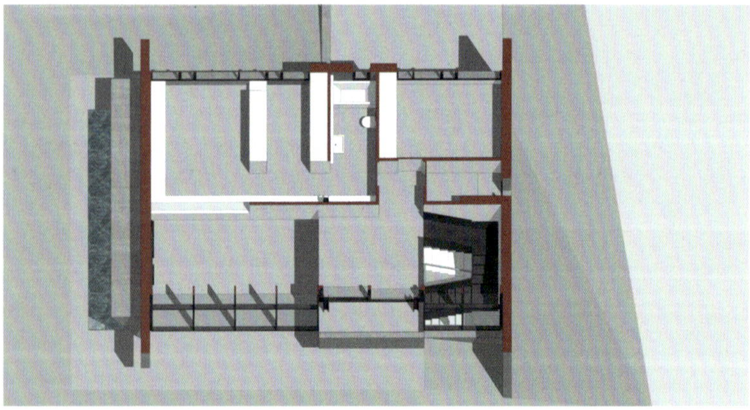

First floor plan

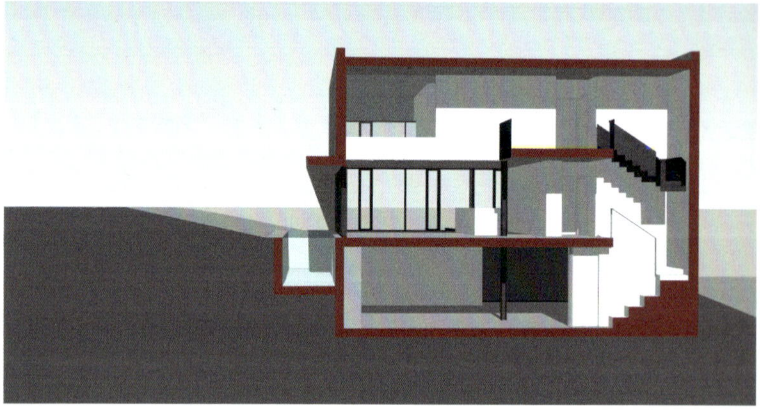

Section

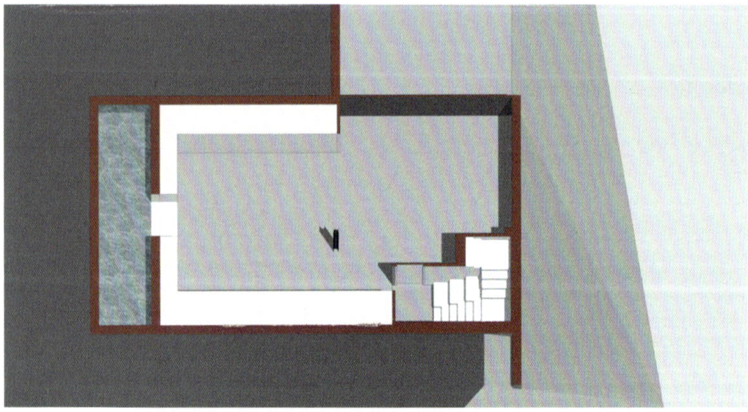

Basement plan

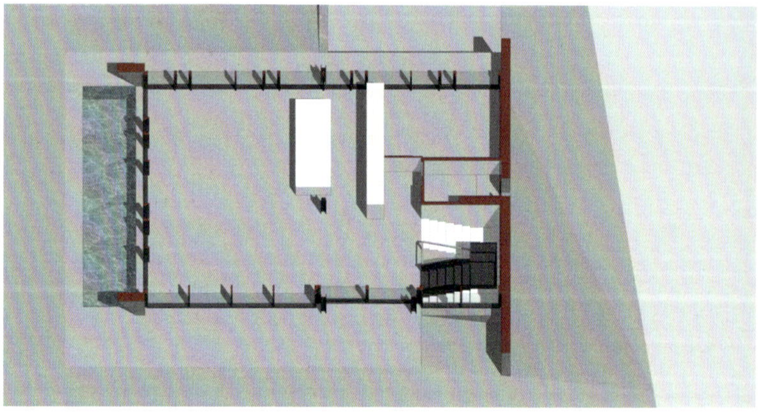

Ground floor plan

# RYUICHI SASAKI ARCHITECTURE +YTRO DESIGN INSTITUTE

**Ryuichi Sasaki + Rieko Okumura with Hidetaka Gonai, Nobumitsu Ohashi**

www.rsa.co.jp

Based in Tokyo, Japan, Ryuichi Sasaki Architecture is one of the most internationally acclaimed firms of its kind in the world. The firm harnesses the experiences of its professionals to design and consult on building types ranging from cultural facilities to commercial facilities, including music halls, apartment complexes, hotels, stores, bars, and housing structures. The firm focuses on the "zeitgeist" of every space that its interventions develop, and leverages continuous reinterpretation and repositioning to achieve excellence in its work.

In 2022, The Architecture Master Prize named Ryuichi Sasaki Architecture as the Firm of the Year Award. The firm is also an eight-time WAF Awards finalist, and was named winner of a Plan Award (Italy) in the Office & Business category. The firm was also anointed Best of Best winner at the Architecture Master Prize Awards in the United States.

Ryuichi Sasaki Architecture mit Sitz in Tokio, Japan, ist eines der international renommiertesten Büros seiner Art weltweit. Das Büro nutzt die Erfahrungen seiner Fachleute, um Gebäude zu entwerfen und zu beraten, die von Kultureinrichtungen bis hin zu kommerziellen Einrichtungen reichen, darunter Musikhallen, Wohnkomplexe, Hotels, Geschäfte, Bars und Wohngebäude. Das Büro konzentriert sich auf den „Zeitgeist" eines jeden Raums, den es gestaltet, und nutzt die kontinuierliche Neuinterpretation und Neupositionierung, um seine Arbeit zu optimieren.

Im Jahr 2022 wurde Ryuichi Sasaki Architecture im Rahmen des Architecture Master Prize als Unternehmen des Jahres ausgezeichnet. Das Büro ist außerdem achtmaliger Finalist bei den WAF Awards und wurde zum Gewinner eines Plan Award (Italien) in der Kategorie Office & Business ernannt. Außerdem wurde das Büro bei den Architecture Master Prize Awards in den Vereinigten Staaten zum Gewinner des Best of Best gekürt.

Basé à Tokyo, au Japon, Ryuichi Sasaki Architecture est l'un des cabinets de ce type les plus réputés au monde. Le cabinet met à profit l'expérience de ses professionnels pour concevoir et conseiller des types de bâtiments allant des installations culturelles aux installations commerciales, y compris des salles de musique, des complexes d'appartements, des hôtels, des magasins, des bars et des structures d'habitation. Le cabinet se concentre sur l'esprit du temps de chaque espace que ses interventions développent, et s'appuie sur une réinterprétation et un repositionnement continus pour atteindre l'excellence dans son travail.

En 2022, l'Architecture Master Prize a décerné à Ryuichi Sasaki Architecture le prix de l'entreprise de l'année. Le cabinet est également huit fois finaliste des WAF Awards, et a été nommé lauréat d'un Plan Award (Italie) dans la catégorie Office & Business. Le cabinet a également reçu le prix Best of Best lors des Architecture Master Prize Awards aux États-Unis.

Con sede en Tokio (Japón), Ryuichi Sasaki Architecture es uno de los estudios de su clase más aclamados internacionalmente. La empresa aprovecha la experiencia de sus profesionales para diseñar y asesorar sobre todo tipo de edificios, desde instalaciones culturales a comerciales, pasando por salas de música, complejos de apartamentos, hoteles, tiendas, bares y viviendas. La empresa se centra en el "espíritu de la época" de cada espacio que desarrollan sus intervenciones, y aprovecha la reinterpretación y el reposicionamiento continuos para lograr la excelencia en su trabajo.

En 2022, The Architecture Master Prize otorgó a Ryuichi Sasaki Architecture el Premio a la Empresa del Año. El estudio también ha sido finalista de los premios WAF en ocho ocasiones, y fue nombrado ganador de un Plan Award (Italia) en la categoría de Oficinas y Negocios. La empresa también fue elegida ganadora del Best of Best en los Architecture Master Prize Awards de Estados Unidos.

# ESCENARIO SHIROKANE

Shirokane, Minato-Ku,Tokyo, Japan

Photos: © Takumi Ota Photography

The location of the plot on a corner with ample visibility and its placement in the lively city of Shirokane determined the desire for this five-story building to constitute an iconic presence in its surroundings. Its envelope is formed by reinforced concrete load-bearing walls that create an expressive play of shadows that change depending on the time of day.
The first floor houses a restaurant, while the next three levels contain two residences per floor. The fifth floor houses a duplex for offices but suitable as a residential unit. The residences feature a flexible layout and have large square openings that recreate the effect of space, light, and wind. The playful use of white and concrete walls in spatial flexibility is based on the idea of minimalism in relation to the building's environment, providing a unique and enriching experience.

Die Lage des Grundstücks an einer Straßenecke mit guter Sicht und seine Lage in der lebhaften Stadt Shirokane bestimmen den Wunsch, dass dieses fünfstöckige Gebäude eine ikonische Präsenz in seiner Umgebung darstellt. Seine Hülle besteht aus bewehrtem Betonmauerwerk, das ein ausdrucksstarkes Spiel von Schatten erzeugt, das sich je nach Tageszeit verändert.
Das Erdgeschoss beherbergt ein Restaurant, während die drei oberen Etagen jeweils zwei Wohnungen pro Etage enthalten. Im fünften Stock befindet sich ein Duplex, der als Büroeinheit, aber auch als Wohnraum genutzt werden kann. Die Wohnungen bieten eine flexible Raumaufteilung und verfügen über große quadratische Öffnungen, die den Effekt von Raum, Licht und Luft nachbilden. Der spielerische Einsatz von weißen und Betonwänden in Bezug auf die räumliche Flexibilität basiert auf dem Minimalismus im Zusammenhang mit der Gebäudeumgebung, was ein einzigartiges und bereicherndes Erlebnis schafft.

L'emplacement du terrain à un coin de rue avec une excellente visibilité et sa situation dans la ville animée de Shirokane ont déterminé le souhait que ce bâtiment de cinq étages constitue une présence emblématique dans son environnement. Sa façade est constituée de murs de charge en béton armé qui créent un jeu expressif d'ombres changeant en fonction de l'heure de la journée.
Le rez-de-chaussée abrite un restaurant, tandis que les trois étages supérieurs contiennent deux appartements par étage. Le cinquième étage abrite un duplex destiné à un usage de bureau mais également adapté à un logement résidentiel. Les appartements offrent une disposition flexible et disposent de grandes ouvertures carrées qui recréent l'effet de l'espace, de la lumière et de l'air. L'utilisation ludique des murs blancs et du béton en relation avec la flexibilité spatiale repose sur le minimalisme en relation avec l'environnement du bâtiment, offrant une expérience unique et enrichissante.

La posición del solar en una esquina con amplia visibilidad y su ubicación en la animada ciudad de Shirokane determinaron la voluntad de que este edificio de cinco plantas constituyese una presencia icónica dentro de su entorno. Su envolvente está formada por muros de carga de hormigón armado que configuran un expresivo juego de sombras que cambia según la hora del día.
La primera planta alberga un local de restauración, mientras que los tres siguientes niveles contienen dos viviendas por planta. En la quinta planta se ubica un dúplex destinado a oficinas pero apto como unidad residencial. Las viviendas plantean una distribución flexible y disfrutan de grandes aberturas cuadradas que recrean el efecto del espacio, la luz y el viento. El uso lúdico de paredes blancas y de hormigón en la flexibilidad espacial se basa en la idea del minimalismo en relación con el entorno del edificio, que proporciona una experiencia única y enriquecedora.

**Awards:**
- **Architecture Master Prize 2021, Best Of Best**
- **German Design Award 2023, Special Mention**
- **The International Architecture Awards 2022, Honorable Mention**
- **The Plan Award 2022, Finalist**
- **Waf Awards 2021, Finalist**

**Project team:**
Architecture team: Ryuichi Sasaki, Rieko Okumura, Gen Sakaguchi, Yuriko Ogura, Shinsaku Karasawa, Hideki Ohashi

**Construction period:**
2020 February to 2020 November

**Total built area:**
345.44 m$^2$

**General contractor:**
Magome Construction Comapany

**Consultants:**
Hidetaka Gonai/Escenario Co., LTD.

**Builder:**
Nobumitsu Ohashi/Shukou Kensetsu Co., LTD

**Building management:**
Kiyoshi Yonemitsu/Alpha Management & Partners CO., LTD.

Elevations

30

Section in perspective

Concrete frame

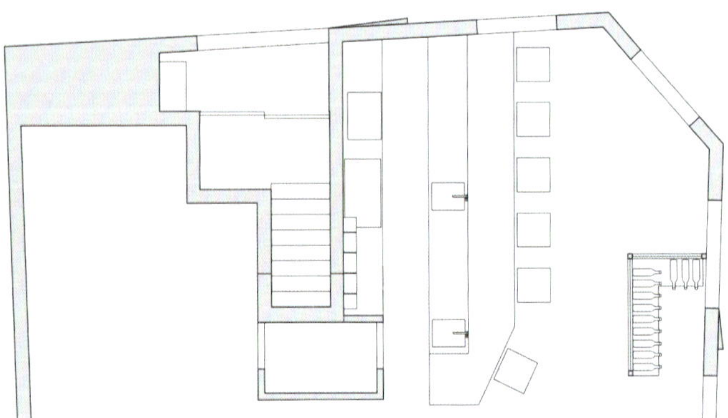

First floor plan

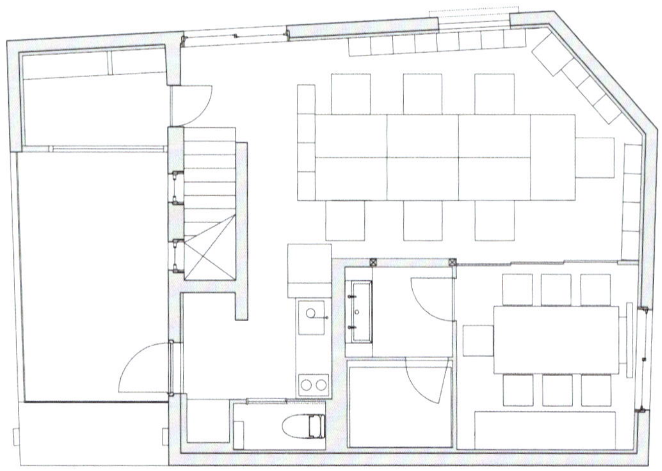

Fifth floor plan

# STU/D/O Architects

**Apichart Srirojanapinyo, Chanasit Cholasuek**

www.stu-d-o.com

Stu/D/O Architects is a young Bangkok-based architectural design studio founded in 2010, whose practice traverses the fields of architecture, urbanism and sustainable design. Grounded in the belief that architecture should consider all layers of physical and cultural distinctness of each site, the office does not adopt a fixed design process, but instead focus on a strong studio culture that pool together fresh ideas to result in new design approaches and possibilities of creating space. Founded under the desire to create architecture that sustains itself and the community along with it, Stu/D/O's work reflects the importance of the human experience within the creation of constructed environments. With its team of passionate architects, designers and engineers, Stu/D/O has designed and is currently involved in both local and international projects across an array of design typologies.

Stu/D/O Architects ist ein junges Architekturbüro mit Sitz in Bangkok, das 2010 gegründet wurde und dessen Tätigkeit sich auf die Bereiche Architektur, Städtebau und nachhaltiges Design erstreckt. Ausgehend von der Überzeugung, dass die Architektur alle charakteristischen physischen und kulturellen Schichten eines jeden Ortes berücksichtigen sollte, verfolgt das Studio keinen festen Entwurfsprozess, sondern konzentriert sich auf eine starke Studiokultur, die frische Ideen zusammenbringt, um neue Designansätze und Raumgestaltungsmöglichkeiten zu schaffen. Die Arbeit von Stu/D/O basiert auf dem Wunsch, eine Architektur zu schaffen, die sich selbst und die Gemeinschaft, die sie begleitet, erhält, und spiegelt die Bedeutung der menschlichen Erfahrung bei der Schaffung gebauter Umgebungen wider. Mit seinem Team aus passionierten Architekten, Designern und Ingenieuren hat Stu/D/O lokale und internationale Projekte verschiedener Design-Typologien entworfen und ist derzeit an diesen beteiligt.

Stu/D/O Architects est un jeune cabinet d'architecture basé à Bangkok, fondé en 2010, dont la pratique couvre les domaines de l'architecture, de l'urbanisme et de la conception durable. Partant du principe que l'architecture doit tenir compte de toutes les caractéristiques physiques et culturelles de chaque lieu, le studio n'adopte pas un processus de conception fixe, mais se concentre sur une forte culture d'atelier qui rassemble des idées fraîches pour donner naissance à de nouvelles approches de conception et à de nouvelles possibilités de création d'espace. Fondé sur le désir de créer une architecture qui se nourrit elle-même et la communauté qui l'accompagne, le travail de Stu/D/O reflète l'importance de l'expérience humaine dans la création d'environnements construits. Avec son équipe d'architectes, de designers et d'ingénieurs passionnés, Stu/D/O a conçu et participe actuellement à des projets locaux et internationaux de diverses typologies de conception.

Stu/D/O Architects es un joven estudio de diseño arquitectónico con sede en Bangkok fundado en 2010, cuya práctica abarca los campos de la arquitectura, el urbanismo y el diseño sostenible. Basado en la creencia de que la arquitectura debe tener en cuenta todos los estratos físicos y culturales distintivos de cada lugar, el estudio no adopta un proceso de diseño fijo, sino que se centra en una sólida cultura de estudio que aúna ideas frescas para dar lugar a nuevos enfoques de diseño y posibilidades de creación de espacios. Fundado bajo el deseo de crear una arquitectura que se sostenga a sí misma y a la comunidad que la acompaña, el trabajo de Stu/D/O refleja la importancia de la experiencia humana en la creación de entornos construidos. Con su equipo de apasionados arquitectos, diseñadores e ingenieros, Stu/D/O ha diseñado y participa actualmente en proyectos locales e internacionales de diversas tipologías de diseño.

# CASA DE ALISA

Nonthaburi, Thailand

Photos: © Sofography, Sky|Ground

The starting concept for this two-floors residence was the use of concrete and its material and structural function. Its spaces are delimited by structural concrete walls that form an austere architecture that directs and frames the views, while visually and acoustically shielding the interior from the surrounding context.
The ground floor houses the communal areas, whose limits are blurred towards the swimming pool and garden, while the upper level contains the more private areas. The main façade features a 37 m long cantilevered plane which acts as a "backdrop" for the rooms on the second floor. The materiality of exposed concrete is used throughout and the texture of its timber formwork is enhanced by light wells and skylights. The simple structural composition of the house optimises construction and assembly time, while reducing the architecture to a minimum.

Das Ausgangskonzept für dieses zweigeschossige Wohnhaus war die Verwendung von Beton und dessen materielle und strukturelle Funktion. Die Räume werden von Betonwänden begrenzt, die eine strenge Architektur bilden, welche die Blicke lenkt und einrahmt, während sie das Innere visuell und akustisch von der Umgebung abschirmt.
Im Erdgeschoss befinden sich die Gemeinschaftsbereiche, deren Grenzen zum Schwimmbad und zum Garten hin verschwimmen, während sich im Obergeschoss die eher privaten Bereiche befinden. Die Hauptfassade weist eine 37 m lange, auskragende Ebene auf, die als „Kulisse" für die Räume im zweiten Stockwerk dient. Die Materialität des Sichtbetons wird durchgängig verwendet, und die Textur der Holzschalung wird durch Lichtschächte und Oberlichter verstärkt. Der einfache strukturelle Aufbau des Hauses optimiert die Bau- und Montagezeit, während die Architektur auf ein Minimum reduziert wird.

Le concept de départ de cette résidence de deux étages était l'utilisation du béton et de sa fonction matérielle et structurelle. Ses espaces sont délimités par des murs structurels en béton qui forment une architecture austère qui dirige et encadre les vues, tout en protégeant visuellement et acoustiquement l'intérieur du contexte environnant.
Le rez-de-chaussée abrite les espaces communs, dont les limites s'estompent vers la piscine et le jardin, tandis que le niveau supérieur abrite les espaces plus privés. La façade principale présente un plan en porte-à-faux de 37 m de long qui sert de « toile de fond » aux pièces du deuxième étage. La matérialité du béton apparent est utilisée partout et la texture de son coffrage en bois est mise en valeur par des puits de lumière et des lucarnes. La composition structurelle simple de la maison optimise le temps de construction et d'assemblage, tout en réduisant l'architecture au minimum.

El concepto de partida de esta residencia de dos plantas fue el uso del hormigón y su función material y estructural. Sus espacios son delimitados por muros estructurales de hormigón que conforman una arquitectura austera que dirige y enmarca las vistas, a la vez que resguarda visual y acústicamente el interior del contexto circundante.
La planta baja alberga las zonas comunes, cuyos límites se difuminan hacia la piscina y el jardín, mientras que el nivel superior contiene las zonas más privadas. En la fachada principal destaca un plano en voladizo de 37 m de longitud que actúa como «telón de fondo» para las estancias de la planta segunda. La materialidad del hormigón visto se utiliza en todos sus aspectos y la textura de su encofrado de madera se realza con pozos de luz y claraboyas. La sencilla composición estructural de la casa optimiza el tiempo de construcción y montaje, a la vez que reduce la arquitectura a su mínima expresión.

**Project team:**
Apichart Srirojanapinyo, Chanasit Cholasuek, Panfan Laksanahut, Win Rojanastien

**Construction period:**
2017-2019

**Total built area:**
1,545 m$^2$

**General contractor:**
D-Innova

**Consultants:**
Lighting designer: in Contrast Design Studio
Structural engineer: Ittipon Konjaisue
Mechanical engineer: MEE Consultants
Consultants: Engineering Plus

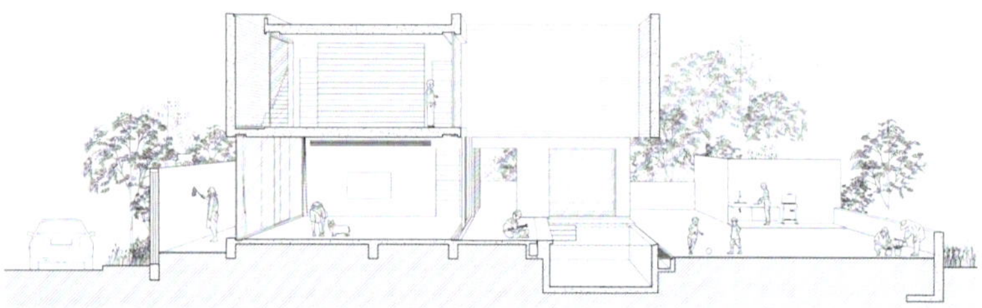

Transversal section

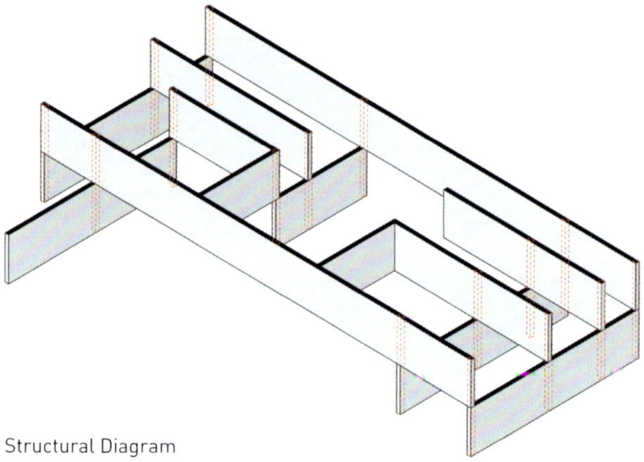

Structural Diagram

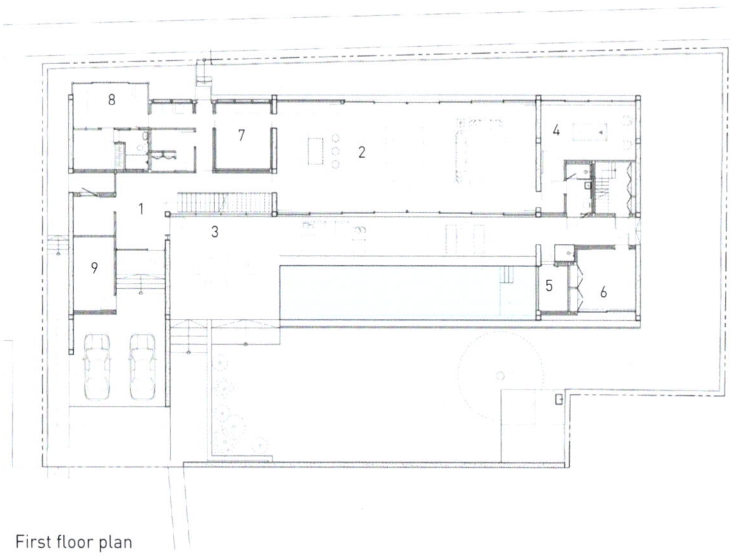

First floor plan

1. Foyer
2. Living/dininig room
3. Outdoor deck
4. Games room
5. Steam room
6. Spa room
7. Thai kitchen
8. Service area
9. Storage

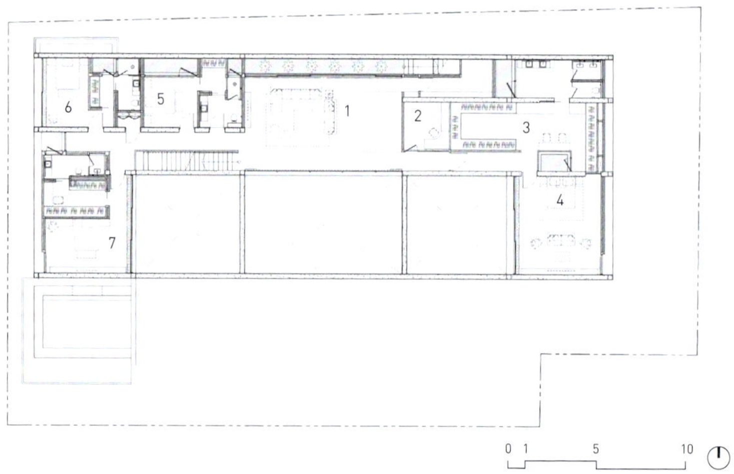

Second floor plan

1. Family living
2. Working room
3. Closet and master bathroom
4. Master bedroom
5. Guest bedroom 1
6. Guest bedroom 2
7. Child room

## TARA

**Heike Pohl, Andreas Zanier**

www.arch-tara.it

Tara is an architecture practice based in Meran (South Tyrol, IT). The two founders, Heike Pohl and Andreas Zanier, met during their studies at the University of Innsbruck. They founded tara in 2011, after gaining different work experiences, both in Italy and abroad. A multidirectional and pragmatic work approach is essential for the tara-team, which currently consists of 9 creatives of different nationalities and backgrounds. Tara deals with planning at 360 degrees, from the urban scale to interior design. They develop tailor-made solutions, starting with a careful analysis of the site and of the client's needs, always aiming to bring additional value to places and people they work with. Over the years, they have gained experience in the design of residential buildings, hotels, public buildings, protected heritage sites, and landscape interventions.

Tara ist ein Architekturbüro mit Sitz in Meran (Südtirol, IT). Die beiden Gründer, Heike Pohl und Andreas Zanier, lernten sich während ihres Studiums an der Universität Innsbruck kennen. Sie gründeten Tara im Jahr 2011, nachdem sie verschiedene Arbeitserfahrungen in Italien und im Ausland gesammelt hatten. Ein multidirektionaler und pragmatischer Arbeitsansatz ist essentiell für das Tara-Team, das derzeit aus 9 Kreativen unterschiedlicher Nationalitäten und Hintergründe besteht. Tara befasst sich mit der Planung von 360 Grad, vom städtischen Maßstab bis zur Innenarchitektur. Sie entwickeln maßgeschneiderte Lösungen, ausgehend von einer sorgfältigen Analyse des Standorts und der Bedürfnisse des Kunden, immer mit dem Ziel, den Orten und Menschen, mit denen sie arbeiten, einen zusätzlichen Wert zu verleihen. Im Laufe der Jahre haben sie Erfahrungen bei der Gestaltung von Wohngebäuden, Hotels, öffentlichen Gebäuden, denkmalgeschützten Stätten und Landschaftseingriffen gesammelt.

Tara est un cabinet d'architecture basé à Merano (Tyrol du Sud, IT). Les deux fondateurs, Heike Pohl et Andreas Zanier, se sont rencontrés lors de leurs études à l'Université d'Innsbruck. Ils ont fondé Tara en 2011, après avoir acquis différentes expériences professionnelles, en Italie et à l'étranger. Une approche multidirectionnelle et pragmatique du travail est essentielle pour l'équipe de Tara, qui compte actuellement 9 créatifs de nationalités et de formations différentes. Tara traite de la planification à 360 degrés, de l'échelle urbaine à la conception intérieure. Ils développent des solutions sur mesure, en commençant par une analyse minutieuse du site et des besoins du client, visant toujours à apporter une valeur ajoutée aux lieux et aux personnes avec lesquels ils travaillent. Au fil des ans, ils ont acquis de l'expérience dans la conception de bâtiments résidentiels, d'hôtels, de bâtiments publics, de sites du patrimoine protégé et d'interventions paysagères.

Tara es un estudio de arquitectura con sede en Meran (Tirol del Sur, IT). Sus dos fundadores, Heike Pohl y Andreas Zanier, se conocieron durante sus estudios en la Universidad de Innsbruck. Fundaron Tara en 2011, tras adquirir diferentes experiencias laborales, tanto en Italia como en el extranjero. Un enfoque de trabajo multidireccional y pragmático es esencial para el equipo de Tara, que actualmente está formado por nueve creativos de diferentes nacionalidades y orígenes. Tara se ocupa de la planificación a 360 grados, desde la escala urbana hasta el diseño de interiores. Desarrollan soluciones a medida, partiendo de un cuidadoso análisis del lugar y de las necesidades del cliente, siempre con el objetivo de aportar un valor añadido a los lugares y personas con los que trabajan. A lo largo de los años, han adquirido experiencia en el diseño de edificios residenciales, hoteles, edificios públicos, sitios patrimoniales protegidos e intervenciones paisajísticas.

## STADELE ROOMS

Lana, Italy

Photos: © David Schreyer

The project "Stadele rooms" forms an addition to the renowned Stadele Restaurant in the village of Lana. The new building, which houses the rooms, is located in a very narrow space between the restaurant and the owner's home, both different in age, function and architectural language. Like a well-studied puzzle piece, the building slots into its densely build context. Freed from all decorative elements, the sharply cut concrete monolith becomes the gem itself. Space-defining balcony boxes climb up its light, velvet-hard concrete façade.
Its interior stands in stark contrast to the exterior: here colors, images and materials unfold exuberantly. Inspired by the adjoining Stadele Restaurant, eight spices form the main themes for the rooms interiors. In the small hotel lobby, the colors and textures of the single spices come together, creating a fascinating blend, reminiscing the atmosphere of an oriental bazaar.

Das Projekt „Stadele Rooms" ist eine Erweiterung des renommierten Restaurants Stadele im Dorf Lana. Das neue Gebäude, in dem die Zimmer untergebracht sind, befindet sich auf engstem Raum zwischen dem Restaurant und dem Wohnhaus des Eigentümers, die sich in Alter, Funktion und Architektursprache unterscheiden. Wie ein gut durchdachtes Puzzlestück fügt sich das Gebäude in den dicht bebauten Kontext ein. Von allen dekorativen Elementen befreit, wird der scharf geschnittene Betonmonolith selbst zum Schmuckstück. An seiner leichten, samtig-harten Betonfassade klettern raumprägende Balkonkästen empor.
Das Innere steht in starkem Kontrast zum Äußeren: Hier entfalten sich Farben, Bilder und Materialien im Überschwang. Inspiriert durch das angrenzende Restaurant Stadele bilden acht Gewürze die Hauptthemen für die Inneneinrichtung der Zimmer. In der kleinen Hotellobby treffen die Farben und Texturen der einzelnen Gewürze aufeinander und bilden eine faszinierende Mischung, die an die Atmosphäre eines orientalischen Basars erinnert.

Le projet « Stadele Rooms » constitue un ajout au célèbre restaurant Stadele dans le village de Lana. Le nouveau bâtiment, qui abrite les chambres, est situé dans un espace très étroit entre le restaurant et la maison du propriétaire, tous deux différents en termes d'âge, de fonction et de langage architectural. Comme une pièce de puzzle bien étudiée, le bâtiment s'insère dans son contexte dense. Libéré de tous les éléments décoratifs, le monolithe en béton coupé net devient lui-même un joyau. Des balcons en boîtes définissant l'espace montent le long de sa façade en béton léger et velouté.
L'intérieur contraste fortement avec l'extérieur : ici, les couleurs, les images et les matériaux se déploient de manière exubérante. Inspiré par le restaurant Stadele voisin, huit épices forment les thèmes principaux de l'intérieur des chambres. Dans le petit hall de l'hôtel, les couleurs et les textures des épices individuelles se mêlent, créant un mélange fascinant, rappelant l'atmosphère d'un bazar oriental.

El proyecto constituye una ampliación del edificio del conocido restaurante Stadele, ubicado en Lana. El nuevo volumen, que alberga las habitaciones, se sitúa en una estrecha parcela entre el restaurante y la casa del propietario, ambos de diferentes épocas, función y lenguaje arquitectónico. Como una pieza de puzzle bien estudiada, el edificio encaja en su densamente edificado contexto, materializándose en un monolito de hormigón liberado de todo elemento decorativo. Por su fachada de hormigón ligero ascienden balcones que definen la composición.
En el interior, los colores, las imágenes y los materiales se despliegan con exuberancia, contrastando con el exterior. Inspiradas en el restaurante contiguo, ocho especias conforman los temas principales del interior de las habitaciones. En el vestíbulo del hotel, los colores y las texturas de las especias se combinan para crear una mezcla fascinante que evoca el ambiente de un bazar oriental.

**Awards:**
**Big SEE Award 2022**

**Project team:**
Heike Pohl, Andreas Zanier, Giulia Basso, Carlo Giannarelli, Filippo Gemmi

**Construction period:**
2017-2021

**Total built area:**
436 $m^2$

**Consultants:**
Gerold Haller, Ema Service

Site plan

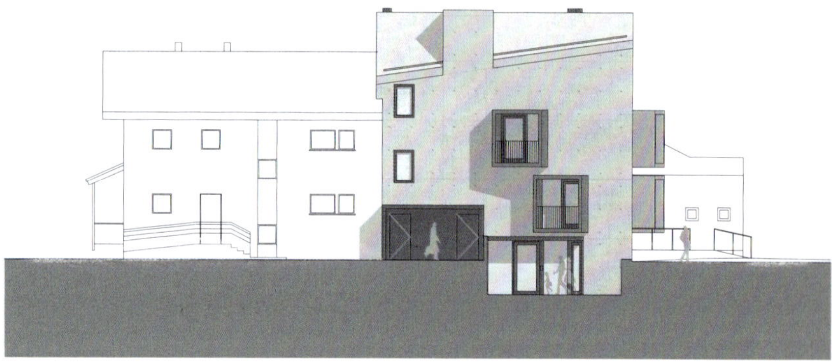

Elevation

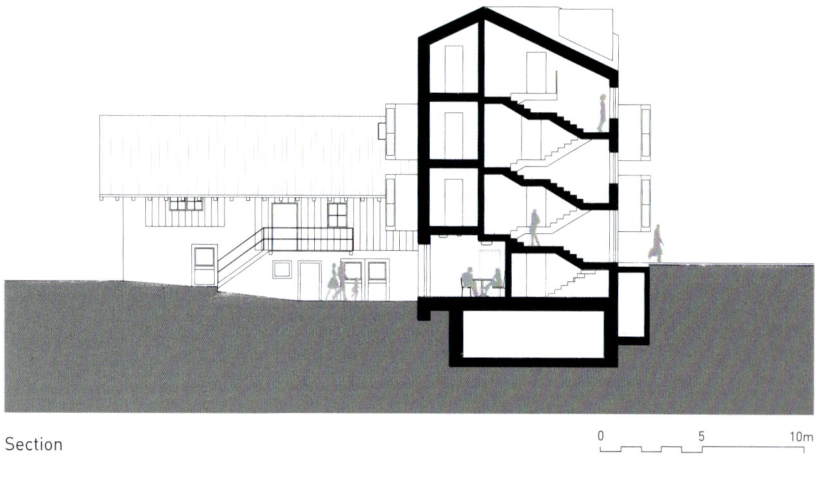


Section

## TETRO

**Carlos Maia, Débora Mendes and Igor Macedo**

www.tetro.com.br

Architecture studio based in Belo Horizonte - Brazil, and working globally, Tetro is formed by the architects Carlos Maia, Débora Mendes, and Igor Macedo. The office's professional practice is based on the careful study of the premises and conditions presented by the location and the client, always seeking for a unique and irreplicable solution to each project. Fundamentals such as integration with nature, use of apparent materials and exploration of empty spaces are characteristics that permeate all the work.

Tetro ist ein weltweit tätiges Architekturbüro mit Sitz in Belo Horizonte (Brasilien), das von den Architekten Carlos Maia, Débora Mendes und Igor Macedo gegründet wurde. Die professionelle Praxis des Büros basiert auf der sorgfältigen Untersuchung der Räumlichkeiten und der Bedingungen, die der Ort und der Kunde vorgeben, wobei für jedes Projekt eine einzigartige und unnachahmliche Lösung gesucht wird. Grundlegende Aspekte wie die Integration mit der Natur, die Verwendung offensichtlicher Materialien und die Erkundung leerer Räume sind Merkmale, die sich durch die gesamte Arbeit ziehen.

Studio d'architecture basé à Belo Horizonte, Brésil, et travaillant dans le monde entier, Tetro est formé par les architectes Carlos Maia, Débora Mendes, et Igor Macedo. La pratique professionnelle du bureau est basée sur l'étude minutieuse des lieux et des conditions présentées par l'emplacement et le client, toujours à la recherche d'une solution unique et irréprochable pour chaque projet. Des principes fondamentaux tels que l'intégration avec la nature, l'utilisation de matériaux apparents et l'exploration des espaces vides sont des caractéristiques qui imprègnent l'ensemble du travail.

Estudio de arquitectura con sede en Belo Horizonte (Brasil), y que trabaja a nivel mundial, Tetro está formado por los arquitectos Carlos Maia, Débora Mendes e Igor Macedo. La práctica profesional del estudio se basa en el estudio cuidadoso de las premisas y condiciones que presentan el lugar y el cliente, buscando siempre una solución única e irreplicable para cada proyecto. Fundamentos como la integración con la naturaleza, el uso de materiales aparentes y la exploración de espacios vacíos son características que impregnan todo el trabajo.

# CAFÉ HOUSE

**Divinópolis, Minas Gerais, Brazil**

Photos: © Luisa Lage

Located in a rural area distinguished by the image of red earth and twisted tree trunks, this project reinterprets the context in which coffee represents an invitation to a long conversation. Trying to connect poetically with the place and its inhabitants, the project aims to represent the characteristics of coffee by drawing references from the beverage itself.
The importance of the earth and air in the quality of coffee is materialized in the thick pigmented concrete side walls framing the views and two thin curved white slabs that "float" over the house. The functional program is divided into two blocks located under these slabs, the social and the intimate, connected by a hallway between two concrete walls. The two volumes are respectfully implanted with the topography and existing trees, creating a stepped garden between them.

Dieses Projekt befindet sich in einer ländlichen Gegend, die durch die rote Erde und die verdrehten Baumstämme gekennzeichnet ist, und interpretiert den Kontext, in dem Kaffee eine Einladung zu langen Gesprächen darstellt, auf eine poetische Weise neu. In dem Versuch, poetisch mit dem Ort und seinen Bewohnern in Verbindung zu treten, zielt das Projekt darauf ab, die Merkmale des Kaffees zu repräsentieren, indem es Referenzen aus dem Getränk selbst zieht.
Die Bedeutung von Erde und Luft für die Qualität des Kaffees wird in den dicken, pigmentierten Betonseitenwänden materialisiert, die die Aussichten einrahmen, und in zwei dünnen gebogenen weißen Platten, die über dem Haus „schweben". Das funktionale Programm ist in zwei Blöcke unter diesen Platten aufgeteilt, das Soziale und das Intime, die durch einen Flur zwischen zwei Betonwänden miteinander verbunden sind. Die beiden Volumina sind respektvoll in die Topografie und die vorhandenen Bäume eingebettet und schaffen einen gestuften Garten zwischen ihnen.

Ce projet est situé dans une région rurale caractérisée par la terre rouge et les troncs d'arbres tordus, et réinterprète de manière poétique le contexte où le café représente une invitation à de longues conversations. Dans une tentative de se connecter poétiquement avec le lieu et ses habitants, le projet vise à représenter les caractéristiques du café en puisant des références de la boisson elle-même.
L'importance de la terre et de l'air pour la qualité du café est matérialisée respectivement par les épais murs latéraux en béton pigmenté encadrant les vues et par deux fines plaques blanches incurvées qui « flottent » au-dessus de la maison. Le programme fonctionnel est divisé en deux blocs situés sous ces plaques, le social et l'intime, reliés par un couloir entre deux murs en béton. Les deux volumes sont intégrés de manière respectueuse dans la topographie et les arbres existants, créant un jardin étagé entre eux.

Situado en una zona rural donde destacan la imagen de la tierra roja y los troncos retorcidos de los árboles, este proyecto reinterpreta a través del diseño un contexto en el cual el café representa la invitación a una larga conversación. Intentando conectar de manera poética con el lugar y con sus habitantes, el proyecto aspira a representar las características del café extrayendo referencias de la propia bebida.
La importancia de la tierra y el aire en la calidad del café se materializó, respectivamente, en los gruesos muros laterales de hormigón pigmentado que enmarcan las vistas y en dos finas losas blancas curvadas que «flotan» sobre la casa. El programa funcional se divide en dos bloques situados bajo estas losas, lo social y lo íntimo, comunicados por un pasillo entre dos muros de hormigón. Los dos volúmenes se implantan de manera respetuosa con la topografía y los árboles existentes, desarrollando entre ellos un jardín escalonado.

**Awards:**
**World Architecture Awards**

**Project team:**
Carlos Maia, Débora Mendes, Igor Macedo.
Collaborators: Bianca de Castro Carvalho, Bruno Bomtempo, Déborah Martins, Diana Oliveira, Giovanna de Giacomo, Gegório Fiorotti, Luisa Lage

**Construction period:**
2020-2023

**Total built area:**
257 m²

**General contractor:**
Somar Engenharia

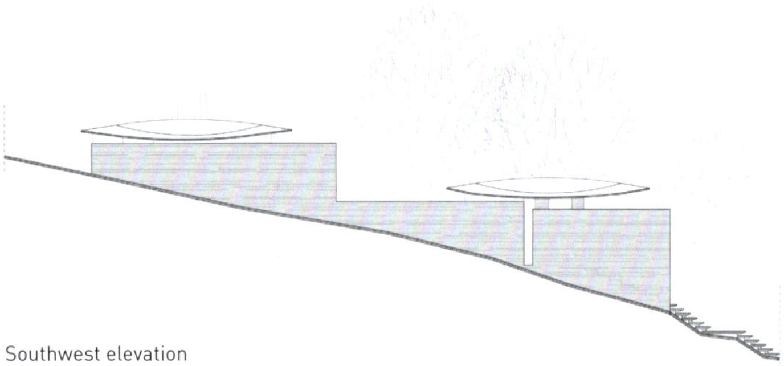

Southwest elevation

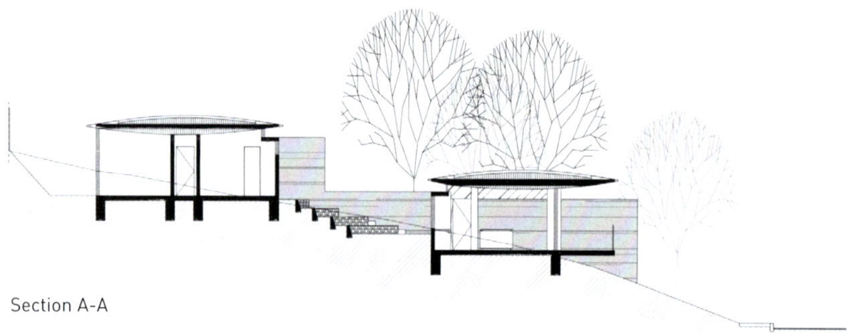

Section A-A

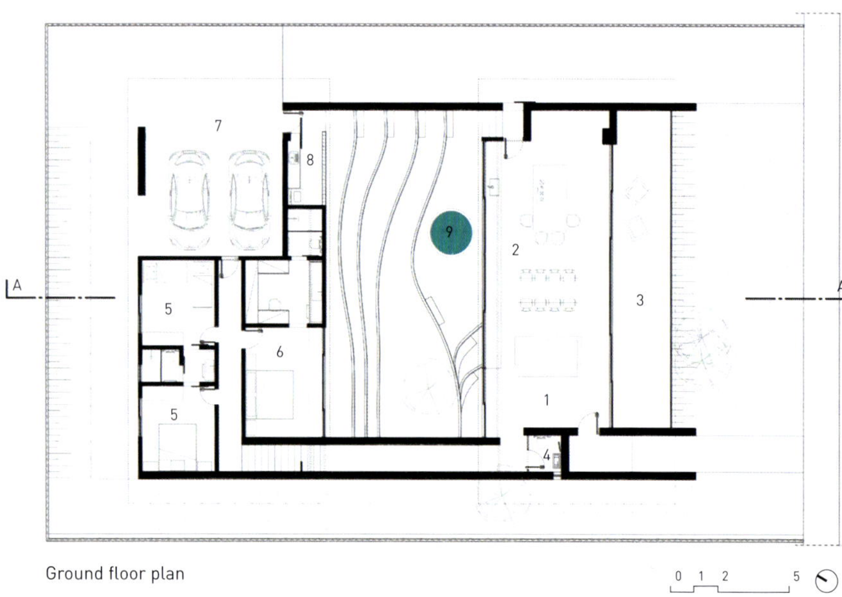

1. Living room
2. Kitchen/dining room
3. Terrace
4. Toilet
5. Demi-suite
6. Master suite
7. Garage
8. Service area
9. Spa

Ground floor plan

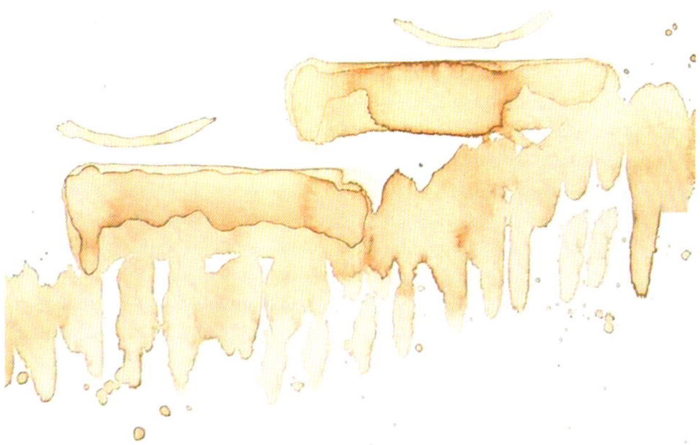

Conceptual watercolour

# WESPI DE MEURON ROMEO Architects

**Markus Wespi, Jérôme de Meuron, Luca Romeo**

www.wdmra.ch

Wespi de Meuron Romeo Architects is an architecture practice based in Caviano, Switzerland, founded in 2002 by Markus Wespi and Jérôme de Meuron, in 2012 Luca Romeo joined.

Architecture,
timelessly self-evident,
interwoven with building culture
and location,
rooted as it has always been,
more discovery than invention,
creating something new out
of old familiar moods,
atmosphere,
light and shadow,
that's what we like.

Wespi de Meuron Romeo Architects

Wespi de Meuron Romeo Architects ist ein Architekturbüro mit Sitz in Caviano, Schweiz, das 2002 von Markus Wespi und Jérôme de Meuron gegründet wurde. 2012 kam Luca Romeo hinzu.

Architektur,
zeitlos klar,
verwoben mit Baukultur und Ort,
verwurzelt, wie sie schon immer war,
mehr Entdeckung als Erfindung,
aus altbekannten Stimmungen etwas Neues
schaffen,
Atmosphäre,
Licht und Schatten,
das ist es, was wir mögen.

Wespi de Meuron Romeo Architects

Wespi de Meuron Romeo Architects est un cabinet d'architecture basé à Caviano, en Suisse, fondé en 2002 par Markus Wespi et Jérôme de Meuron, rejoint en 2012 par Luca Romeo.

Architecture,
une évidence intemporelle,
entrelacée avec la culture de la construction
et l'emplacement,
enracinée comme elle l'a toujours été,
plus de découverte que d'invention,
créer quelque chose de nouveau à partir
d'anciennes ambiances familières,
l'atmosphère,
la lumière et l'ombre,
c'est ce que nous aimons.

Wespi de Meuron Romeo Architects

Wespi de Meuron Romeo Architects es un estudio de arquitectura con sede en Caviano, Suiza, fundado en 2002 por Markus Wespi y Jérôme de Meuron y al que en 2012 se incorporó Luca Romeo.

Arquitectura,
atemporalmente evidente,
entrelazada con la cultura de la construcción
y la ubicación,
arraigada como siempre ha estado,
más descubrimiento que invención,
creando algo nuevo a partir de viejos estados
de ánimo familiares,
atmósfera,
luz y sombra,
eso es lo que nos gusta.

Wespi de Meuron Romeo Architects

# NEW HOUSE IN SAN NAZZARO

**San Nazzaro, Italy**

Photos: © Giacomo Albo architect/photographer

**Project team:**
Markus Wespi, Jérôme de Meuron, Luca Romeo,

**Construction period:**
2020-2021

**Total built area:**
180 m$^2$

**General contractor:**
Walzer costruzioni SA

**Consultants:**
Engineer: Pianifica Ingegneri Consulenti SA
Building physics: IFEC Consulenze SA

The irregular shape of this house was determined by the configuration of the plot and the distances to its boundaries. This irregular shape encloses a rectangular floor plan that houses the living spaces and interstitial courtyards located between the two figures.
The morphology of the terrain and the shape of the building make it look like an archaic rock. This impression is reinforced by the rough washed concrete surfaces, the climbing plants on the facades and the few small square openings in the walls. Towards the upper street, the building presents itself as a discreet, closed, single-storey structure. On the valley side, the house is perceived as a larger, stepped volume. Both the living/dining room with open-plan kitchen on the upper floor and the rooms on the middle floor open onto the inner courtyards through fully glazed enclosures which ensure that natural light enters.

Die unregelmäßige Form dieses Hauses wurde durch die Konfiguration des Grundstücks und die Abstände zu seinen Grenzen bestimmt. Diese unregelmäßige Form umschließt einen rechteckigen Grundriss, in dem die Wohnräume und einige Zwischenhöfe untergebracht sind, die zwischen den beiden Figuren liegen.
Die Morphologie des Geländes und die Form des Gebäudes lassen es wie einen archaischen Felsen erscheinen. Dieser Eindruck wird durch die rauen Waschbetonflächen, die Kletterpflanzen an den Fassaden und die wenigen kleinen quadratischen Öffnungen in den Wänden noch verstärkt. Zur oberen Straße hin präsentiert sich das Gebäude als unauffälliger, geschlossener, eingeschossiger Baukörper. Zur Talseite hin wird das Haus als größeres, gestuftes Volumen wahrgenommen. Sowohl das Wohn-/Esszimmer mit offener Küche im Obergeschoss als auch die Räume im mittleren Geschoss öffnen sich zu den Innenhöfen durch vollverglaste Einbauten, die für natürlichen Lichteinfall sorgen.

La forme irrégulière de cette maison a été déterminée par la configuration du terrain et les distances par rapport à ses limites. Cette forme irrégulière renferme un plan rectangulaire qui abrite les espaces de vie et quelques cours interstitielles situées entre les deux figures.
La morphologie du terrain et la forme du bâtiment le font ressembler à un rocher archaïque. Cette impression est renforcée par les surfaces en béton lavé brut, les plantes grimpantes sur les façades et les quelques petites ouvertures carrées dans les murs. Vers la rue supérieure, le bâtiment se présente comme une structure discrète, fermée et de plain-pied. Du côté de la vallée, la maison est perçue comme un volume plus grand, en gradins. Le salon/salle à manger avec cuisine ouverte à l'étage supérieur et les chambres à l'étage intermédiaire s'ouvrent sur les cours intérieures au moyen de clôtures entièrement vitrées qui garantissent l'entrée de la lumière naturelle.

La forma irregular de esta casa vino determinada por la configuración de la parcela y las distancias a sus límites. Esta forma irregular encierra una planta rectangular que alberga los espacios habitables y unos patios intersticiales situados entre ambas figuras.
La morfología del terreno y la forma del edificio hacen que este parezca una roca arcaica. Esta impresión se ve reforzada por las rugosas superficies de hormigón lavado, las plantas trepadoras de las fachadas y las escasas y pequeñas aberturas cuadradas de los muros. Hacia la calle superior, el edificio se presenta como una discreta estructura cerrada de una sola planta. En el lado del valle, la casa se percibe como un volumen más grande y escalonado. Tanto el salón-comedor con cocina abierta de la planta superior como las habitaciones de la planta intermedia se abren a los patios interiores mediante cerramientos totalmente acristalados que garantizan la entrada de luz natural.

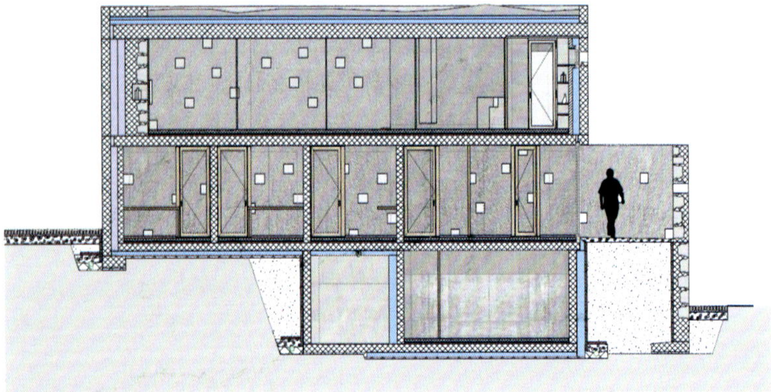

Section 1

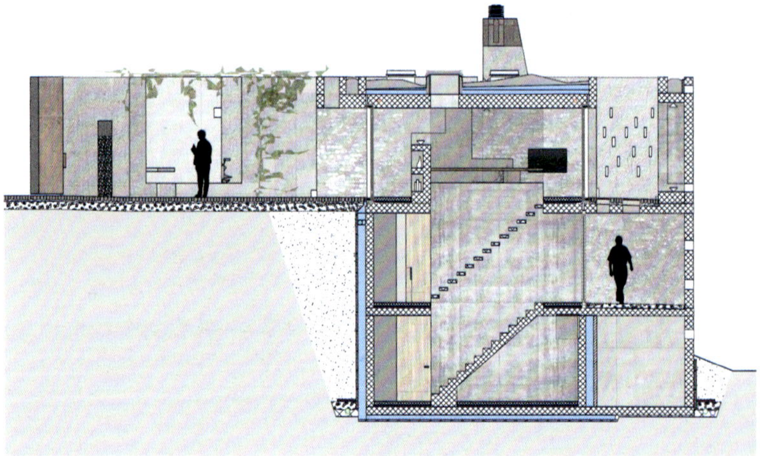

Section 2

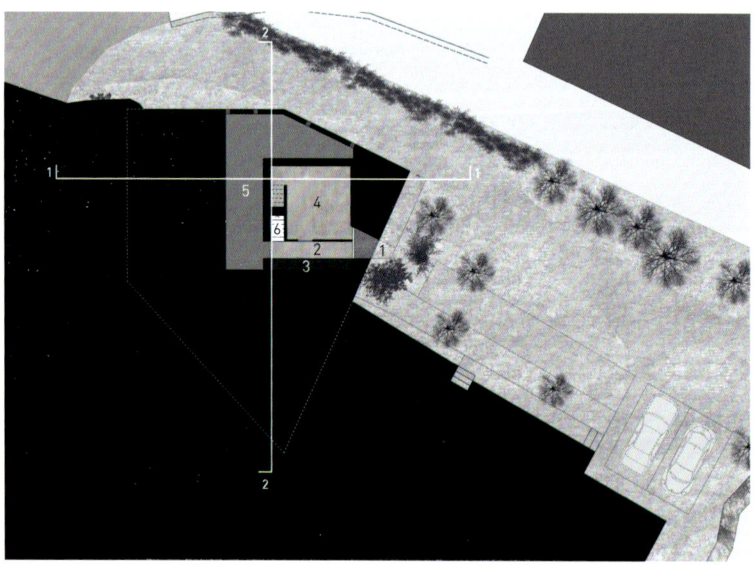

First floor plan

1. Secondary entrance
2. Corridor
3. Cupboards
4. Washroom
5. Technique/storage
6. Stairs

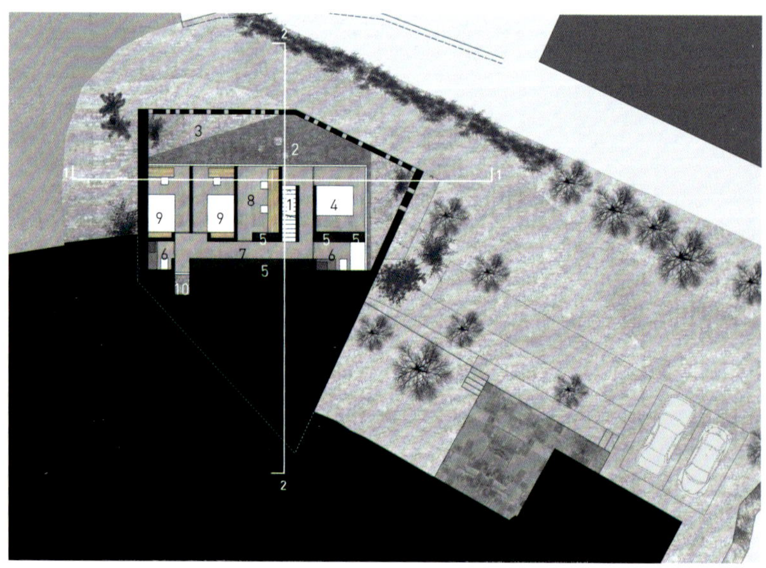

Second floor plan

1. Stairs
2. Covered courtyard
3. Open courtyard
4. Master bedroom
5. Cupboards
6. Bathroom
7. Corridor
8. Studio
9. Sleepingroom
10. Lightwell

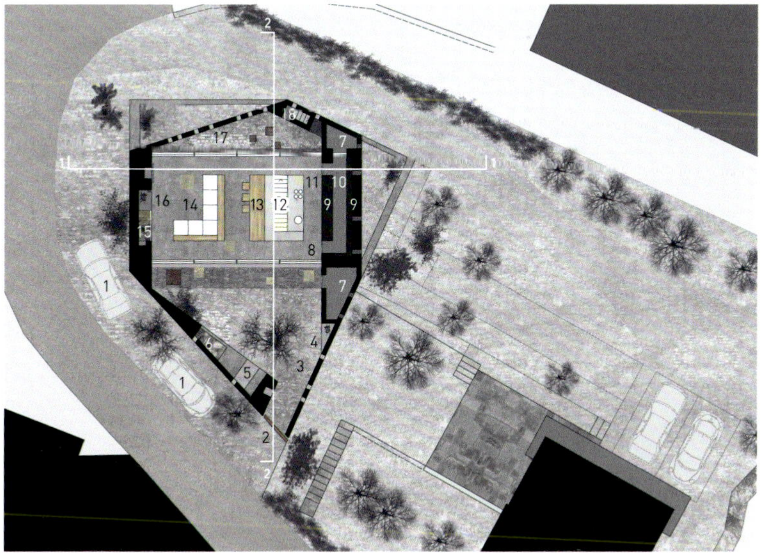

Third floor plan

1. Forecourt / parking
2. Access to the house
3. Main courtyard
4. Outdoor fireplace
5. Outdoor table
6. Outdoor bathtube / fountain
7. Storage
8. Main entrance
9. Cupboards
10. Backside kitchen
11. Kitchen
12. Stairs
13. Dining
14. Living
15. Bathtube
16. Fireplace
17. Courtyard
18. Stairs to the roof

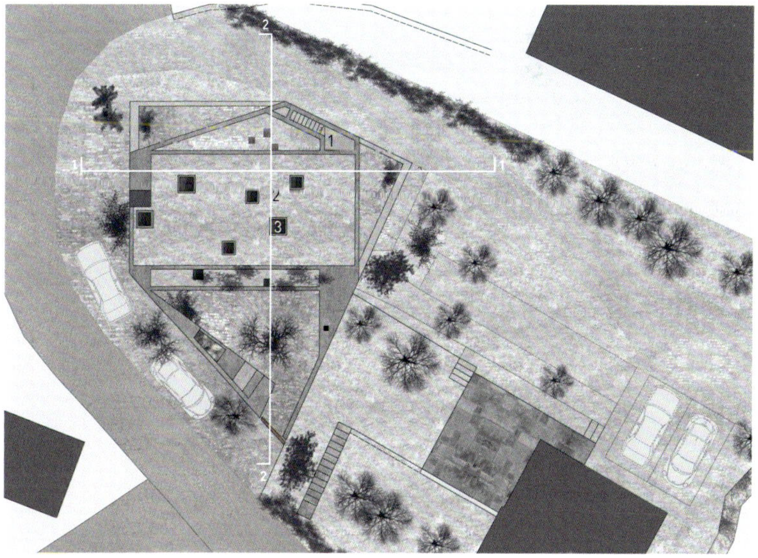

Roof plan

1. Lookout terrace
2. Green roof
3. Skylights

# WILD BÄR HEULE Architekten AG

**Thomas Wild, Sabine Bär, Ivar Heule**

www.wildbaerheule.ch

Following an attitude rather than developing a formal style.
Sabine Bär, Thomas Wild, and Ivar Heule lead this office founded in Zurich in 1988 as Wild-Bär+Wild, operating under its current name since 2009.
Regardless of the functional typology of the building and its formal expression, each project begins with a central idea that guides the design throughout its development, influenced by the location, economic factors, and regulations. A general concept that they like to call "the book of a movie."
Approaching each new task with freshness allows them to continuously adopt new perspectives. Unconventional perspectives that bring a breath of fresh air through their neutrality regarding typology. Critical perspectives that always question established requirements and goals. In the end, they write books that the client could never have dreamed of.

Einer Haltung folgen, statt einen formalen Stil zu entwickeln.
Sabine Bär, Thomas Wild und Ivar Heule leiten das Büro, welches 1988 als Wild-Bär+Wild in Zürich gegründet wurde und seit 2009 unter dem heutigen Namen firmiert.
Losgelöst von der typologischen Bauaufgabe und vom formalen Ausdruck, wird zu Beginn jedes Entwurfes eine Leitidee geformt. Eine Idee, die den Entwurf durch seine Entwicklung hindurch trägt. Geformt wird diese durch die treibenden Hauptakteure der Ökonomie, des Baugesetzes und dem Ort. Ein übergeordnetes Thema, das sie gerne als „Buch zum Film" betiteln.
Frisch an jede neue Aufgabe heranzugehen, erlaubt es sie, immer wieder neue Perspektiven einzunehmen. Unkonventionelle Perspektiven, die aufgrund ihrer Neutralität bezüglich der Typologie oft frischen Wind mitbringen. Kritische Perspektiven, die stets von neuem hinterfragen und gestellte Anforderungen und Wünsche überdenken. Um schlussendlich Bücher zu schreiben, von denen der Kunde nicht zu träumen wagt.

Suivre une attitude plutôt que développer un style formel.
Sabine Bär, Thomas Wild et Ivar Heule dirigent ce cabinet fondé à Zurich en 1988 sous le nom de Wild-Bär+Wild, et qui porte son nom actuel depuis 2009.
Indépendamment de la typologie fonctionnelle du bâtiment et de son expression formelle, chaque projet démarre avec une idée centrale qui guide la conception tout au long de son développement, influencée par l'emplacement, les facteurs économiques et les réglementations. Un concept général auquel ils se réfèrent comme « le livre d'un film ».
Aborder chaque nouvelle tâche avec fraîcheur leur permet d'adopter en permanence de nouvelles perspectives. Des perspectives non conventionnelles qui apportent un souffle d'air frais par leur neutralité vis-à-vis de la typologie. Des perspectives critiques qui remettent toujours en question les exigences et les objectifs établis. Au final, ils écrivent des livres que le client n'aurait jamais rêvé.

Seguir una actitud en lugar de desarrollar un estilo formal.
Sabine Bär, Thomas Wild e Ivar Heule dirigen este despacho fundado en Zúrich en 1988 como Wild-Bär+Wild y que desde 2009 opera bajo su actual nombre.
Independientemente de la tipología funcional del edificio y de su expresión formal, al iniciar cada proyecto se genera una idea central que guía el diseño a lo largo de su desarrollo y que está influenciada por el emplazamiento y por factores económicos y normativos. Un concepto general al que se refieren como «el libro de una película».
Abordar cada nueva tarea con frescura les permite adoptar continuamente nuevas perspectivas. Perspectivas poco convencionales que aportan un soplo de aire fresco por su neutralidad respecto a la tipología. Perspectivas críticas que siempre cuestionan los requisitos y objetivos establecidos. Al final, escriben libros que el cliente nunca habría soñado.

# WOHNTURM, WINTERTHUR

Winterthur, Switzerland

Photos: © Roger Frei, Zürich

On a small 400 $m^2$ plot stands this slim four-story building with a tower-like appearance, set on a slightly elevated concrete platform. Upon this solid base rises a lightweight steel and glass facade, stabilized by an open concrete tower visible from the exterior, containing the staircase, and on which the artist Beni Bischof has engraved linguistic traces. The building's rooftop houses a shared terrace.
The steel and glass cladding of the facade evokes Winterthur's industrial tradition and, at the same time, represents an uncommon finish in residential construction. The four identical residences were designed for open-minded and self-sufficient residents. Inside, everything revolves around the central black plywood piece that serves as a kitchen, storage space, room divider, and ingenious piece of carpentry all in one.

Auf einer kleinen Parzelle von 400 $m^2$ steht dieses schlanke, turmartige viergeschossige Gebäude auf einer leicht erhöhten Betonplattform. Über diesem massiven Sockel erhebt sich eine leichte Stahl-Glas-Fassade, stabilisiert durch einen nach aussen offenen Sichtbetonturm, der das Treppenhaus enthält und auf dem der Künstler Beni Bischof sprachliche Spuren eingraviert hat. Auf dem Dach des Gebäudes befindet sich eine gemeinsame Terrasse.
Die Verkleidung der Fassade mit Stahl und Glas erinnert an die Winterthurer Industrietradition und ist gleichzeitig eine im Wohnungsbau selten verwendete Ausführung. Die vier identischen Wohnungen sind für aufgeschlossene, autarke Bewohner konzipiert. Im Innern dreht sich alles um die zentrale schwarze Sperrholzeinheit, die Küche, Stauraum, Raumteiler und geniales Tischlerstück in einem ist.

Sur un petit terrain de 400 $m^2$ se dresse ce bâtiment élancé de quatre étages, en forme de tour, sur une plate-forme en béton légèrement surélevée. Une façade légère en acier et en verre s'élève au-dessus de cette base massive, stabilisée par une tour en béton apparent ouverte sur l'extérieur, qui contient l'escalier et sur laquelle l'artiste Beni Bischof a gravé des traces linguistiques. Le toit du bâtiment abrite une terrasse commune.
Le revêtement en acier et en verre de la façade évoque la tradition industrielle de Winterthur et, en même temps, est une finition rarement utilisée dans la construction résidentielle. Les quatre logements identiques sont conçus pour des résidents ouverts d'esprit et autonomes. À l'intérieur, tout tourne autour de l'unité centrale en contreplaqué noir qui est à la fois une cuisine, un espace de rangement, un séparateur de pièces et une pièce de menuiserie ingénieuse.

En una pequeña parcela de 400 metros cuadrados se alza este esbelto edificio de cuatro plantas con apariencia de torre, asentado sobre una plataforma de hormigón ligeramente elevada. Sobre esta base maciza se levanta una fachada ligera de acero y cristal, estabilizada por una torre de hormigón visto abierta al exterior que contiene la escalera y sobre la que el artista Beni Bischof ha grabado huellas lingüísticas. La cubierta del edificio alberga una terraza compartida.
El revestimiento de acero y cristal de la fachada evoca la tradición industrial de Winterthur y, al mismo tiempo, constituye un acabado poco utilizado en la edificación residencial. Las cuatro viviendas idénticas se diseñaron para residentes de mente abierta y autosuficientes. En su interior, todo gira en torno al mueble central de madera contrachapada de color negro que es cocina, espacio de almacenamiento, separador de ambientes e ingeniosa pieza de carpintería, todo en uno.

**Awards:**
**Prixforix 2021, best architects 20**

**Project team:**
Andreas Meiler, Christa Lippuner

**Construction period:**
2016-2017

**Total built area:**
Volume 1,600 $m^3$

**Consultants:**
Construction management: Robauen GmbH, Winterthur
Facade: Krapf AG, Engelburg

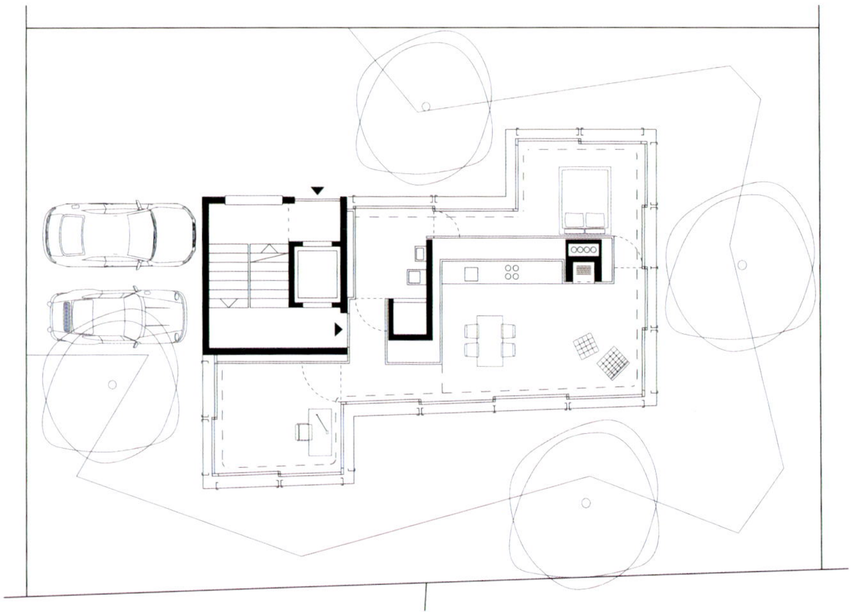

Ground floor plan

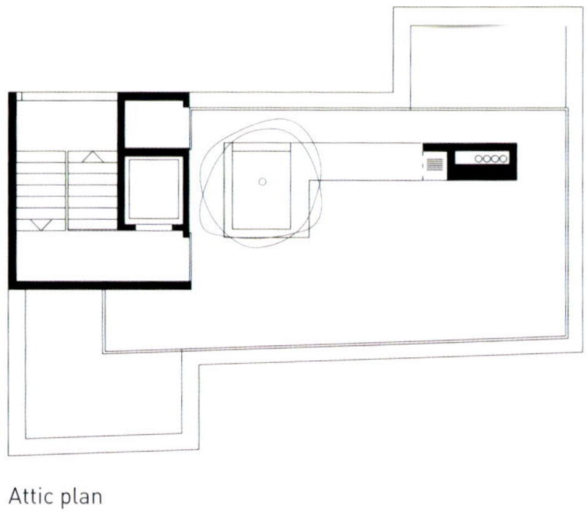

Attic plan

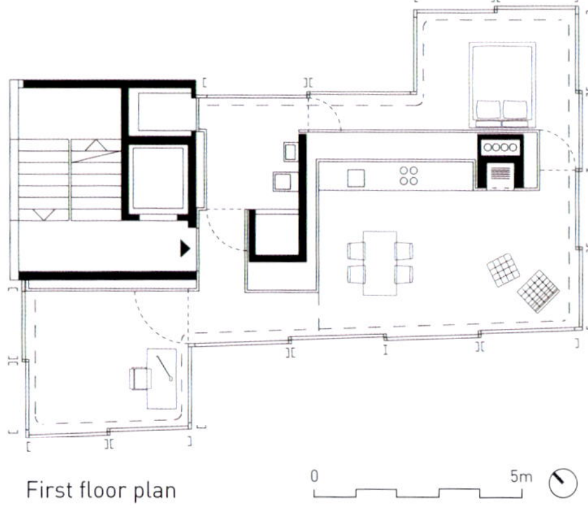


First floor plan

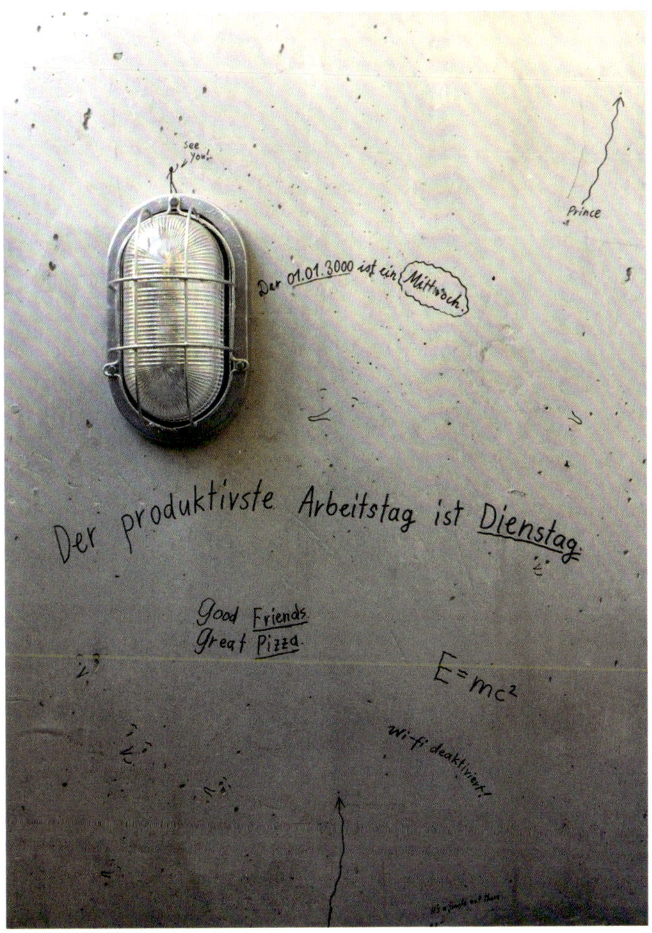
Der 01.01.3000 ist ein Mittwoch.
Prince
Der produktivste Arbeitstag ist Dienstag.
Good Friends.
Great Pizza.
E=mc²
Wi-fi deaktiviert!

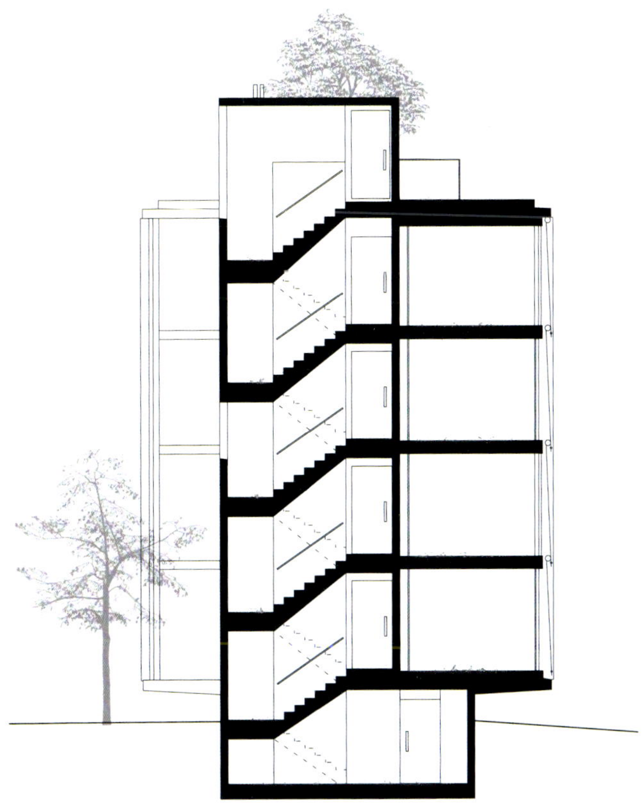

Section

# HOCHHAUS AUF DEM GLASI QUARTIER, BÜLACH
# WOHNHOCHHAUS MIT 74 EIGENTUMSWOHNUNGEN

Bülach, Switzerland

Photos: © Roger Frei, Zürich

This 60 m tall tower is located in a former industrial area where a new residential neighborhood with over 500 flats is being built. Elevated 35 m above its neighbors and with an asymmetric hexagonal footprint, it will serve as the landmark of the new area and will house 74 residences on 18 floors.
The skyscraper features a classic composition with a base and cornice. Its curtain wall facades form a regular grid that conceals double-height spaces on the access floor and in the residences. The intertwined elements of the curtain wall provide depth to the facades, where the generated shadows, along with fluted double columns and corbels, become ornaments. The symmetrical composition of the facade adds calmness to the ensemble. The open corners of the building host the outdoor spaces of the residences, making it clear that this is a place for living, not working.

Dieser 60 m hohe Turm steht in einem ehemaligen Industriegebiet, in dem ein neues Wohnquartier mit mehr als 500 Wohnungen gebaut wird. Mit einer Höhe von 35 Metern über den Nachbarn und einem asymmetrischen sechseckigen Grundriss wird es das Wahrzeichen des neuen Quartiers sein und 74 Wohnungen auf 18 Etagen beherbergen.
Das Hochhaus hat eine klassische Komposition mit Sockel und Gesims. Seine Vorhangfassaden bilden ein regelmäßiges Raster, das die doppelt so hohen Räume des Eingangsgeschosses und der Wohnungen verdeckt. Die ineinander greifenden Elemente der Vorhangfassade verleihen den Fassaden Tiefe, wobei die erzeugten Schatten zusammen mit den kannelierten Doppelsäulen und Kragsteinen zur Ornamentik werden. Die symmetrische Komposition der Fassade bringt Ruhe in das Ganze. Die offenen Ecken des Gebäudes beherbergen die Außenwohnbereiche und machen deutlich, dass dies ein Ort zum Leben und nicht zum Arbeiten ist.

Cette tour de 60 mètres de haut est située dans une ancienne zone industrielle où un nouveau quartier résidentiel de plus de 500 appartements est en cours de construction. S'élevant à 35 mètres au-dessus de ses voisins et présentant un plan hexagonal asymétrique, elle sera le point de repère du nouveau quartier et abritera 74 appartements sur 18 étages.
Le gratte-ciel présente une composition classique avec un socle et une corniche. Ses façades en mur-rideau forment une grille régulière qui masque les espaces à double hauteur de l'étage d'entrée et des appartements. Les éléments entrelacés du mur-rideau ajoutent de la profondeur aux façades, où les ombres générées, ainsi que les colonnes à double cannelure et les corbeaux, deviennent des ornements. La composition symétrique de la façade apporte du calme à l'ensemble. Les angles ouverts du bâtiment abritent les espaces de vie extérieurs, indiquant clairement qu'il s'agit d'un lieu de vie et non de travail.

Esta torre de 60 metros de altura se ubica en una antigua zona industrial en la que se construye un nuevo barrio residencial con más de 500 pisos. Elevada 35 metros por encima de sus vecinos y con una planta hexagonal asimétrica, constituirá el punto de referencia de la nueva zona y albergará 74 viviendas en 18 plantas.
El rascacielos presenta una composición clásica con zócalo y cornisa. Sus fachadas de muro cortina constituyen una malla regular que enmascara los espacios a doble altura de la planta de acceso y de las viviendas. Los elementos entrelazados del muro cortina aportan profundidad a las fachadas, en las que las sombras generadas, junto a las columnas dobles estriadas y las ménsulas, se convierten en ornamento. La composición simétrica de la fachada aporta calma al conjunto. Las esquinas abiertas del edificio albergan los espacios exteriores de las viviendas, dejando claro que éste es un lugar para vivir y no para trabajar.

**Awards:**
**Best Architects 24**

**Project team:**
Andreas Meiler, Christian Keller, Per Nussbaumer, Nikolas Schlick, Joan Carles Pallàs Hernàndez, Maximilian Richter

**Construction period:**
2019-2022

**Total built area:**
Volume 42,200 $m^3$

**General contractor:**
Steiner AG, Zürich

**Consultants:**
Free space concept: Studio Vulkan, Zürich
Facade planner: PSS Engineering AG, Chur

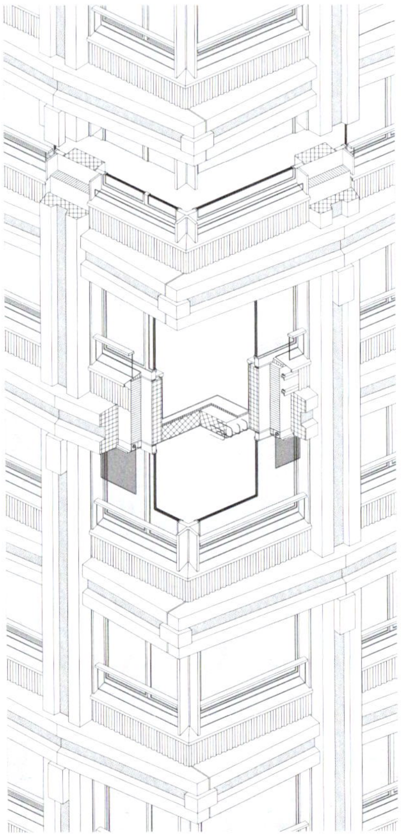

Axonometric detail

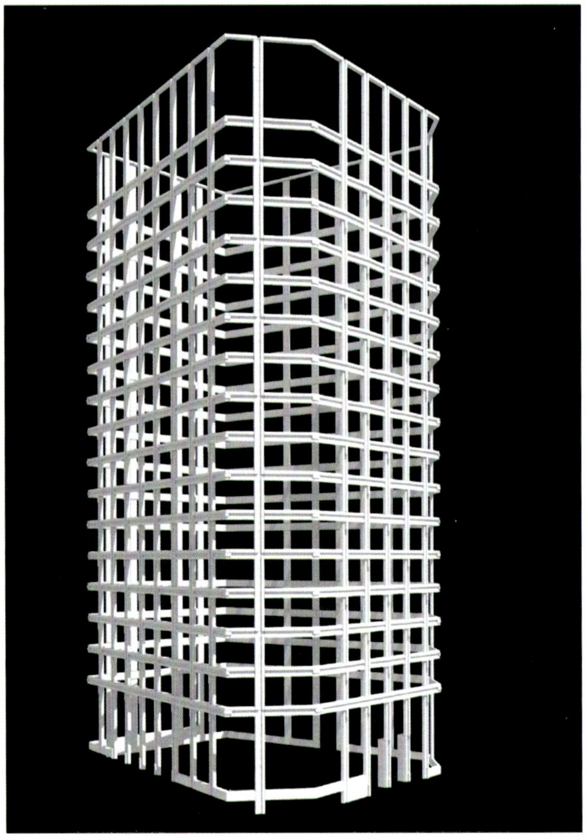

3D visualization

F

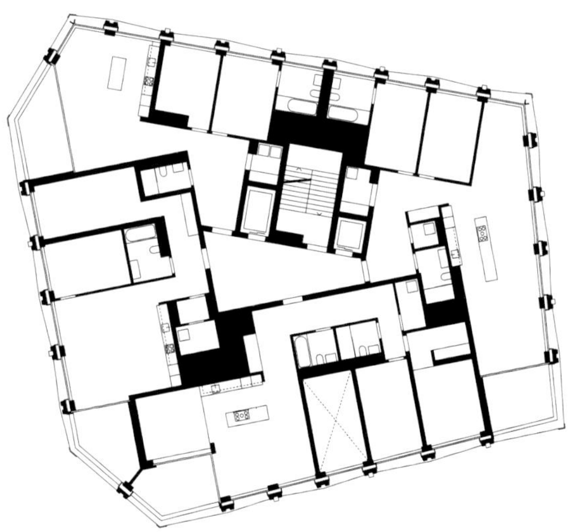

13th/15th/17th floor plan

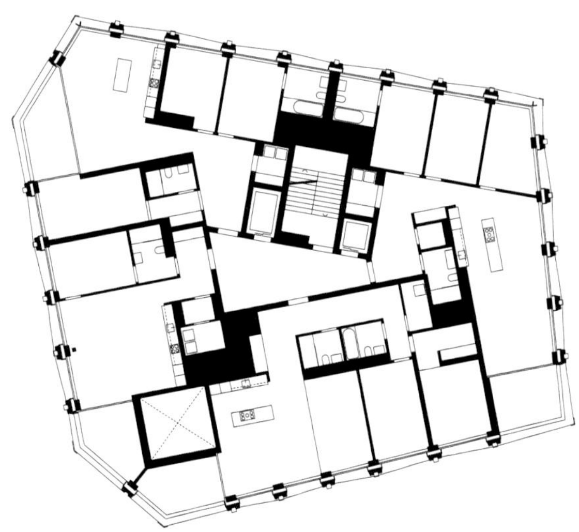


14th/16th floor plan

## XRANGE Architects

**Grace Cheung AIA**

www.xrange.net

Founded 2003 in Taipei by architect Grace Cheung and industrial designer and serial entrepreneur Royce YC Hong, XRANGE works on multiple scales, with a scope and diversity of projects encompassing masterplans, architecture, landscape, installations and products. Steered by the founders' extensive international background and cultural fluency, XRANGE's work is characterized by concise strategic thinking, bold forms and distinctive material attitude shaped by local contexts. Inspired by constraints unique to every project, XRANGE's architecture strives for original solutions that create meaning and place for users. With unwavering commitment to purpose and performance, XRANGE takes an essential and adaptive design approach, capitalizing on minimal means to realize works that are grounded without compromising human and environmental factors, spatial experience, design innovation and the soul of craft.

XRANGE wurde 2003 in Taipeh von der Architektin Grace Cheung und dem Industriedesigner und Serienunternehmer Royce YC Hong gegründet. Das Büro arbeitet in verschiedenen Maßstäben, wobei die Bandbreite und Vielfalt der Projekte Masterpläne, Architektur, Landschaft, Installationen und Produkte umfasst. Die Arbeit von XRANGE zeichnet sich durch prägnantes strategisches Denken, kühne Formen und eine unverwechselbare, von lokalen Kontexten geprägte Materialität aus und wird durch den umfassenden internationalen Hintergrund und die kulturelle Kompetenz der Gründer gelenkt. Die Architektur von XRANGE ist inspiriert von den Zwängen, die jedes Projekt mit sich bringt, und strebt nach originellen Lösungen, die für die Nutzer einen Sinn und einen Ort schaffen. Mit einem unerschütterlichen Bekenntnis zu Zweck und Leistung verfolgt XRANGE einen essentiellen und adaptiven Designansatz und nutzt minimale Mittel, um Werke zu realisieren, die geerdet sind, ohne menschliche und ökologische Faktoren, räumliche Erfahrung, Designinnovation und die Seele des Handwerks zu beeinträchtigen.

Fondé en 2003 à Taipei par l'architecte Grace Cheung et le designer industriel et entrepreneur en série Royce YC Hong, XRANGE travaille sur de multiples échelles, avec une diversité de projets englobant des plans directeurs, l'architecture, le paysage, les installations et les produits. Guidé par la vaste expérience internationale et la fluidité culturelle des fondateurs, le travail de XRANGE se caractérise par une pensée stratégique concise, des formes audacieuses et une attitude matérielle distinctive façonnée par les contextes locaux. Inspirée par les contraintes propres à chaque projet, l'architecture de XRANGE vise des solutions originales qui créent du sens et un lieu pour les utilisateurs. Avec un engagement inébranlable envers la finalité et la performance, XRANGE adopte une approche de conception essentielle et adaptative, capitalisant sur des moyens minimes pour réaliser des œuvres ancrées sans compromettre les facteurs humains et environnementaux, l'expérience spatiale, l'innovation en conception et l'âme de l'artisanat.

Fundada en 2003 en Taipei por la arquitecta Grace Cheung y el diseñador industrial y empresario en serie Royce YC Hong, XRANGE trabaja a múltiples escalas, con un alcance y una diversidad de proyectos que abarcan planes maestros, arquitectura, paisaje, instalaciones y productos. Dirigido por la amplia experiencia internacional y la fluidez cultural de los fundadores, el trabajo de XRANGE se caracteriza por un pensamiento estratégico conciso, formas audaces y una actitud material distintiva moldeada por los contextos locales. Inspirándose en las limitaciones propias de cada proyecto, la arquitectura de XRANGE busca soluciones originales que creen significado y lugar para los usuarios. Con un compromiso inquebrantable con el propósito y el rendimiento, XRANGE adopta un enfoque de diseño esencial y adaptable, aprovechando los medios mínimos para realizar obras sin comprometer los factores humanos y ambientales, la experiencia espacial, la innovación en el diseño y el alma de la artesanía.

# WANDERING WALLS

**Hengchun Township, Pingtung County, Taiwan**

Photos: © Kuo-Min Lee, Lorenzo Pierucci Studio, Studio Millspace

At the top of a hill facing the ocean, amidst meadows and acacia forests, steep and curvilinear in-situ concrete walls blur the boundaries between architecture and landscape to define the public and private spaces of this refuge.
A structural system of flat slabs and concrete walls built with wooden formwork allowed for the vertical misalignment of load-bearing walls. These walls enter and exit the three floors independently, subject to views and the arrangement of rooms and wind barriers, forming suspended vertical spaces and courtyards.
Inspired by the natural beauty of the surroundings, the design creates a sense of stillness and permanence with a single architectural element and a minimal palette of materials, defining architecture with curved walls that "wander" and are simultaneously structure and form, interior and exterior, exterior and interior, all at once.

Auf einer dem Meer zugewandten Hügelkuppe, zwischen Wiesen und Akazienwäldern, lassen steile, geschwungene Wände aus Ortbeton die Grenzen zwischen Architektur und Landschaft verschwimmen, um die öffentlichen und privaten Räume dieses Refugiums zu definieren.
Ein strukturelles System aus Flachdecken und Betonwänden, die mit einer Holzschalung errichtet wurden, ermöglichte es, die tragenden Wände vertikal zu verschieben. Diese Wände betreten und verlassen die drei Stockwerke unabhängig voneinander, abhängig von den Aussichten und der Anordnung der Räume und Windschutzwände, und bilden so schwebende vertikale Räume und Höfe.
Inspiriert von der natürlichen Schönheit der Umgebung schafft der Entwurf mit einem einzigen architektonischen Element und einer minimalen Materialpalette ein Gefühl der Stille und Beständigkeit und definiert die Architektur mit gebogenen Wänden, die „wandern" und gleichzeitig Struktur und Form, Innen und Außen, Außen und Innen sind.

Au sommet d'une colline face à l'océan, entre prairies et forêts d'acacias, des murs abrupts et curvilignes en béton coulé sur place brouillent les frontières entre l'architecture et le paysage pour définir les espaces publics et privés de ce refuge.
Un système structurel de dalles plates et de murs en béton construits avec un coffrage en bois a permis de désaligner verticalement les murs porteurs. Ces murs entrent et sortent indépendamment des trois étages, en fonction des vues et de la disposition des pièces et des brise-vent, formant des espaces verticaux suspendus et des cours.
Inspiré par la beauté naturelle de l'environnement, le projet crée un sentiment d'immobilité et de permanence avec un seul élément architectural et une palette minimale de matériaux, définissant l'architecture avec des murs courbes qui « errent » et sont à la fois structure et forme, intérieur et extérieur, extérieur et intérieur, tout à la fois.

En la cima de una colina frente al océano, entre praderas y bosques de acacias, unos muros escarpados y curvilíneos de hormigón in situ desdibujan los límites entre arquitectura y paisaje para definir los espacios públicos y privados de este refugio.
Un sistema estructural de losa plana y muros de hormigón construidos con encofrados de madera permitió desalinear verticalmente los muros de carga. Estos muros entran y salen de las 3 plantas de forma independiente, supeditados a las vistas y a la disposición de las habitaciones y de las barreras contra el viento, formando espacios verticales suspendidos y patios.
Inspirado en la belleza natural del entorno, el diseño crea una sensación de quietud y permanencia con un único elemento arquitectónico y una mínima paleta de materiales, definiendo la arquitectura con muros curvos que «deambulan» y que son simultáneamente estructura y forma, interior y exterior, exterior e interior, todo a la vez.

**Awards:**
- **ArchDaily Best Architectural Projects of 2022**
- **2022 Rethinking The Future Awards, Hospitality (built), Third Award**

**Project team:**
Grace Cheung, Royce Hong, Emily Lin, Peihsuan Hsu, Jason Chen, Miriam Park, Sonia Pan, Beatrice Cordella, Edgar Navarrete

**Construction period:**
2016-2019

**Total built area:**
490 $m^2$

**Consultants:**
Structural engineers: Top Technic Engineering consultants Co., Ltd.
Lighting design: Unolai Lighting Design & Associates

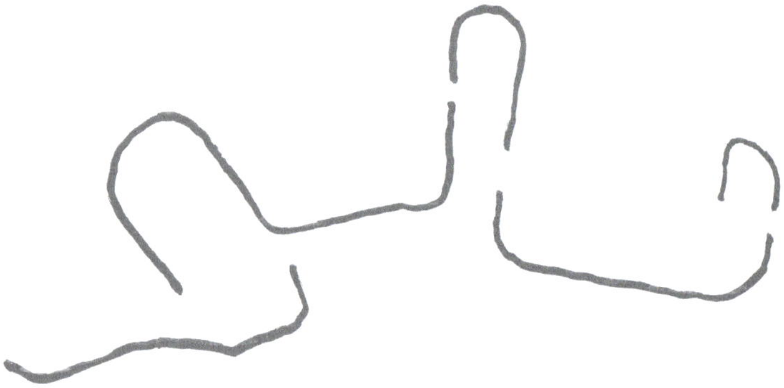

Concept sketch

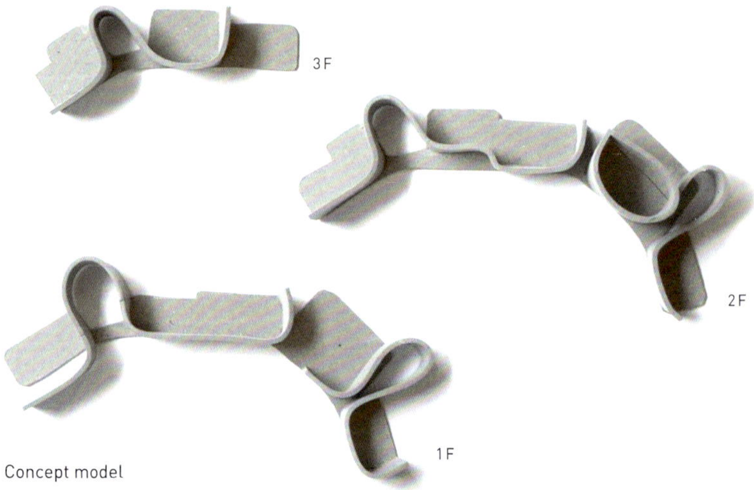


Concept model

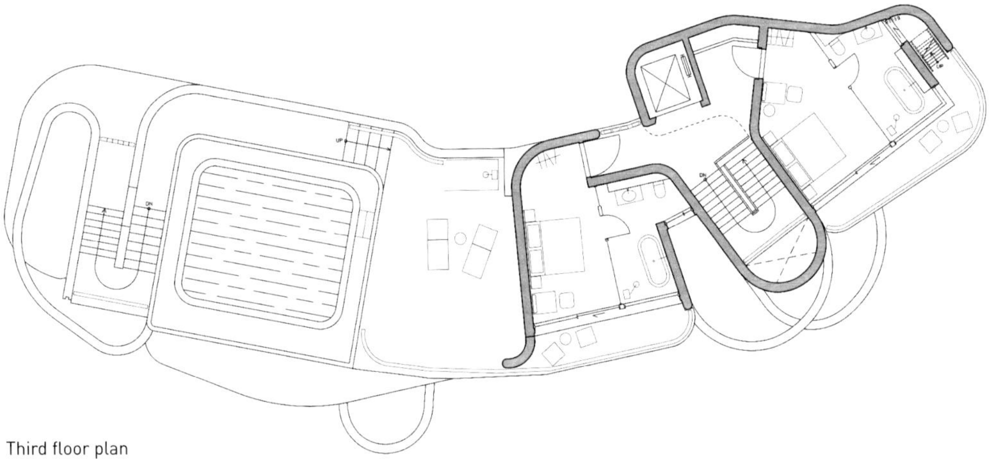

Third floor plan

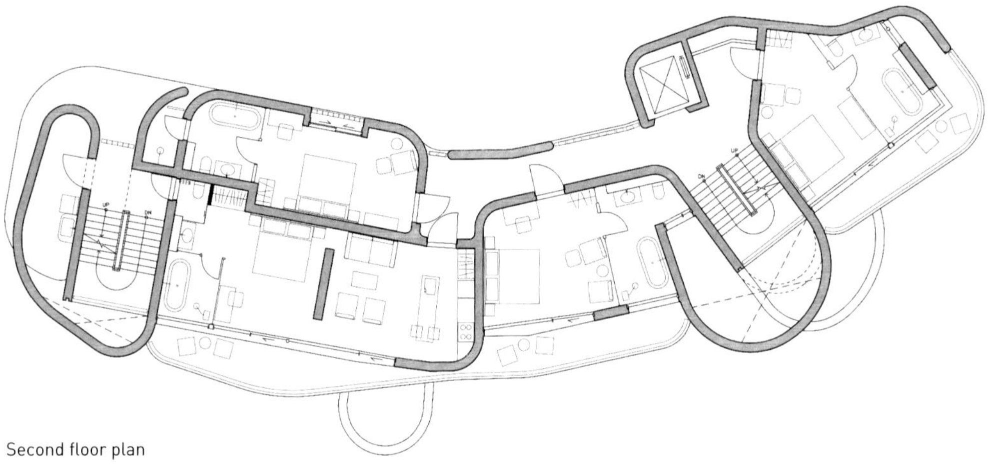

Second floor plan

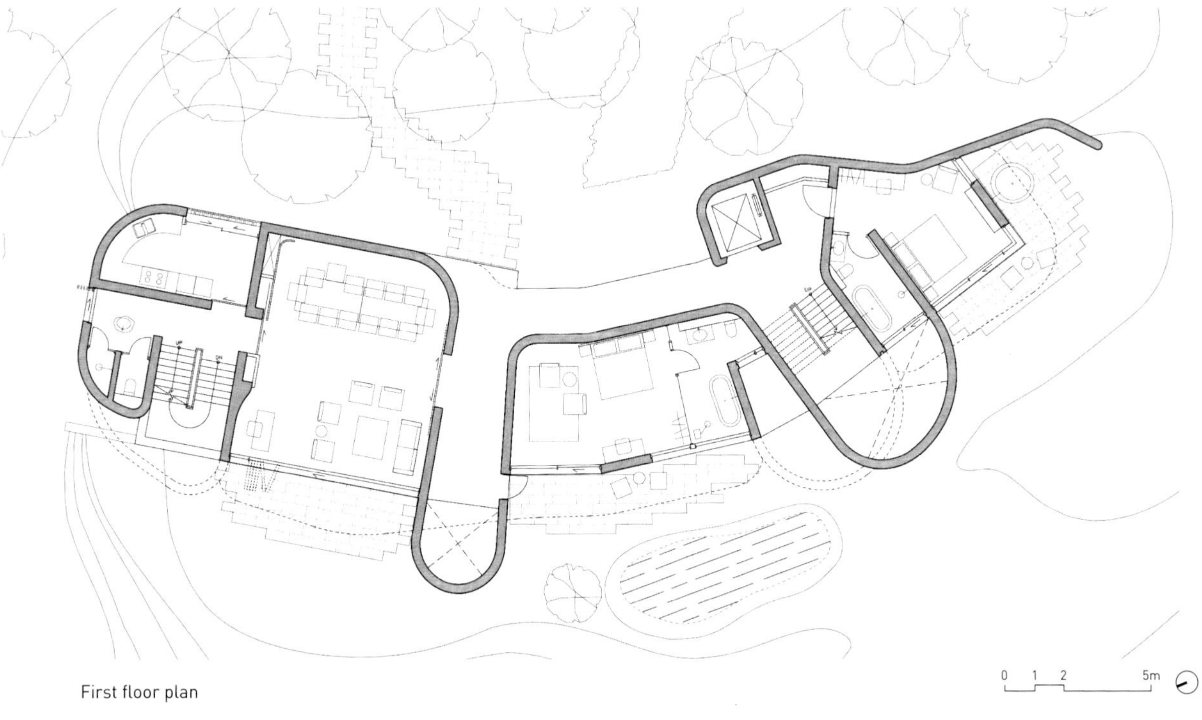

First floor plan